GU00792827

Disk Instructions

The enclosed diskette contains the full text of the 120 precedents set out in th
the text of a chosen precedent to one of five popular word processing package
formats provided are:

ASCII
IBM DCA
Word Perfect 4.2 or higher
Wordstar 3.3 or higher
Microsoft Word

A simple menu system allows you to select the format you want to create, and to extract a particular precedent for conversion.

Preparing the conversion program for use on a hard disk system
Whilst it is not essential, it is probably a good idea to make a new directory on your hard disk for the data file and conversion program:

From the C: prompt type :
MKDIR \DAVIES

Change directory to the newly created directory

CD \DAVIES

Copy all files from the diskette into the new directory

COPY a:*.*

The conversion program is ready for use - but first put the diskette away in a safe place.

Preparing the conversion program for use on a floppy disk
First make a working copy of the *Davies* diskette.

Place a new floppy in drive A: and format it with the command:
FORMAT a: /s (The /s extension tells MSDOS to copy certain system files to the newly formatted floppy)

Place the distribution diskette in drive B:, and type:
COPY *.*b:

Put the distribution diskette away in a safe place and label your new working diskette.

Running the conversion program
If you are using a hard disk system, make sure you are in the DAVIES directory - if you are using a twin floppy disk system, ensure that the working disk you have created is in the A: drive.
At the prompt type:
DWP

A menu appears on your screen. Use your cursor keys to highlight the conversion you wish to use, then press:
<RETURN>

You are prompted to enter the number of the precedent you want to convert to your chosen format; type in a number from 1 to 120.

The conversion takes a few seconds - a box appears which tells you the file name your chosen precedent has been written to. You can now copy this file to whichever directory or floppy disk you normally use for word processing documents.

Other file formats
If your word processor is not listed above, don't give up. Most word processing systems have a utility that will allow you to convert from one of the formats listed above.

Other disk formats
The disks are available in other formats. For more information contact Data Text (UK), Cobbarn House, Eridge Green, Tunbridge Wells, Kent, TN3 9LA - Tel (0892) 861222.

Copyright
The data from *Will Precedents and Inheritance Tax (4th edition)* is the copyright of Butterworth Law Publishers Ltd. The conversion program is the copyright of Data Text (UK).

Will Precedents and Inheritance Tax

Will Precedents and Inheritance Tax

Fourth Edition

D. T. Davies R.D., F.T.I.I.
Solicitor of the Supreme Court
Formerly Senior Partner of Penningtons

Butterworths
London, Dublin and Edinburgh
1991

United Kingdom	Butterworth & Co (Publishers) Ltd, 88 Kingsway, LONDON WC2B 6AB and 4 Hill Street, EDINBURGH EH2 3JZ
Australia	Butterworths Pty Ltd, SYDNEY, MELBOURNE, BRISBANE, ADELAIDE, PERTH, CANBERRA and HOBART
Canada	Butterworths Canada Ltd, TORONTO and VANCOUVER
Ireland	Butterworth (Ireland) Ltd, Dublin
Malaysia	Malayan Law Journal Sdn Bhd, KUALA LUMPUR
New Zealand	Butterworths of New Zealand Ltd, WELLINGTON and AUCKLAND
Puerto Rico	Equity de Puerto Rico, Inc, HATO REY
Singapore	Malayan Law Journal Ltd, SINGAPORE
USA	Butterworths Legal Publishers, AUSTIN, Texas; BOSTON, Massachusetts; CLEARWATER, Florida (D & S Publishers); ORFORD, New Hampshire (Equity Publishing); ST PAUL, Minnesota; and SEATTLE, Washington

A CIP Catalogue record for this book is available from the British Library.

ISBN 0 406 11783 7

Typeset by Kerrypress Ltd, Luton, Bedfordshire
Printed and bound in Great Britain by Mackays of Chatham, PLC, Chatham, Kent

Preface

The third edition of this book was published in 1988 and took account of the fundamental changes to the law of inheritance tax, formerly called capital transfer tax, by the Finance Act 1986. That Act introduced into the Inheritance Tax Act 1984, the title of which having then been changed from the Capital Transfer Tax Act 1984, the concepts of potentially exempt transfers and property subject to a reservation.[1]

Since 1988, the changes in inheritance tax law have not been technical or difficult. Nevertheless, a very practical change resulted from the Finance Act 1988 whereby there are at present two bands only in the table of rates of inheritance tax.[2] The first is the nil% band, at present £140,000.[3] The second is the 40% band on the value of a person's estate, irrespective of its value above the upper limit of the nil% band.[2] When coupled with the availability of the exemption for gifts between husbands and wives, the will practitioner has great scope for advising on the mitigation of inheritance tax and other taxes by means of imaginative will drafting.

The competitiveness of tax mitigation by will drafting has increased because of the contrasting consequences caused by the Finance Act 1989, section 124. Thereby, the overall availability of capital gains tax hold-over relief, for lifetime gifts and disposals not at arm's length, ceased to have effect.[4] Thus, except in limited circumstances, a lifetime gift gives rise to an immediate charge to capital gains tax possibly at 40%.

As in the case of previous editions, this book eschews tax mitigation arrangements involving complexity and artificiality in favour of those which are straightforward and clearly sanctioned within the terms of our taxing legislation. Nevertheless, it is accepted that to assist future tax saving it is often necessary to draft wills in a manner which is complex. Hence, the drafting of wills and the giving of advice are matters which need continuing knowledge and experience.

It is recognised that, irrespective of the complexity of the subject matter, endeavour must be made to draft wills in as understandable a manner as the circumstances allow and to give clients written explanations in language which itself is not legalistic. This edition has been written with those factors in mind.

Butterworths have added a new feature to this book. With it, at no additional cost, is included a disk by which precedents and forms can be called up by keying in the appropriate number.[5]

1 Dealt with respectively in ch 5, B and D, pp 46 and 48 below.
2 See IHTA 1984, Sch 1.
3 For the twelve months from 6 April 1991.
4 See 6 of S of ch 5, p 65 below.
5 The matter of the disk is also referred to on p 5 below.

I have continued to derive great help from many fellow practitioners and members of my profession. I have also been particularly fortunate, as general editor, to study and learn from the expert contributions of the seven editors of *Butterworths Wills, Probate and Administration Service*. Until recently Richard Oerton was, apart from being its author, the editor of its Wills Division. I wish to thank him for all the personal help and advice he has given to me. He has the gift of being able to analyse and penetrate the complexities of current legislation and then to draft in a manner which is complete and yet as straightforward as those complexities allow.

I have recently retired from Penningtons, after forty-four years. I would again like to thank my partner Lesley Lintott. She and I worked closely together and this edition reflects the many discussions we have had. She has succeeded Richard Oerton as the wills editor of *Butterworths Wills, Probate and Administration Service*.

I wish to thank my friend Ralph Ray whose energy continues unabated. He has the art, displayed by his writings and lectures, to convert the complexities of modern taxation into practical solutions. My daughter, Emma, who was articled to him, is an associate of his firm, Wedlake Saint. I am very indebted to her for the many and various discussions we have had. She and I have checked the proofs of this edition including its subject matter.

It is always appropriate to refer to the Capital Taxes Office. Its function is central to the smooth administration of inheritance tax. The members of my profession and many others are much indebted to the Controller, Mr Brian Kent, who has always taken great trouble to attend meetings and explain and discuss matters of inheritance tax. His staff's reputation for courtesy and help continues to be well merited. The booklet *Inheritance Tax*, IHT I, a new edition of which was issued by the Inland Revenue in January 1991 is a lucid commentary on inheritance tax.

This will be the last edition of this book of which I am the author and editor. Accordingly, I wish to end on a very personal note. I wish to thank my wife, Pauline, for her tireless efforts over the years in typing and retyping the manuscripts of this and the earlier three editions, over and beyond her domestic and many outside preoccupations. Not only has she given me great support and encouragement but her expressions of views on matters within this book have been practical and important.

The law is stated as at 30 September 1991.

David T. Davies

The Barn
Shortgrove
Newport
Essex
CB11 3TX

1991

Contents

PART IV.   POST-DEATH DEEDS AND MISCELLANEOUS PRECEDENTS

APPENDIX.   IHT TABLES

Table of Statutes

References in this Table to *Statutes* are to Halsbury's Statutes of England (Fourth Edition) showing the volume and page at which the annotated text of an Act may be found.

List of Cases

Abbreviations and definitions

The Finance Act 1986, section 100, states that capital transfer tax *shall* be known as inheritance tax. That section also states that the Capital Transfer Tax Act 1984 *may* be cited as the Inheritance Tax Act 1984. The newer title of that Act is used in this book.

While the policy adopted, for ease of reading, is mentioned at the end of Chapter 1, it is particularly emphasised that generally:[1]

a) references to IHT are to inheritance tax, and

b) references to Parts, chapters, sections, sub-sections, Schedules, paragraphs etc are, unless otherwise stated, to those contained in the Inheritance Tax Act 1984, as subsequently amended.

The following are the principal expressions used in the 1984 Act with a short summary of the meaning to be attached to them:

'Transfer of value'	A disposition made by a person as a result of which the value of his estate after the disposition is less than it would be but for the disposition.
'Chargeable transfer'	A transfer of value which is made by an individual but which is not an exempt transfer, including one which started as a PET (see below).
'Exempt transfer'	A transfer which is exempt from IHT. Some exempt transfers are exempt for both lifetime transfers and transfers on death, such as transfers between spouses, and others are exempt for lifetime transfers only, such as the £3,000 annual exemption.
'Potentially Exempt Transfer' (PET)	A transfer which is not an exempt transfer and which is a gift by an individual to another individual or into an interest in possession trust or into an accumulation and maintenance trust or a disabled trust but which becomes a chargeable transfer in the event of the donor not surviving the gift by seven years.

---

1 Chapter 11 is about the Inheritance (Provision for Family and Dependants) Act 1975 and chapter 13 about the Enduring Powers of Attorney Act 1985. In those chapters the references will be to those statutes.

Part I

Chapter 1
Introduction

A. Purpose and objectives

The purpose behind this book is to act as a practitioner's manual. Its objectives are as follows:

1) to assist those who, by reason of their existing experience of preparing wills, can use it for quick and ready reference;
2) to assist those of less experience to prepare satisfactory drafts of wills, and give appropriate advice, thereby gaining experience and confidence; and
3) to be of more general interest and to emphasise that the making of wills, given appropriate circumstances, is not an end in itself but can also be regarded as a fundamental part of an adult's financial and taxation affairs.

The comprehensive family will,[1] with a memorandum directed to capital tax mitigation[2] and a letter of explanation,[3] is central to this book. It is structured with the object of enabling future tax, particularly inheritance tax, to be saved, whether the testator's spouse survives or not. That precedent is of some length and is in a form which can be moulded to meet particular sets of circumstances. Chapter 8, 'Considerations in framing the trusts of the residuary estate',[4] is written with that will precedent in mind.

In order to limit but at the same time to concentrate its scope, this book is not intended to be a definitive one on the law of wills or to contain a complete range of unusual clauses which need isolated drafting. In the latter respects the well-known precedent books can be consulted.[5] Nor is the book intended to be an exposition on inheritance tax.[6] Nevertheless, it seeks to explain in some detail relevant aspects of the inheritance tax legislation in relation to lifetime gifts and gifts on death and to cover those matters which have a bearing on the drafting of wills. In fact, in the obtaining of instructions and the giving of testamentary advice it may well become clear that the testator does not appreciate the likely impact of inheritance tax on his assets in the event of his death nor the possibility that by making regular gifts and taking other action including by will, that impact can be mitigated. Above all else, the object of any will must be to give effect to the testator's wishes so far as the law allows and accordingly it is incumbent on the adviser in his capacity

---

1 Form 1, p 127 below.
2 Form 2, p 135 below.
3 Form 3, p 140 below.
4 See p 88 below.
5 Eg *Williams on Wills* (6th edn) and Division A of *Butterworths Wills Probate and Administration Service*.
6 For instance, though the subject is discussed where relevant, there is no separate treatment about IHT on settlements without interests in possession and the Inheritance Tax Act 1984, Part III Ch III.

as draftsman to recognise the testamentary legal principles involved, apart from any relevant aspects of the general law.

A will draftsman owes a duty of care to his testator. In *Ross v Caunters*[7] it was decided that the presence of that duty is extended to persons whom the testator intends to benefit under his will. In that case the solicitors had prepared a will for a testator and sent it to him, but did not warn him that it should not be witnessed by the spouse of a beneficiary.[8] The bequest to that beneficiary was thus void and the beneficiary sued the solicitors for negligence, which was admitted. The issue was whether the solicitors owed the beneficiary a duty of care. Sir Robert Megarry V-C held that the three constituent elements of the tort of negligence existed on the facts – there was a duty, there was a breach of that duty and there was loss suffered as a consequence. This not being the case concerning the giving of wrong advice or the making of an untrue statement, it was not necessary for the plaintiff to have placed reliance upon the solicitors' skill. He summarised the duty thus:[9]

'A solicitor who is instructed by his client to carry out a transaction that will confer a benefit on an identified third party owes a duty of care towards that third party in carrying out that transaction, in that the third party is a person within his direct contemplation as someone who is likely to be closely and directly affected by his acts or omissions that he can reasonably foresee that the third party is likely to be injured by those acts or omissions.'

According to a New Zealand case, *Gartside v Sheffield Young & Ellis*,[10] a solicitor may be liable to a testator's intended beneficiary if, as the result of the solicitor's unreasonable delay in preparing a will, the testator dies without executing it, as a result of which the intended beneficiary loses his benefit. Provided that the will draftsman discharges his duty of care to the testator in a proper and prompt manner, in relation to the obtaining of instructions, the giving of advice and the drafting and execution of the will, there can be no scope for any post-death claims against the will draftsman by a disgruntled beneficiary or by any other person.

B. Outline

The succeeding chapters, being Part I of the book, continue in chapter 2 with the background to the making of a will and general matters which need early consideration and advice. Chapters 3, 4, 5 and 6 cover matters of inheritance tax, particularly in relation to death, and the exemptions and reliefs that are available including those for lifetime transfers. Chapter 5 is in fact directed to what can conveniently be described as tax planning and chapters 6 and 7 deal with will drafting and relevant implications of inheritance tax including those in respect of the matrimonial home. Chapter 8 deals with considerations in framing the residuary trusts of wills and has form 1[1] in contemplation. Chapter 9 covers post-death variations and disclaimers, which subject the will draftsman needs to be aware of. There follow three chapters of general importance, being chapter 10, domicile and allied matters, chapter 11, the Inheritance (Provision for Family and Dependants) Act 1975, and chapter 12, testamentary matters concerning children. Chapter 13 is on enduring powers of

7 [1980] Ch 297, [1979] 3 All ER 580.
8 Thus falling foul of the Wills Act 1837, s 15.
9 [1980] Ch 297 at 322-323, [1979] 3 All ER 580 at 599.
10 [1983], NZLR 37 (NZCA). In *Smith v Claremont Haynes & Co* (1991) Times, 3 September a solicitor was held to be liable in negligence because his failure to act promptly in preparing a will for a testator in poor health who died deprived two intended beneficiaries of their expectations.

attorney which is a subject suitable to be discussed with a testator when he is making his will.

Part II contains complete will precedents including the comprehensive will,[1] the memorandum directed to capital tax mitigation,[2] and the letter of explanation,[3] previously referred to.

Part III contains precedents of forms, clauses and aids, to assist the making and completion of most wills.

Part IV includes precedents of post-death deeds of variation and of a disclaimer. There are also precedents, not of a testamentary nature, which may be of assistance to the will draftsman in relation to lifetime tax planning.

Lastly, the appendix contains inheritance tax tables.

The will precedents, forms and the other precedents in Parts II, III and IV have together been numbered consecutively to facilitate the use of the precedents disk with this book. Accordingly, the precedents and forms can be called up by keying in the appropriate number.

c. Abbreviations etc

The Finance Act 1986, section 100, provides that capital transfer tax *shall* be known as inheritance tax. That section also states that the Capital Transfer Tax Act 1984 *may* be cited as the Inheritance Tax Act 1984. The latter title of the Act is used in this book.

For the purpose of limiting repetition, references to inheritance tax are shortened to IHT and references in this book, unless otherwise stated, to parts, chapters, sections, sub-sections, schedules and paragraphs are to those in the Inheritance Tax Act 1984, as subsequently amended. In the statutes, gifts, devises, bequests and legacies are commonly described as transfers of value (whether lifetime or on death) and chargeable transfers. Nevertheless, the former expressions are often used in this book, for ease of explanation.

Narrative and drafting can become pedestrian and tedious when there is a continuous use of such expressions as 'him or her', 'he or she', 'testator or testatrix' and indeed 'husband or wife'. For the purposes of the purist and possibly the Sex Discrimination Act 1975 it is stated that the contents of this book have the benefit of section 61 of the Law Property Act 1925, so that, unless the context otherwise requires, the masculine includes the feminine and vice versa. The general assumption is that it is the husband who wishes to benefit his wife when a reverse disposition from the wife to the husband will have similar effect.

There is also the assumption that the persons concerned, particularly husbands and wives, are domiciled in England, except when distinctions to the contrary are mentioned.

Chapter 2
General considerations

A. Introduction and need for a will

English testamentary law confers freedom of disposition, though there are curbs and limitations. These include the existence of the Inheritance (Provision for Family and Dependants) Act 1975,[1] and matters of law such as the rule against perpetuities. The right to make a will should be exercised by every adult of normal mental capacity even when the amount of assets is small. A will can deal with important matters, other than testamentary gifts, such as the appointment of executors of the testator's personal choice, the appointment of testamentary guardians and the inclusion of funeral and burial wishes. The absence of a will creates a void and a vacuum. The presence of a will obviates any futile search for one. In fairness to the deceased's family, and possibly even more so where there are no very close relatives, by nominating the executors it makes clear who are to be responsible for arranging the funeral and generally taking over the deceased's affairs, including business ones. Various technical reasons can be given for the making of a will even when the testator, apart from matters already referred to, wants only to record that the same persons are to benefit in the same manner as would otherwise have been the case were he to die intestate. In fact, it is unlikely that after discussion and advice a testator will find the intestacy provisions[2] entirely satisfactory. By his will he can, for example, state the substitutional gifts that are to take effect in the event of a joint calamity affecting himself and any of the primary beneficiaries. Where there is a life interest or there are young children who are to benefit, any statutory powers, such as those in relation to investment, can if desired be enlarged. A will can appoint guardians of infant children.[3]

B. Requirements and form

The present law for the making of wills is governed largely by the Wills Act 1837 as amended. Essential requirements for a valid will, unless it is a privileged will, are as follows:

    a) the testator must be of full age and capacity;[4]
    b) the will must be in writing;[5]

---

1 See ch 11, p 110 below.
2 See J of this chapter, p 13 below.
3 See ch 12, p 115 below.
4 See C of this chapter.
5 Wills Act 1837, s 9.

c) the testator must intend the document to be his will and know and approve its contents.[6]

A privileged will may be made by a member of the armed forces in actual military service or by a seaman at sea by virtue of section 11 of the Wills Act 1837 and the Wills (Soldiers and Sailors) Act 1918. Such persons, even though under the age of majority, may make a testamentary disposition of real or personal property without complying with any formal requirements; such a will may be nuncupative (ie oral) provided it is made with a testamentary intention.[7]

The formal requirements for the execution of a valid will (other than a privileged will) under English law are contained in the Wills Act 1837, section 9. To use the wording of that section:

No will shall be valid unless—

a) it is in writing, and signed by the testator, or by some other person in his presence and by his direction:[8] and

b) it appears that the testator intended by his signature to give effect to the will: and

c) the signature is made or acknowledged by the testator in the presence of two or more witnesses present at the same time: and

d) each witness either—
   i) attests and signs the will: or
   ii) acknowledges his signature,
   in the presence of the testator (but not necessarily in the presence of any other witness),

but no form of attestation shall be necessary.

Although the inclusion of an attestation clause is not a legal requirement, the absence of a satisfactory clause, which would have shown that the last two requirements had been complied with, will cause complication following the death. In those circumstances the registrar of the Family Division will require formal evidence as to due execution, before admitting the will to probate.[9]

c. Testamentary capacity[10]

As a matter of general principle, so that the draftsman can be satisfied that he is implementing the testator's own wishes and that there is no doubt about the testator's testamentary capacity, the draftsman should deal direct with the client and not accept instructions through someone else.

To make a will or codicil the testator must be of testamentary capacity at the time of its execution. The draftsman must do his best to satisfy himself that the testator has this capacity. The essentials were summarised by Cockburn CJ in *Banks v Goodfellow*[11] as follows:

6 See C of this chapter.

7 *Re Jones* [1981] Fam 7, [1981] 1 All ER 1, for example, involved a nuncupative will, held to be valid, by a soldier engaged in counter-terrorist military duties in Northern Ireland who died of wounds. *Re Rapley's Estate* [1983] 3 All ER 248, [1983] 1 WLR 1069 contains a careful consideration of when a mariner or seaman might be considered to be at sea.

8 See comment in *Williams on Wills* (6th edn) p 98.

9 Non-Contentious Probate Rules 1954, SI 1987/2024 r 12.

10 *Williams on Wills* (6th edn) p 24 is of help on this subject.

11 [1870] LR 5 QB 549 at 565.

'It is essential to the exercise of such a power that a testator shall understand the nature of the act and its effects; shall understand the extent of the property of which he is disposing; shall be able to comprehend and appreciate the claims to which he ought to give effect; and, with a view to the latter object, that no disorder of the mind shall poison his affections, pervert his sense of right, or prevent the exercise of his natural faculties – that no insane delusion shall influence his will in disposing of his property and bring about a disposal of it which, if the mind had been sound, would not have been made.'

Templeman J in *Re Simpson*[12] asked that what he had to say should be brought to the attention of as many practitioners as possible. His statement read as follows:

'When a question of testamentary capacity is raised it falls on the Chancery Division of the High Court to ascertain the powers of memory and rational thought of a testator at the date he made his will. The dispute as to his state of mind is often bitter, protracted and expensive. It is sometimes difficult to put in its proper perspective evidence given in good faith, which derives from the testator's condition before he made his will, or derives from the testator's condition after he made his will. Sometimes the testator creates confusion by making contradictory promises; sometimes his friends and relations are blind to his failings or exaggerate his eccentricities.

In the case of an aged testator or a testator who has suffered a serious illness, there is one golden rule which should always be observed, however straightforward matters may appear, and however difficult or tactless it may be to suggest that precautions be taken: the making of a will by such a testator ought to be witnessed or approved by a medical practitioner who satisfied himself of the capacity and understanding of the testator, and records and preserves his examination and finding.

There are other precautions which should be taken. If the testator has made an earlier will this should be considered by the legal and medical advisers of the testator and, if appropriate, discussed with the testator. The instructions of the testator should be taken in the absence of anyone who may stand to benefit, or who may have influence over the testator.

These are not counsels of perfection. If proper precautions are not taken injustice may result or be imagined, and great expense and misery may be unnecessarily caused.'

A patient within the meaning of the Mental Health Act 1983, provided he has testamentary capacity, is not precluded from making a valid will.[13]

The Mental Health Act 1983, section 96(1)(d), enables the Court of Protection to order the execution of a will for a patient who has not testamentary capacity.[14]

---

12 (1977) 121 Sol Jo 224.

13 *Heywood and Massey Court of Protection* (11th edn) ch 14, p 185, is of assistance on practice and procedure.

14 Ibid, ch 14, p 189ff. *Re Davey* [1980] 3 All ER 342, [1981] 1 WLR 164 and *Re D (J)* [1982] Ch 237, [1982] 2 All ER 31 show circumstances under which the Court of Protection can direct a will to be executed for a patient and the principles to be taken into account. It was reported in the *Law Society's Gazette*, 1 May 1991, that in the Court of Protection Mr. Justice Hoffman had effectively written a will for a mentally handicapped woman of 75, who was unaware that she had an estate worth £1.6m. He said the court would work on the assumption that the woman was 'a normal decent person acting in accordance with contemporary standards of morality' and wished to divide her money between relatives and health charities that had helped her. The matter was brought to the court by the official solicitor and the decision made public because of its importance in setting guidelines.

The donor under an enduring power of attorney cannot confer on his attorney power to make a will on his behalf.[15]

D. Dissolution or annulment of testator's marriage to beneficiary

Prior to 1983 divorce or nullity had no effect on a will.

Section 18A of the Wills Act 1837 (inserted by the Administration of Justice Act 1982, section 18(2)) provides as follows:

(1) Where, after a testator has made a will, a decree of a court of civil jurisdiction in England and Wales dissolves or annuls his marriage or his marriage is dissolved or annulled and the divorce or annulment is entitled to recognition in England and Wales by virtue of Part II of the Family Law Act 1986,—

    a) the will shall take effect as if any appointment of the former spouse as an executor or as the executor and trustee of the will were omitted; and

    b) any devise or bequest to the former spouse shall lapse, except in so far as a contrary intention appears by the will.

(2) Sub-section (1)(b) above is without prejudice to any right of the former spouse to apply for financial provision under the Inheritance (Provision for Family and Dependants) Act 1975.

(3) Where—

    a) by the terms of a will an interest in remainder is subject to a life interest; and

    b) the life interest lapses by virtue of sub-section (1)(b) above,

    the interest in remainder shall be treated as if it had not been subject to the life interest and, if it was contingent upon the termination of the life interest, as if it had not been so contingent.'

Section 18A applies if the testator dies after 31 December 1982 (1982 Act sections 73(6) and 76(11)). It reverses the rule in force prior to 1983.

Judicial separation has no effect on a will. Nevertheless, it has on an intestacy if the decree is in force and the separation is continuing at the intestate's death; in that case the surviving spouse takes no beneficial interests on intestacy.[16]

E. Foreign aspects and domicile[17]

There is a foreign aspect where the testator has property situated outside England and Wales or is domiciled outside England and Wales.

Under private international law, as it applies to wills, the primary distinction is between movables and immovables and *not* between personalty and realty.[18] As a general rule, a will of movables is governed by the law of the testator's domicile and a will of immovables by the lex situs.

---

15 Ch 13, p 119 below is about the enduring power of attorney.

16 Matrimonial Causes Act 1973, s 18(2).

17 On the principles for ascertaining domicile, see generally ch 10, p 103 below.

18 Accordingly, English law accepts that all interests in land in England are in fact immovable property, including mortgages over land, leasehold property and freehold property which is not yet sold but which is subject to a trust for sale and a beneficial interest in the proceeds of sale thereof. When there is a conflict between the lex situs and the lex forum the former controls whether an interest is immovable or movable property.

a) PERSONAL TESTAMENTARY CAPACITY OR ABILITY

Movables. Governed by the law of testator's domicile, probably as at the time of the making of the will rather than as at the time of his death.

Immovables. Governed by the lex situs.

b) FORM IN RELATION TO BOTH MOVABLES AND IMMOVABLES

The Wills Act 1963, and similar law introduced in other countries which assented to and implemented the Hague Convention on the Conflict of Laws relating to the Form of Testamentary Dispositions, was aimed at rationalising generally throughout the world the formalities for the execution of wills. Under section 1 of the 1963 Act a will of movable or immovable property is to be treated as properly executed if its execution conformed to the internal law in force in the territory where it was executed, or in the territory where, at the time of its execution or of the testator's death, he was domiciled or had his habitual residence, or in a state of which, at either of those times, he was a national. Under section 2(1)(b) a will of immovable property is also properly executed if its execution conformed to the internal law in force in the territory where the property was situated.[19] Reference should also be made to the next sub-chapter F on international wills.

c) MATERIAL OR ESSENTIAL VALIDITY[20]

Movables. Governed by the law of the testator's domicile at the time of his death.

Immovables. Governed by the lex situs.

d) CONSTRUCTION IN RELATION TO BOTH MOVABLES AND IMMOVABLES

This is governed by the law intended by the testator, intention being expressed or arising by implication. In the absence of expressed intention the presumption is that the law of the testator's domicile, at the time of the execution of the will, shall apply. Nevertheless, when construing a will of immovables, if the dispositions are not allowed by the lex situs then to such extent the lex situs prevails.

e) DOCTRINE OF RENVOI

This can arise when English law refers a matter, such as one of succession, to the law of a foreign country, but that law would refer it to English law. This could arise, for example, in the case of foreign immovables owned by a testator who either was domiciled in England or was a British subject. The practical operation of the doctrine gives rise to difficulties and reference should be made to the leading text books.[1]

Arising from the foregoing commentary, when there are foreign immovables such as a house, it is to be recommended that a separate will should be made in such respect drafted by a lawyer of the particular country. When there are foreign movables, consideration should also be given to the making of a foreign will for administrative convenience.

The possibility of there being community of property on marriage should be

---

19 Regarding the revocation of a will, see Wills Act 1963, s 2(1)(c) and *Williams on Wills* (6th edn) p 144.
20 This expression applies to such matters as whether the testator must leave a fixed proportion of his assets to his widow and children, whether a gift to a charity is valid, the application of the rules against perpetuities and accumulation and whether a gift to an attesting witness is valid.
1 Dicey and Morris *The Conflict of Laws* (11th edn) ch 5, Cheshire and North *Private International Law* (11th edn) Ch 5, *Theobald on Wills* (14th edn) pp 21-23.

considered when an English girl is to marry a man domiciled abroad.[2] While, in those countries[3] where community of property applies, there are differing systems, the principle is that all the property of both spouses forms a joint unseverable pool and on the death of the first to die that pool is divisable equally between the survivor and the estate of the deceased irrespective of the proportions of their contributions to the pool. All systems, nevertheless, permit of ante-nuptual contracts to negate or vary the operation of the community of property effects that would otherwise apply on marriage. An English fiancée with an absence of means might welcome community of property, while an heiress might not.[4]

The subject of domicile, including in relation to IHT, is covered in chapter 10, commencing at page 103 below. At the time of the making of the will it is well to remember that, on a death, the Capital Taxes Office will require, where it is claimed that the deceased was domiciled outside the United Kingdom according to general law at the time of his death, with Inland Revenue Account Form IHT 201, a schedule to be filed stating the circumstances relied upon to establish his domicile in the particular country, state or province, as the case may be, and giving a short history of the deceased's life commencing with his domicile of origin. Evidence should be adduced, where possible, by two persons closely related to or well acquainted with the deceased, one preferably without financial interest in the estate.[5] If, notwithstanding section 1 of the Domicile and Matrimonial Proceedings Act 1973, in the case of a deceased wife, a dependant domicile outside the United Kingdom is claimed, a short history of her husband's life commencing with his domicile of origin would need to be supplied with a statement of her relevant activities since 31 December 1973.[5]

F. International wills in relation to form

The Administration of Justice Act 1982, sections 27 and 28, gives legislative effect in the United Kingdom to the Annex to the Convention on International Wills, which Annex is set out in Schedule 2 to the Act.

The statutory provisions are to come into force on such day as the Lord Chancellor and the Home Secretary by order jointly appoint.[6]

The Annex set out in Schedule 2 to the Act gives the details of the formal requirements. If those requirements are complied with, such a will, *as regards form*, is to be valid irrespective particularly of the place where it is made, of the location of the assets and of the nationality, domicile or residence of the testator. It is to be appreciated that this form of international will is to be accepted in addition to the existing forms of will in each country. It is evident that such a will could be of

2 It is settled that the consequences of marriage are governed by the law of the domicile of the husband at the time of the marriage: *Re Egerton's Will Trusts* [1956] Ch 593, [1956] 2 All ER 817. Once that is settled no subsequent change of domicile affects the position: *De Nicols v Curlier* [1900] AC 21.

3 These include many European countries, several of the States of the USA and under Roman-Dutch law applied in South Africa.

4 A very useful commentary on community of property is in Law Commission Working Paper No 42 Part 5.

5 See IHT 210 *Instructions for the completion of Inland Revenue Account Forms 200 and 201 used where the deceased died on or after 18 March 1986* at 2.1.3.

6 Those provisions will come into force only after ss 23 to 26 (registration of wills) have done so. No date for the latter has been fixed.

particular help where a testator has assets in more than one of the signatory countries.

The formalities prescribed are that the will is to be in writing in any language, by hand or by any other means, and it need not be written by the testator himself. The testator must declare in the presence of *two* witnesses and of a person authorised to act in connection with international wills that the document is his will and that he knows its contents. It is stated that the testator need not inform the witnesses, or the authorised person, of the contents of the will. In the presence of the witnesses and the authorised person the testator is to sign or acknowledge his previously made signature. The witnesses and the authorised person are required there and then to attest the will by signing in the presence of the testator. All the signatures are to be placed at the end of the will and, when there is more than one sheet, the sheets are to be numbered and each signed. The date is to be noted at the end of the will by the authorised person.

The formalities accordingly envisage a crucial role to be played by 'the authorised person'. He is required to attach to the will a certificate in the form prescribed by Article 10 establishing in detail that the required obligations have been complied with. In continental countries he is to be a notary. Section 28 of the 1982 Act states that the persons authorised to act in the United Kingdom are solicitors and notaries public.

G. Knowledge of personal circumstances[7]

It is assumed that in making a will for a testator the solicitor will already have, and if not will obtain most conveniently at a meeting, personal details of the testator such as details of his wife and her relative age, his family and former marriages.

The solicitor should also seek to gauge the personal inclinations and philosophy and indeed foibles of the testator since, though it is the wishes of the testator that must prevail and be appropriately worded, it is for the solicitor to advise and guide. Generally these days the wording of wills is severely practical and has an absence of sentiment, but there is no reason against the inclusion of personal wording and clauses, which do not cut across the legal effect of the will, yet record deeper and more personal feelings and sentiments.

H. Knowledge of financial circumstances[8]

To enable the solicitor to give advice, the testator should supply full information about the nature and extent of his assets and financial interests. This is important since those matters could bear on the terms of the will. They will also enable any calculations to be made with regard to the likely impact of IHT on his death. Such information as emerges may lead to arrangements to mitigate the IHT liability, by

---

7 Although it is the case that wills are specifically excluded from the general restriction relating to the preparation of instruments contained in the Solicitors Act 1974, s 22, it is assumed that it will in fact be a solicitor who will be in direct contact with the testator for the purpose of advice and of drafting the will. Quite apart from the complexities of drafting, it would be foolish for a person other than a qualified lawyer to undertake the responsibilities for advice when the present legislation provides that reliefs from IHT and other taxes may depend upon the precise wording used in a will and on the dispositions made by the testator.

8 See Form 9, p 156 below, for assets questionnaire.

lifetime transfers. Because of the nature of IHT it is important that the solicitor should also have details of the assets of the other spouse whether or not the latter is making a will at the same time.

I. Inheritance tax and capital gains tax

Chapter 3, page 16 below, covers IHT on death and chapter 5, page 45 below, refers to the principles of IHT in relation to lifetime gifts.[9]

There is no capital gains tax (CGT) liability on death. Under the Capital Gains Tax Act 1979, section 49(1)(a) there is a deemed acquisition of the assets of the deceased person, at their value on death, by his personal representatives. Nevertheless, by section 49(1)(b) there is no disposal by the deceased person and thus no CGT liability because such a liability is only as the result of a disposal. Under section 49(4) beneficiaries take assets, from the personal representatives, without a CGT liability being incurred, at the personal representatives' deemed acquisition values, which are the values on death. Apart from specific legacies this latter provision can also apply to assets appropriated to satisfy cash legacies and to a distribution of assets as part of a share of residue. The sale of property by personal representatives is a disposal for CGT purposes.[10] For the purposes of calculation of the CGT liability, the IHT valuation will be the personal representatives' acquisition price.[11]

J. Intestacy provisions

Should a person die without leaving a will, the Administration of Estates Act 1925, section 46 contains the manner of distribution of his assets.

I. WHEN THE INTESTATE LEAVES A SPOUSE
    a) Where there are issue, the surviving spouse is entitled to:
        i) The personal chattels;[12]
        ii) A net sum of £75,000[13] with interest at 6%[14] from death until payment; and
        iii) A life interest in one half of the rest of the estate which one half is held, subject to such life interest, on the statutory trusts[15] for the issue. The other half is immediately held on the statutory trusts[15] for the issue.

---

9 See, in particular, A of ch 5, p 45 below.
10 Personal representatives are subject to capital gains tax at 25%. For the year of assessment in which an individual dies and for the next two following years of assessment, Capital Gains Tax Act 1979, s 5(1), (4) to (5), which gives relief for the first £5,500 (this figure being subject to indexation each 6 April) of chargeable gains, applies to his personal representatives in the same way as it applies to a living person: s 5(6) and Sch 1, para 4.
11 Capital Gains Tax Act 1979, s 153.
12 As defined by the Administration of Estates Act 1925, s 55(1)(x).
13 This figure is the result of an increase under the Family Provision (Intestate Succession) Order 1987 (SI 1987/799), made by virtue of the Family Provisions Act 1966, s 1(3) in relation to the estate of a person dying on or after 1 June 1987.
14 Administration of Justice Act 1977, s 28 amended the Administration of Estates Act 1925, s 46(1) to enable the Lord Chancellor to prescribe by Order the appropriate rate of interest. The Administration of Justice Act 1977 (Commencement No 2) Order 1977 (SI 1977/1490) brought s 28 into operation on 15 September 1977. The Intestate Succession (Interest and Capitalisation) (Amendment) Order 1983 (SI 1983/1374) which came into operation on 1 October 1983 altered the rate of interest from 7% to 6%.
15 See Administration of Estates Act 1925, s 47.

   b) Where there are no issue, but there are certain other close relatives (ie one or both parents, or brothers and sisters or their issue) the surviving spouse is entitled to:

     i) The personal chattels;[12]

     ii) A net sum of £125,000[13] with interest at 6%[14] from death until payment; and

     iii) One half of the rest of the estate absolutely. The other half goes to the close relatives in the order stated in section 46.

   c) Where there are no issue and there are no such close relatives the surviving spouse takes the whole estate.

The surviving spouse can require capitalisation of his or her life interest,[16] which will arise where the deceased also left issue, and elect to have a capital sum paid.[17] Election to this effect must usually be made within twelve months of representation being granted.

There is special provision under the Second Schedule to the Intestates Estates Act 1952, in relation to the matrimonial home. If resident there at the intestate's death, the surviving spouse may require the personal representatives to appropriate the interest of the intestate in the matrimonial home in or towards satisfaction of any absolute interest of the surviving spouse, including the capitalised value of a life interest. The house is valued at the date of appropriation, not death.[18] Election must generally be made within twelve months of representation being granted. *Re Phelps, Wells v Phelps*[19] lays down that the surviving spouse has the right to require the appropriation of the matrimonial home, although the value of it exceeds the value of the absolute interest of the surviving spouse in the intestate's estate, with payment of equality money by the surviving spouse.

2. THE RIGHTS OF THE ISSUE

If the intestate leaves a spouse, the rest of the estate (including ultimately that part subject to the life interest of the surviving spouse) goes on the statutory trusts[15] to the issue. This means that it will be held for all the children living at the death of the intestate who attain eighteen or marry in equal shares. Issue, living at the intestate's death, of any child who died before the intestate take, by substitution, the share that their parent would have taken had that parent attained a vested interest, provided they attain eighteen or marry. If there is no surviving spouse, the whole of the estate goes on the statutory trusts[15] to the issue.

3. THE RIGHTS OF PARENTS

If the intestate leaves a spouse but no issue who attain a vested interest, the

16 Article 3 of the Intestate Succession (Interest and Capitalisation) Order 1977 (SI 1977/1491) governs the calculation of the capital value of a life interest. The Tables scheduled to the Order provide a multiplier which, when applied to the appropriate part of the residuary estate, produces the capital value. There are separate Tables for surviving husbands and wives (owing to the different expectations of life of the two sexes) and the variables in each Table are the age of the surviving spouse and prevailing rate of interest on medium term Government Stocks, determined by an index compiled by the *Financial Times*, the Institute of Actuaries and the Faculty of Actuaries.

17 Administration of Estates Act 1925, s 47A. Ss 17 and 45 provide that such an election by the surviving spouse is not a transfer of value for IHT purposes and for such purposes the surviving spouse, in effect, is treated as having been entitled to the capital sum instead of the life interest.

18 *Robinson v Collins* [1975] 1 All ER 321, sub nom *Re Collins, Robinson v Collins* [1975] 1 WLR 309.

19 [1980] Ch 275, [1979] 3 All ER 373, CA.

parents are entitled to half of any surplus over the spouse's £125,000[13] legacy. If there is neither surviving spouse nor issue they take the whole estate. If both parents are living, they take in equal shares.

4. THE RIGHTS OF BROTHERS AND SISTERS OF THE WHOLE BLOOD

If the intestate leaves a spouse but no issue who attain a vested interest and no parents, the brothers and sisters of the whole blood are entitled to half of any surplus over the spouse's £125,000[13] legacy on the statutory trusts.[15] If there is no spouse, they take the whole estate.

5. THE RIGHTS OF OTHERS

The Table in section 46 prescribes the sequence of entitlement where there are none of the foregoing close relatives: namely brothers and sisters of the half blood on the statutory trusts,[15] grandparents in equal shares, uncles and aunts of the whole blood on the statutory trusts,[15] and uncles and aunts of the half blood on the statutory trusts.[15] The final beneficiary in the event of none of the foregoing being entitled is the Crown or Duchy of Lancaster or Duchy of Cornwall who take the estate as bona vacantia. However they may at their discretion provide for persons who were dependant on the intestate whether related or not and for other persons for whom the intestate might reasonably have been expected to make provision.[20]

The unsevered interest of a deceased joint tenant, which therefore passes, by survivorship, to the other joint tenant, does not form part of the estate of an intestate.

The intestacy provisions can apply where the deceased had a foreign domicile. They can produce curious results as in *Re Collens*.[1]. In that case the widow was entitled to her statutory legacy out of the intestate's English immovable property despite her substantial benefits from assets situate in the place of his domicile, there being no relevant provisions for hotchpot under the English law of intestacy.

In 1988 the Law Commission produced a Working Paper ('Distribution on Intestacy' WP No 108) which considered how property of an intestate should be distributed and invited comments. The matter and results were subsequently placed before the Lord Chancellor whose decisions are awaited.

20 It is also possible that such a person could, in those circumstances, have a claim under the Inheritance (Provision for Family and Dependants) Act 1975, which is dealt with in ch 11. See in particular the categories of possible claimants under (d) and (e), p 111 below.

1 [1986] Ch 505, [1986] 1 All ER 577.

Chapter 3
Inheritance tax on death

A. Background and basis of IHT

Section 4(1) states that on the death of any person tax shall be charged as if, immediately before his death, he had made a transfer of value and the value transferred by it had been equal to the value of his estate immediately before his death.

Under section 5(1), a person's estate is the aggregate of all the property[1] to which he is beneficially entitled,[2] except that the estate of a person immediately before his death does not include excluded property.[3] In determining the value of a person's estate at any time his liabilities at that time shall be taken into account, except as otherwise provided.[4]

The pattern of the IHT legislation is that *lifetime* transfers of value made by the transferor during the period of seven years before his death, unless they are exempt transfers[5] or dispositions of excluded property[3] or dispositions stated not to be transfers of value,[6] give rise to a charge to IHT on a cumulative basis starting with a nil% band for amounts or values of up to £140,000[7] – this figure for the period to 5 April 1992 will be subject to annual adjustment as mentioned in the next paragraph – and thereafter the rate is 40% irrespective of the amounts or values over £140,000. The calculation of IHT on each additional chargeable transfer commences in the table at the point where the aggregate of the values of the chargeable transfers made during the prior seven years ended. Because of section 4(1), the IHT charge on death, being deemed to take place immediately prior thereto, is calculated accordingly. Thus, if a person during the prior seven years made an aggregate total of chargeable transfers of a value of £100,000 and leaves an estate of £150,000 IHT on his death is calculated by reference to the rates that then apply between £100,000 and £250,000.

By section 8, each 6 April the IHT rate bands are adjusted, for the purposes of the following twelve months, having regard to changes in the retail price index. This is subject to Parliament's overriding right to determine otherwise. Before each 6 April, the Treasury is required, by statutory instrument, to make an order specifying the amounts in the table which is in Schedule I. The 1991 order is Inheritance Tax (Indexation) Order 1991 (SI 91/1735).

1 'Property' is defined in s 272 as including rights and interests of every description.
2 Under s 49(1) a person beneficially entitled to an interest in possession in settled property is also treated for IHT purposes as beneficially entitled to the property in which the interest subsists.
3 'Excluded property' is defined in s 6.
4 S 5(3).
5 See ch 1 of part 11.
6 See, for example, s 11 in relation to dispositions for maintenance of family.
7 By the Finance Act 1988 the IHT rate bands were reduced to two and are now as mentioned in the text. Sch 1 contains the table of rates of IHT.

B. Potentially exempt transfers and gifts with reservation

The Finance Act 1986, in the case of lifetime gifts on or after 18 March 1986, made fundamental changes which will be dealt with in chapter 5. The following comments in the next two paragraphs are therefore brief.

By section 3A, a gift which when made was not a chargeable transfer can become a chargeable transfer if the transferor does not survive its making by seven years. Thus, not only will the gift itself become chargeable to IHT but, by reason of cumulation, that will also adversely affect the IHT paid on subsequent chargeable transfers and the IHT liability on death.

By the Finance Act 1986, section 102(3), if, immediately before the death of the donor, there is any property which he has previously gifted and is property subject to a reservation, it is to be treated as property to which he was beneficially entitled immediately before his death. Thus it will be aggregated with all such other property for the purposes of arriving at the total IHT liability. For property subject to a reservation, reference should be made to sub-chapter D of chapter 5.

The Finance Act 1986, section 104, empowers the Board of Inland Revenue, by statutory instrument, to make regulations for the avoidance of death charges and double cumulation otherwise arising as the result of the transferor's death. For example, sub-section 1(b) refers to an individual who disposes of property by a transfer of value which is or proves to be a chargeable transfer, possibly because he does not survive its making by seven years, and the circumstances are also such that the gifted property proves to be property subject to a reservation for the purposes of section 102. The Inheritance Tax (Double Charges Relief) Regulations 1987, SI 1987/1130, came into force on 22 July 1987 and provide for the avoidance, to the extent specified, of double charges to IHT arising with respect to specific transfers of value made, and other events occurring, on or after 18 March 1986. In principle these Regulations preserve the higher amount of IHT but also eliminate the double charges and double cumulation as the result of the transferor's death. Helpfully, the schedule to the Regulations provides examples of their application to the respective sets of circumstances they cover.

C. Meaning of person's estate and excluded property

As has previously been mentioned, under section 5(1), a person's estate is the aggregate of all the property[8] to which he is beneficially entitled,[9] except that the estate of a person immediately before his death does not include excluded property. As stated in the previous sub-chapter, it will also include 'property subject to a reservation'. As stated in the last but one paragraph of this sub-chapter, it will also include the underlying settled property in which he has an interest in possession, principally by being entitled as of right to current income.[9] As IHT is charged on the value of the deceased's estate immediately before his death, this would therefore include his interest as a joint tenant where having died his interest passes, by survivorship, to the other joint tenant. In contrast, property falling into his estate after his death is not included as part of it for IHT purposes. Section 5(2) states that a person who has a general power which enables him, or would if he were sui juris enable him, to dispose of any property *other than settled property*, or to charge money on

8 See note 1 above.
9 See note 2 above.

any property *other than settled property*, shall be treated as beneficially entitled to the property or money; and for this purpose 'general power' means a power or authority enabling the person by whom it is exercisable to appoint or dispose of property as he thinks fit. Property held in a fiduciary capacity is excluded.[10]

Section 6 describes the main categories of excluded property. First, property is excluded property if it is situated outside the United Kingdom and the person entitled to it is an individual domiciled outside the United Kingdom despite taking into account the extended definition of domicile in section 267. Subject to the necessity of deciding the situs of an asset which in most cases will not be difficult,[11] the domicile[12] of the person at the relevant time, including at his death, is crucial. If the donor/deceased is then domiciled in the United Kingdom, all his assets so 'gifted', wherever in the world they may be, are subject to IHT. If he is not so domiciled, IHT will be charged only on such of his gifted assets as are in this country. Secondly, property is excluded property where securities have been issued by the Treasury subject to a condition authorised by section 22 of the Finance (No 2) Act 1931 (or section 47 of the Finance (No 2) Act 1915) for exemption from taxation so long as the securities are in the beneficial ownership of persons neither domiciled nor ordinarily resident in the United Kingdom. For the foregoing, 'domicile' means domicile under the general law and does not have the extended meaning given to it by section 267. Thirdly, national savings certificates and certain other forms of 'small' savings are excluded property when the person beneficially entitled is domiciled in the Channel Islands or the Isle of Man. The deemed domicile provisions of section 267 do not apply for this purpose. Finally, excluded property, by cross reference to section 155(1), includes emoluments and tangible movable property of members of visiting forces.

Additionally, a reversionary interest, which is defined under section 47, is excluded property if owned by the donor/deceased unless it has been acquired by him or by a person previously entitled to it at any time, for a consideration in money or money's worth;[13] or it is one to which the settlor or his spouse is or has been beneficially entitled;[14] or it is the interest expectant on the determination of what can be summarised as a lease for life.[15]

Section 49(1) states that a person beneficially entitled to an interest in possession[16] in settled property shall be treated, for IHT purposes, as beneficially entitled to the property in which the interest subsists. The charge to IHT on death is assessed after taking into account his cumulative total of lifetime transfers, during the preceding seven years. There is no charge on the death of a discretionary object under a settlement or on any addition to or removal from the class of persons eligible to benefit.[17]

---

10 See remarks of the Financial Secretary to the Treasury, Official Report, Standing Committee A, 4 February 1975, cols 629/30.
11 See *Capital Taxes Encyclopaedia, Division F.3*. Double taxation conventions may have an effect on what otherwise would be, for example, the situs of property and the domicile of a person, for IHT purposes and can also override the extended definition of domicile under s 267; see p 107 below.
12 See ch 10, p 103 below. See also note 11 above regarding double taxation conventions.
13 S 48(1)(a).
14 S 48(1)(b).
15 S 48(1)(c) and s 43(3).
16 See next sub-chapter D.
17 See, for example, IR Consultative Document *Capital Transfer Tax and Settled Property* (August 1980) at 2.2.3 on p 5.

The underlying trust capital in which a person enjoyed a life interest in possession is on death equated to and aggregated with his free estate. The combined liability for IHT will be apportioned pro rata between the two sets of assets.[18] Nevertheless where, on the death of a person entitled to a life interest, the trust capital reverts to the settlor or devolves on the United Kingdom domiciled spouse of the settlor, during the lives of either of such persons, or to the widow or widower within two years of the settlor's death, the trust capital is left out of account for IHT purposes.[19] These exceptions do not apply if the reversionary interest was acquired by such persons for a consideration in money or money's worth.[20]

Under section 200(1) the personal representatives are the liable parties for IHT in respect of the free estate and the trustees in respect of the settled property.[1]

D. What is an interest in possession in settled property

The last but one paragraph of C, above, states simply that a person beneficially entitled to an interest in possession in settled property shall be treated, for IHT purposes, as entitled to the property in which the interest subsists. The Inheritance Tax Act 1984 does not define 'interest in possession'. This matter is of great importance, in relation to settled property, not only on whether there is a charge to IHT on death under section 4(1), in the same way as a person's free estate, but also because, trusts with an interest in possession and trusts without an interest in possession are charged to IHT under different regimes.

On 12 February 1976 by a press notice the Inland Revenue gave their interpretation of the meaning of interest in possession in the following terms:

'. . . An interest in possession in settled property exists where the person having the interest has the immediate entitlement (subject to any prior claim by the trustees for expenses or other outgoings properly payable out of income) to any income produced by that property as the income arises; but a discretion or power, in whatever form, which can be exercised after income arises so as to withhold it from that person negatives the existence of an interest in possession. For this purpose a power to accumulate income is regarded as a power to withhold it, unless any accumulation must be held solely for the person having the interest or his personal representatives. On the other hand, the existence of a mere power of revocation or appointment, the exercise of which would determine the interest wholly or in part (but which so long as it remains unexercised does not affect the beneficiary's immediate entitlement to income) does not in the Board's view prevent the interest from being an interest in possession.'

While any future case law will need to be watched it is generally accepted that the House of Lords' decision in *Pearson v IRC*[2] confirmed the foregoing interpretation of the Inland Revenue. Accordingly what would otherwise be an interest in possession cannot exist when trustees have, for example, the right by reason of a trust or power to accumulate or divert income in priority to the income rights of the life tenant. It would seem that administrative rights, as opposed to dispositive ones, to apply income 'in or towards the payment or discharge of any duties, taxes, costs, charges,

---

18 S 265.
19 S 54(1) and (2).
20 S 54(3) and s 53(5) and (6).
 1 See the precise provisions of s 200(1).
 2 [1981] AC 753, [1980] STC 318, HL.

fees or other outgoings . . . payable out of or charged upon *the capital* . . .'3 would not prevent the life tenant having an interest in possession for IHT purposes.

E. Exemptions and reliefs

The most important exemption from liability to IHT, including on death, is for transfers between spouses.4 That exemption does not, however, apply when the transferor spouse is, but the transferee spouse is not, domiciled in the United Kingdom. It applies to all other permutations of their respective domicile. When the transferee spouse is not so domiciled the exemption is limited to an aggregate value of £55,0005 and on death such amount would be reduced to the extent that it had been so absorbed by lifetime transfers during the previous seven years. Additionally, the nil% band would be available to the extent that it had not been absorbed.

There is IHT exemption in the case of gifts to charities.6 A charity is only within the exemption if it is established in the United Kingdom. There is a similar exemption for gifts to certain political parties,7 for gifts to housing associations,8 for gifts for national purposes, such as to main museums and galleries, any local authority, any government department and any university,9 and for gifts for public benefit, being gifts to various non profit-making organisations so approved by the Treasury and subject to undertakings; the emphasis in the latter respect being on property of outstanding scenic, historic or scientific interest or outstanding architectural or aesthetic interest.10

There are IHT exemptions and reliefs in respect of works of art, historic buildings, etc, business property, agricultural land and woodlands.11

The exemptions under sections 19, 20, 21 and 22 (£3,000 annual exemption, £250 small gifts, normal expenditure out of income and marriage gifts) are not available on death.12

F. Valuation

Section 160 governs the valuation of a person's assets, including on death, and states that, except as otherwise provided, the value of an asset, shall be the price13 which it might reasonably be expected to fetch if sold in the open market at the time in question.14 Nevertheless, such price shall not be assumed to be reduced on the ground that the whole property is (deemed) to be placed on the market at one and

---

3 [1981] AC 753 at 775B, [1980] STC 318 at 325H, HL.
4 S 18(1).
5 S 18(2).
6 S 23.
7 S 24.
8 S 24A.
9 S 25(1) and Sch 3.
10 S 26.
11 See generally ch 4, p 31 below.
12 Ss 19(5), 20(3), 21(5) and 22(6).
13 The price means the gross price without deduction for costs of sale. The exception is that there can be some allowance for additional administration expenses where foreign property is valued on death: s 173. The familiar 'quarter up' rule for quoted securities applies.
14 This principle is modified when the asset would fetch a higher price if sold in conjunction with 'related property' see H, p 22 below.

the same time. For the purpose of deciding the open market value, certain assumptions need to be made, as in the case of estate duty valuations in the past. There will be an assumption that there is such an open market, if only a hypothetical one, with willing (but not anxious) sellers and willing buyers (including persons to whom the property has a special attraction such as a sitting tenant), and that assets would be sold in the way likely to produce the best result. Thus, if an asset would produce a higher price if sold in separate lots such would be the basis of its valuation. Even though assets cannot in fact be sold in the open market, such as shares in private companies subject to prohibitions or restrictions or rights of pre-emption under the Articles of Association, there will nevertheless be an assumption that they are freely marketable but that the assumed purchaser will not be able to re-sell except in the restricted market. Section 168 contains assumptions about the availability of information in determining the open market price of unquoted shares or securities.

In the case of an asset abroad, it may be frozen by reason of exchange control or other overseas government law. Nevertheless, the following concessions are available:

a) the asset is valued with an allowance for the restrictions; and
b) it is permissible to defer payment of IHT in respect of the asset until the proceeds are received.[15]

By section 171 any changes in the value of a person's estate, by reason of his death, and which either add to the property comprised in his estate *or* increase or decrease that value are to be taken into account, subject to certain exceptions. Thus, for example, there would be included the money payable, on death,[16] under a life policy and excluded the value of an annuity, purchased from a life office, which ceased to be payable on the person's death. The exceptions include the termination on the death of any interest, such as a life interest in settled property, and the passing of any interest by survivorship, such as the interest of a joint tenant.[17]

By section 163(1), where by a contract made at any time the right to dispose of any property has been excluded or restricted, then, in determining the value of the property the exclusion or restriction is to be taken into account only to the extent (if any) that consideration in money or money's worth was given for it. Mutual arrangements between partners could reasonably contain sufficient commercial consideration.

The ordinary valuation rules may subsequently be adjusted in certain circumstances, summarised as follows:

a) When qualifying investments (shares or securities quoted on a recognised stock exchange etc) owned by a deceased person are sold within twelve months after his death and a loss is realised on such sale, such loss can be deducted from the value of his estate on death with the result that the IHT payable is recalculated by reference to the sale proceeds and not the value at the date of death: sections 178 to 189.
b) Similar relief is given in the case of land and interests in land sold within three years after death: sections 190 to 198.
c) The related property provisions are covered shortly[18] and can require a greater

---

15 See IR 1(1988) in respect of extra-statutory concessions, F6.
16 The valuation provisions of s 167 do *not* apply in the event of maturity on death; see sub-s (2).
17 S 171(2).
18 At H below.

value to be placed on a particular asset than its value when taken alone. The special rules are displaced and the actual sale proceeds can be substituted for the artificial value provided the sale takes place within three years after the death: section 176.

In the case of business and agricultural property, subject to the conditions being complied with, there are special reliefs under sections 103 to 114 and sections 115 to 124B respectively.[19]

G. Quick succession relief

Section 141 provides quick succession relief on death where the value of a person's estate was increased by a chargeable transfer ('the first transfer'), whether a lifetime transfer or one on death, made not more than five years before his death, irrespective of whether or not the property which resulted in that increase was then owned by the deceased.

The relief is an IHT credit against the IHT payable on the second chargeable transfer, being the one arising on death, under section 4(1). The IHT credit is a percentage, in accordance with the scale below, of the IHT paid on the first transfer. When the first transfer was part of a larger transfer, to the deceased and others, it is necessary to ascertain what proportion it bore to the total. It is also necessary to remember that IHT, on the first transfer, went to the Inland Revenue and accordingly did not increase the deceased's estate. If the estate taxable on death includes both free estate and settled property the benefit of the IHT credit needs to be apportioned between them.

The scale of relief is as follows:

Period between original transfer and subsequent death	Tax credit available on second transfer, as a percentage of the tax on the first transfer
One year or less	100%
Between one and two years	80%
Between two and three years	60%
Between three and four years	40%
Between four and five years	20%
More than five years	Nil%

H. Valuation of related property

Under section 161 regard has to be had to the principles of the valuation of 'related property'.[20] Such paragraph provides that where the value of any property comprised in a person's estate would be less than the appropriate portion of the value of the aggregate of that and any related property, it shall be treated as the appropriate portion of the value of that aggregate. This applies between husband and wife. For example, in the case of the valuation of their respective interests in the matrimonial home it does not matter for IHT purposes whether they are beneficially entitled as joint tenants or as tenants in common since the value of each interest will be

---

19 See the particular sub-chapters B and C of ch 4, p. 31 below.
20 Apart from s 161, property in a life tenant's estate and settled property in which he has a life interest are effectively related having regard to s 49(1) despite the fact that they are held under different titles.

the appropriate portion of the property's market value. It could well apply to their shares in private companies, their adjoining land and their collections or groups of chattels. It could also apply where husband and wife possess freehold and leasehold interests, or separate interests under a trust, in the same property. Related property also includes property which is or has been within the preceding five years either (i) the property of a charity, or held on charitable trusts only or (ii) the property of a body mentioned in sections 24, 25 or 26 (political parties, heritage bodies etc), and became so on a transfer of value which was made by him or his spouse after 15 April 1976 and was exempt to the extent that the value transferred was attributable to the property.

1. Liabilities

Liabilities are taken into account and deducted against a person's estate.[1] Except in the case of a liability imposed by law, a liability is only to be taken into account to the extent that it was incurred for a consideration in money or money's worth.[2] Where a debt or liability is secured on an asset, it is treated as reducing the value of that asset.[3] Accordingly for example, where agricultural property is charged any agricultural property relief available will be restricted to the net value of the property after deducting the amount of the charge. Reasonable funeral expenses may be deducted[4] and no account need be taken of any death grant paid.

Additionally the Finance Act 1986, section 103, contains rules to decide whether any particular debts (and incumbrances) incurred or created on or after 18 March 1986[5] can in fact be taken into account in determining the value of a person's estate immediately before their death for the purposes of section 5. Any such debt is abated in whole or in part if any part of the consideration for the debt was either (a) property derived from the deceased[6] (or property representing that property[7]) or (b) was given by any person among whose resources there was at any time property derived from the deceased.[8] In the case of both (a) and (b) property is not derived from the deceased where the deceased's disposition was not a transfer of value and not part of associated operations.[9] In the case of (a), because of the wide definition of property derived from the deceased,[7] it is not necessary for the deceased's disposition to have been made in favour of the creditor with whom the deceased's debt is incurred. In the case of (b), a debt is not disallowed to the extent that consideration for the debt exceeded the value of all property derived from the deceased.[10] Also, property derived from the deceased which has not been given to facilitating the creation of the debt is ignored.[11]

1 S 5(3).
2 S 5(5).
3 S 162(4).
4 S 172. The Inland Revenue have published a Statement of Practice, SP7/87, which expands the interpretation of the term 'reasonable funeral expenses' to include the cost of tombstone or gravestone. IR1 1988, Inland Revenue Extra-Statutory Concessions, at F1 states that a reasonable amount for mourning for the family and servants is allowed as a funeral expense.
5 Finance Act 1986, s 103(6).
6 Ibid, s 103(1)(a).
7 Ibid, s 103(3).
8 Ibid, s 103(1)(b).
9 Ibid, s 103(4).
10 Ibid, s 103(2)(a).
11 Ibid, s 103(2)(b).

Where a person in his lifetime discharges a debt which would otherwise be disallowed under the Finance Act 1986, section 103, he is treated as having made a PET equal in value to the money or money's worth so paid or applied.[12]

The conclusion to be drawn from these section 103 provisions is that persons should avoid borrowing from those to whom they have made or have in mind to make gifts.

J. Transitional provisions covering former spouse estate duty relief

Under pre 1975 estate duty law, duty was not paid in respect of settled property if duty had already been paid (or would have been but for the fact that it was sufficiently small) in respect of it since the date of the settlement, on the death of the other party to the marriage, unless the surviving spouse was at the time of his or her death or at any time during the continuance of the settlement competent to dispose of the settled property. Hence the popularity by persons of substance of limiting, under their wills, their spouses to a life/income interest which would, while not saving estate duty on their death, save estate duty on the spouse's subsequent death. Paragraph 2 of Schedule 6 carries forward into the IHT legislation the benefit of the former exemption under the Finance Act 1894, section 5(2), as modified by the Finance Act 1914, section 14(a), by providing that where one party to a marriage has died before 13 November 1974 and the other party dies after 12 March 1975 the potential estate duty exemption should have similar effect for IHT purposes, by leaving *out of account* the value of the relevant settled property.[13] In the light of *IRC v Coutts & Co*[14] the exemption also extends to any apportionment of income to the date of death whether or not under the Apportionment Act 1870 and to any dividend or interest payable after the death in respect of a period wholly within the deceased's lifetime. The effect of the exemption is that the value of the settled property is ignored in ascertaining the aggregable value of the other party's estate, being that of the surviving spouse, under section 4(1), for the purposes of IHT on death. It is thus non-aggregable with the free estate of the deceased's surviving spouse. Nevertheless, the settled property remains part of the estate under section 4(1); it is the value of it, not the settled property, which is left out of account. Accordingly, the settled property may be taken into account in valuing other property liable to IHT contained in the overall estate. That could, for example, include another fractional share in the same property or another parcel of shares in the same company where the value of the whole exceeds the value of the two shares or parcels, taken separately.

K. Chargeable transfers made within seven years prior to death

The above reference to chargeable transfers is to those which are chargeable when made in contrast to gifts which when made are not chargeable transfers but become so if the transferor does not survive their making by seven years.

Such chargeable transfers are of limited categories. The main one is a gift into a discretionary trust. A gift to a company or club is also such a chargeable transfer.

12 Ibid, s 103(6).
13 Sch 6, para 2.
14 [1964] AC 1393, [1963] 2 All ER 722.

If the transferor dies within seven years of making such a chargeable transfer, that transfer becomes taxable at the death rates then in force. The additional IHT is the difference between the tax due at the death rates and tax already paid which will have been at half death rates. The tax due at the death rates is calculated with the benefit of the rate scales in force at the time of death[15] and with the benefit of taper relief,[16] but not so as to reduce the tax already paid. Thus, there cannot be any repayment.[17]

L. Time for payment, instalments and interest

Under section 226(1), IHT on death is due six months after the end of the month in which the death occurs although it is the case that personal representatives without making payment cannot obtain a grant of representation.

Under sections 227 and 228 when on death IHT is payable in respect of:

  i) any land (including buildings)[18] whether freehold or leasehold and whether situated in the United Kingdom or abroad; or
 ii) shares or securities of a company which gave the deceased control[19] of the company immediately before his death; or
iii) unquoted shares or securities if the Board of Inland Revenue are satisfied that the IHT attributable to their value cannot be paid in one sum without undue hardship; or
 iv) unquoted shares or securities if the IHT on them and other instalment-option property is not less than 20% of the total IHT; or
  v) unquoted shares worth more than £20,000 which are not less than 10% of the company's share capital or, if they are ordinary shares, not less than 10% of the nominal value of the ordinary share capital; or
 vi) the net value of a business or an interest in a business, including a profession or vocation, but not a business carried on otherwise than for gain, such as a hobby. This does not include individual assets of a business as distinct from the business as a whole,

it may be paid, if the personal representatives so elect, by ten equal yearly instalments, the first instalment being due six months after the end of the month in which the death occurred. If the property is subsequently sold, the unpaid IHT becomes payable forthwith.[20]

There is, under section 229, a further category for payment of IHT by instalments in respect of woodlands and this is dealt with in sub-chapter E of chapter 4.

Under section 233 interest at present at 8% pa is payable on outstanding IHT.[1]

---

15 Sch 2, para 2.
16 S 7(4).
17 S 7(5).
18 Despite the equitable doctrine of conversion under which land held on trust for sale is treated as personalty, the Inland Revenue regard the land as being the particular asset.
19 S 269.
20 S 227(4).
 1 FA 1989, s 178 and SI 1989/1297 (the Taxes (Interest Rate) Regulations 1989) lay down the procedure and formulae for calculating revenue interest rates. Under an Order issued by the Inland Revenue on 19 April 1991 the rate of interest was 9%. By an Order issued on 28 June 1991 it became 8%. That rate was confirmed by the Order issued on 20 September 1991. In line with frequent changes in market rates, it is to be anticipated that the rate of interest will change frequently.

No income tax relief is available in respect of interest on overdue tax.[2] Under section 234 instalments are interest free, until they become due, for IHT in respect of:

a) shares or securities falling within categories (ii) to (v) above. Nevertheless shares in an investment or property company (whether a dealing or holding company) qualify only if either the company is primarily a holding company of companies which themselves are not investment or property companies or it is a market maker or discount house in the United Kingdom; or

b) a business or interest in a business falling within category (vi) above; or

c) land which qualifies for relief for agricultural property, in respect of which see sub-chapter C of chapter 4.

M. Accountability

Under section 200(1) the personal representatives are primarily accountable and liable for the payment of IHT on their deceased's free estate and in respect of land in the United Kingdom which was comprised in a settlement which devolves upon or vests in them. Under section 216 the personal representatives are required to deliver to the Board of Inland Revenue before the expiration of the period of twelve months from the end of the month in which the death occurs or, if it expires later, the period of three months beginning with the date on which they first act as such an account specifying to the best of their knowledge and belief all appropriate property and its value.[3] Nevertheless, under section 256(1)(a) the Board has power to make regulations dispensing with the delivery of accounts.[4]

Under section 226(2), the personal representatives are required on delivery of their account to pay all the tax for which they are liable. Section 109 of the Supreme Court Act 1981 stipulates that no grant of representation is to be made except on the production of an account showing by means of a prescribed form of receipt or certification that the IHT has been paid or none is payable.

Under section 204(1)(a) the liability of the personal representatives is limited to the assets received by them or which they might have received but for their own neglect or default. Thus, they may have some measure of protection such as in the case of a deceased's foreign property.

N. Miscellaneous exemptions

Sub-chapter C of this chapter deals with excluded property. There are also the following miscellaneous exemptions:

Section 152—where an annuity is payable to the deceased's widow, widower or dependant under an approved retirement annuity contract or trust scheme, and the deceased had an option to have a sum of money paid instead to his personal representatives, the deceased is not treated as having been beneficially entitled to that sum;

---

2 S 233(3).
3 S 216(6)(a).
4 See SI 1991/1248. These regulations which take on from earlier ones dispense with the need to deliver an account for IHT purposes on death where (subject to specified exceptions) the gross value of the deceased's estate does not exceed £125,000. This new limit applies from 1 July 1991 to estates of persons who died on or after 1 April 1991.

Section 153—certain overseas pensions;

Section 154—death as the result of active service.[5] There is no charge in the case of death when the person dies of a wound, accident or disease caused while on active service against an enemy or any other service of a warlike nature. The exemption applies to any member of the armed forces or various listed ancillary bodies. By concession there is similar relief for the estates of members of the Royal Ulster Constabulary who die from injuries caused in Northern Ireland by terrorist activity. It is for the Ministry of Defence to issue certificates in qualifying cases;

Section 157—certain non-residents' bank accounts;

Sections 158 and 159—these provide for double taxation and unilateral reliefs and are covered in chapter 10.

o. Benefits under superannuation schemes

The IHT exemptions in relation to benefits under approved pension schemes are covered under sections 151 and 152. Knowledge of a testator's pension and death in service benefits are important for reviewing his financial position and the benefits available for his family. The following guidance note was issued by the Capital Taxes Office in 1988.

'Inheritance Tax on benefits under superannuation schemes

These notes replace those that were issued to explain the practice of the Capital Taxes Office regarding liability to Capital Transfer Tax on benefits payable under the rules of employees' retirement benefits schemes and superannuation funds and under retirement annuity contracts and trust schemes approved under section 226/226A of the Taxes Act.

They outline the effect on such benefits of Inheritance Tax (IHT) introduced by the FA 1986 and refer in particular to section 151 of the IHTA 1984, as extended to approved personal pension arrangements by section 98(4) of the Finance (No 2) Act 1987.

(A) Payments to the deceased's legal personal representatives

(1) Payments that are legally due to the legal personal representatives, and cannot be withheld from them at the discretion of any person exercisable after the death, form part of the deceased's estate and are taxable as such (subject to any spouse exemption under section 18 of the IHTA 1984 having regard to the devolution of the deceased's estate under his will or intestacy). Payments made to the legal personal representatives in exercise of a discretion exercisable after the death are not treated as part of the deceased's estate for tax purposes on his death.

(2) Payments which are taxable as at (1) above are not regarded as property comprised in a settlement and where they are paid over to duly constituted legal personal representatives those representatives (not the trustees of the fund) are liable to tax. They should include the value of the payments in the personal representatives' account of the deceased's estate.

5 Although a case in connection with estate duty, *Barty-King v Ministry of Defence* [1979] 2 All ER 80, [1979] STC 218 gives useful guidance. See also observation about question 25 of form 9, p 160 below.

(3) Where payments are made to the duly constituted legal personal representatives, the person making them need not send a separate notification to the Capital Taxes Office.

(B) Where the deceased had a general power of nomination

(1) Where the deceased had a general power to nominate a benefit to anyone he wished and had not exercised his power irrevocably in his lifetime the benefit forms part of the estate for Inheritance Tax purposes and is taxable as such subject again to any "spouse" exemption under section 18.

(2) The legal personal representatives are liable for any tax.

(3) Where the deceased's power of nomination is restricted to a specified class of persons which does not include himself, failure to exercise the power irrevocably in his lifetime will not give rise to a tax liability on death unless under the rules of the fund or scheme the benefit then forms part of his estate.

(4) Where the deceased had at the time of his death an option to have a sum of money paid to his legal personal representatives, that sum of money will normally be taxed as part of his estate. Where however an annuity is payable to the deceased's widow, widower or dependant under a contract or trust scheme approved under sections 226 or 226A of the Taxes Act or (before the commencement of that Act) under section 22 of the Finance Act 1956 or under Chapter 11 of Part I of the Finance (No 2) Act 1987 and the deceased had an option to have a sum of money paid to his legal personal representative tax is not charged (section 152 of the Inheritance Tax Act 1984).

(C) Annuities which continue to be payable after the deceased's death

(1) Provided that the Scheme or Fund under which it is payable is one mentioned in sections 151(1) and 151(1A) of the IHTA 1984 a pension or annuity continuing after the deceased's death will not give rise to a tax liability in connection with his death unless the continuing pension or annuity results from the settlement or other application of a lump sum benefit (see s 151(2)(b)).

(2) If however the continuing pension or annuity is payable as of right to the deceased's legal personal representatives it will be taxable (see paragraph (A) above).

(D) Gratuitous transfers of value

(1) Inheritance Tax is not considered to be chargeable under section 3(1) of the IHTA 1984, as a gratuitous transfer of value, on the contributions (made either directly or by a reduction in the remuneration which he would otherwise have received) by a member to provide any benefit to another person payable under retirement benefit or superannuation schemes, trusts, contracts or arrangements the main or substantial object of which is to make provision for a person on his own retirement. (As to the surrender of part of the benefit to which the member would himself have been entitled see (E) below.)

(2) The statement in paragraph 1 above does not extend to any *separate* provision made by a member for his dependants or otherwise, for example under a group life insurance scheme operated in conjunction with superannuation arrangements, even if the scheme or other provision is arranged and administered by or in

co-operation with the employer. Nor does it extend to a contract under section 226A of the Taxes Act.

Premiums paid by the member on a policy on his life effected under a scheme of this kind or under such a contract may be chargeable to tax as gratuitous transfers of value although the transfers will commonly qualify for exemption under section 21 of the IHTA as normal expenditure out of income.

(3) In practice contributions (other than those provided as at (*E*)) payable under ordinary pension or superannuation schemes for members of the kind referred to in paragraph 1 above will automatically be regarded as covered by the statement in this paragraph if the scheme is one to which section 151 applies (see ss.151(1) and 151(1A)). The tax position of contributions to and benefits arising from any other scheme will be considered individually when a transfer of value, which is not a potentially exempt transfer, occurs.

(*E*) Dispositions by nominations or surrender of benefits

(1) Where
   (a) a member provides for a pension to another
      (i) by irrevocably surrendering part of his own pension, or
      (ii) by giving up a right to receive a lump sum (or part of it) payable to him on retirement or to his legal personal representatives on death
   or
   (b) he irrevocably nominates such a lump sum

he will prima facie have made a potentially exempt transfer if his disposition is after March 17, 1986; (prior to that, between March 26, 1974 and March 17, 1986, a prima facie chargeable transfer would have arisen). If the potentially exempt transfer subsequently becomes a chargeable transfer the value transferred will be determined by the "loss" to the member at the date the disposition is made and therefore will normally be less than the value of the pension or lump sum ultimately paid to the beneficiary.

A disposition of this nature could in appropriate circumstances be an exempt transfer under:
   (a) section 18 (Transfers between spouses)
   (b) section 19 (Values not exceeding £3,000)
   (c) section 20 (Small gifts to same person)
   (d) section 11 (Dispositions for maintenance of family)

(2) The *revocable* exercise of a power of nomination over a lump sum benefit will have the same Inheritance Tax consequences except that the disposition will be treated as taking effect at the latest time at which the member could have revoked his nomination (*e.g.* his retirement or his death).

(*F*) Termination of a pension or annuity

(1) Section 151 provides exemption on the termination on death or otherwise of a pension or annuity payable under a scheme or fund to which sections 151(1) or 151(1A) applies. For this purpose a pension payable without proportion to the date of death is regarded as terminating on the death.

(2) Section 151(2)(b) and 151(3) make it clear that the exemption does not apply to the termination of an interest under a trust of a *lump sum* benefit payable under a scheme or fund and section 58(2) and section 151(6) that it does not

extend to a discretionary payment made out of a benefit which, having become payable, becomes comprised in a settlement. If a lump sum benefit is settled (for example, in the exercise of discretionary powers as to the disposal of a death benefit) claims for tax may arise on the termination of an interest in possession under the settlement or, if there are no interests in possession in the settled property, on the various chargeable events described in Chapter III, Part III of the IHTA 1984.

(3) Where a lump sum benefit is converted into a pension under the rules of the scheme or fund then normally neither the conversion nor the cesser of that pension will give rise to a tax charge. If however the lump sum benefit is surrendered to provide a pension for some other person then paragraph (*E*) above will apply.

(G) Payments made in exercise of a discretion

Where a lump sum benefit payable under a scheme or fund within sections 151(1) or 151(1A) is distributed or settled in exercise of a discretion neither such distribution nor the making of a settlement will give rise to a liability to tax.

(H) Implications of the provisions on gifts with reservation

As explained in the Press Release of July 9, 1986 (now Statement of Practice 10/86), the provisions introduced by section 102 of the FA 1986 do not affect the former Estate Duty practice regarding gifts with reservation. Benefits under tax-approved superannuation arrangements that would have been exempt from capital transfer tax will also be exempt from inheritance tax even if they involve gifts with reservation.'

P. Accident insurance benefits

Enquiry should also be made of a testator whether his employers have effected an accident insurance policy which is available to provide benefits for himself or his dependants. The Revenue have made it clear that section 10(1) provides that there will not be a 'transfer of value' where the employer and employee are at arm's length and not connected with each other and where there is no intention to confer a gratuitous benefit. Where the employer and employee are connected there will be no liability if the payment was such as might reasonably be expected between non-connected persons. In many cases the payment will be covered by the exemption in section 12(1), as being allowable as a deduction in computing the taxable profits of a trade, profession or vocation, so that no question of an IHT liability can arise. If a payment not covered by section 12(1) is allowable for income tax or corporation tax purposes, the Revenue will accept that this of itself establishes that the requirements of section 10(1) are met.

Chapter 4
Inheritance tax exemptions and reliefs for works of art etc, business property, agricultural property and woodlands

A. Conditional exemption for works of art, historic buildings etc

Sections 30 to 35 provide a comprehensive code, under which conditional exemption from IHT can be obtained, in respect of transfers of what is conveniently described as heritage property which is designated by the Treasury as being of national interest etc.[1] Subject to what is said in the next paragraph, this legislation applies to both lifetime transfers and transfers on death, in particular testamentary gifts. It does not apply to a transfer of value to the extent to which it is an exempt transfer under sections 18 or 23 (gifts to spouses or charities),[2] and thus such a gift is ineligible for conditional exemption. If conditional exemption was given on an occasion before the gift to the spouse or charity it will be necessary for them to give a further undertaking otherwise there will be a chargeable event referable to the earlier occasion.

Despite this legislation applying to lifetime transfers as well as transfers on death, changes to section 30, introduced by the Finance Act 1986 in relation to potential exempt transfers (PETs), limits the possible application for conditional exemption in respect of lifetime transfers of heritage property. As sub-chapter B of chapter 5 explains, where there is a PET which in particular includes an absolute gift of property by an individual to another individual there is no IHT liability on the making of it and consistent with that, section 30(3B) provides that no claim for conditional exemption may be made under that section until the transferor has died. It follows that a possible claim for conditional exemption in respect of lifetime transfers is generally limited to gifts into a discretionary trust which is not an accumulation and maintenance trust[3] or to a company. Section 30(3C), in the event of the transferor not surviving the making of his PET by the period of seven years, precludes a claim for conditional exemption where during that period the gifted property has been disposed of by sale.

It will also be recognised, as explained in sub-chapter D of chapter 5, that gifted property subject to a reservation including a PET is treated as property to which the transferor was beneficially entitled immediately before his death and accordingly subject to the charge to IHT; and that equally applies where the gift, irrespective of when it was made, was one of heritage property.

To enable a claim for conditional exemption to be made for a transfer on death, there is no requirement that the deceased owned the particular asset for a minimum period.

Where there is a lifetime transfer which is not a PET or a PET where the transferor

---

1 The Inland Revenue have issued a useful booklet 'Capital Taxation and The National Heritage' (IR 67). 'How to make a claim' (IR 88) can be obtained from the Capital Taxes Office.
2 S 30(4)
3 Thus complying with the conditions of s 71.

dies within the next seven years or a transfer of gifted property subject to a reservation or where the reservation or benefit is given up within seven years of death, exemption can be claimed only if:[4]

    i) the transferor (or his spouse or the two of them together) have been beneficially entitled to the property for at least six years preceding the transfer: or

    ii) the transferor acquired the property on a death upon which it was conditionally exempt from IHT or capital transfer tax.

By the Finance Act 1985, section 95, the Board of Inland Revenue took over responsibilities of the Treasury for capital tax reliefs with effect from 25 July 1985. Hence, there will be references to the Board rather than to the Treasury where the latter is referred to in the legislation.

Conditional exemption can apply as the result of the Board's designation[5] of the following categories of assets:[6]

    a) any pictures, prints, books, manuscripts, works of art, scientific collections or other things not yielding income which appear to the Board to be of national,[7] scientific, historic or artistic interest;

    b) any land (as opposed to the buildings erected on the land unless they qualify, on their own merits, under the next category) which in the opinion of the Board is of outstanding scenic or historic or scientific interest;[8]

    c) any building for the preservation of which special steps should in the Board's opinion be taken because of its outstanding historic or architectural interest;

    d) any adjoining land which in the Board's opinion is essential for the protection of the building's character and its amenities; and

    e) any object which in the Board's opinion is historically associated with the building.

The conditions require a claim to be made[9] and an indemnity to be given by such person as the Board thinks appropriate in the circumstances.[10] When the object is within category (a) above the required undertaking[11] is that until the person beneficially entitled to it dies or it is disposed of, whether by sale or gift or otherwise:

    i) it will be kept permanently in the United Kingdom and will not leave it temporarily except for a purpose and a period approved by the Board; and

    ii) such steps as are agreed between the Board and the person giving the undertaking, and are set out in it, will be taken for the preservation of the object and for securing reasonable access to the public.

In the exceptional case, when documents under category (a) contain information which for personal or other reasons ought to be treated as confidential the Board may exclude those documents from the public access requirements.[12]

Where the asset is within categories (b), (c), (d) or (e) above the required

---

4 S 30(3).

5 S 31(1A) provides that when the transfer in relation to which the claim for designation is made is a PET which has proved to be a chargeable transfer, the question whether any property is appropriate for designation shall be determined by reference to circumstances existing after the death of the transferor.

6 S 31(1).

7 S 31(5).

8 This can include horticultural, arboricultural or silvicultural interest.

9 S 30(1)(a).

10 S 30(1)(b).

11 S 31(2).

12 S 31(3).

undertaking[13] is that, until the person beneficially entitled to it dies or it is disposed of, whether by sale or gift or otherwise, such steps as are agreed between the Board and the person giving the undertaking and are set out in it will be taken—

i) in the case of land within category (b) above, for the maintenance of the land and the preservation of its character, and

ii) in the case of any other property, for the maintenance, repair and preservation of the property and, if it is an object falling within category (e) above, for keeping it associated with the building concerned,

and for securing reasonable access to the public.

In the case of amenity land within category (d) above, additionally 'supportive undertakings' must be given[14] in respect of:

i) the building whose character and amenities the land protects;

ii) any other qualifying essential amenity land which lies between the building and the land for which exemption is sought; and

iii) any other qualifying essential amenity land which, in the opinion of the Board, is physically closely connected with either the claimed area of land or the outstanding building.

On death, it is understood to be the practice of the Board to accept an undertaking initially from the personal representatives who are requested to report subsequently when exempted items have been allocated to the beneficiaries who can then give their own undertakings, consequently enabling the personal representatives to be released from theirs. Where the personal representatives seek conditional exemption, the IHT self-assessment arrangements cannot be used and accordingly the IHT account form needs to be delivered to and assessed by the Capital Taxes Office before application for probate can be made.[15]

IHT becomes payable on conditionally exempted property if a chargeable event occurs.[16] Such event occurs if:

a) the undertakings are broken in any material respect;[17]

b) the property is disposed of in any way[18] other than as follows:

i) the ownership passes on *death* and the transfer is itself conditionally exempt (that is that the undertakings previously given are renewed by the new owner);[19]

ii) the disposal is a *lifetime* transfer and the undertakings previously given are renewed;

iii) the disposal is a bequest or gift which is exempt from IHT under some other provision such as exemptions for transfers between spouses or for transfers to charities or to bodies within section 26, provided that the undertakings previously given are renewed by the new owner;

iv) the property is bequeathed, given or sold by private treaty to a body listed in Schedule 3 to the 1984 Act;[20]

v) the property is offered and accepted in lieu of IHT.[1]

---

13 S 31(4).
14 S 31(4A) etc.
15 See statement in *Law Society's Gazette* September 1970, p 605.
16 S 32(1).
17 S 32(2).
18 S 32(3).
19 S 32(5).
20 S 32(4)(a).
 1 S 32(4)(b).

Section 207 contains details of the persons liable for the payment of IHT when there is a chargeable event under section 32 in relation to conditionally exempt property.

Once conditional exemption has been obtained a subsequent gift of conditionally exempt property, either during lifetime or on death, on which conditional exemption is *not* claimed will result in two charges to IHT. The first will be under section 32 as 'a chargeable event'. The second will be under the general IHT chargeable provisions relating to gifts and transfers generally; here IHT is payable in the normal way by reference to the circumstances of the transferor at the time of the gift. The IHT payable on the latter will be allowed as a credit against the IHT payable in respect of the chargeable event.[2] If the chargeable event is also the occasion of a capital gains tax charge under the Capital Gains Tax Act 1979, section 147, the amount on which IHT is chargeable is reduced by the capital gains tax payable.

The amount of the IHT, when there has been a chargeable event under section 32, is governed by section 33. It is based on the value of the property at *that* time[3] and at the following rate(s) of tax:[4]

i) If the relevant transferor is alive, the rate(s) that would be applicable to that amount in accordance with section 7(2) (that is at lifetime being one-half of normal rate(s) in Schedule 1) if it were the value transferred by a chargeable event at *that* time. Nevertheless, any earlier PETs made by the relevant transferor are left out of account and the charge is not revised if those earlier PETs later prove to be chargeable because that person dies within seven years after making them.[5]

ii) If the relevant transferor is dead, but his transfer was a lifetime transfer, then the same lifetime rate(s) still apply but are those which would have been applicable if the amount had been added to and formed the highest part of the value transferred on his death. However, if the relevant transferor's transfer was on his death, then the amount is likewise added as a top slice and the normal rate(s) on death apply.[6]

The relevant transferor is identified under section 33(5), as follows:

a) if there has been only one conditionally exempt transfer before the chargeable event, he is the person who made it;

b) if there have been two or more and the last one was before, or only one of them was within, the period of thirty years ending with the chargeable event, he is the person who made the last of those transfers;

c) if there have been two or more transfers within such thirty-year period, he is that person who made whichever of those transfers the Revenue may select.[7] In this case, the effect of section 34 may mean that the relevant transferor whose figures are used, for calculating the IHT liability, is not the same person as the last transferor whose cumulative total is adjusted upwards.

There is a clearing of the slate each time a chargeable event occurs,[8] because no conditionally exempt transfer is considered if it occurred, even within the thirty-

2 S 33(7)(a).
3 S 33(1)(a).
4 S 33(1)(b).
5 S 33(1)(b)(i).
6 S 33(2)(a).
7 It has been stated that selection will be on the basis of greatest yield to the Exchequer.
8 S 33(6).

year period, before a previous chargeable event, or before a transfer to a Schedule 3 body or the property is accepted in satisfaction of IHT.

This legislation only has effect in respect of transfers of value made after 6 April 1976.[9] It will not in general affect the treatment of property left out of account for estate duty by virtue of the Finance Act 1930, section 40, as amended,[10] or under the Finance Act 1975, sections 31 to 34,[11] unless and until a conditionally exempt transfer is made under the new provisions. The legislation ensures that on the sale of an object left out of account for estate duty the charge will not be negated by an intervening transfer on death after 6 April 1976, for which conditional exemption does not run.[12]

If heritage property is held in a trust under which there is an interest in possession, conditional exemption may be claimed on the same terms as for heritage property owned absolutely, on the death of the person with the interest in possession or when that interest otherwise ceases.

If heritage property is held upon trusts in which there is no interest in possession, thus a discretionary trust, exemption may be claimed when it ceases to be held on those trusts, such as when it is distributed to a beneficiary or when an interest in possession is created over it, provided that the heritage property has been held by the trustees for at least six years.[13] If heritage property which is held upon no interest in possession trusts was conditionally exempt on or before the time when it became settled there will be exemption from the ten-year anniversary charge under section 64. If such property has not previously enjoyed conditional exemption, because, for example, the trustees themselves bought it, it may nevertheless be exempted from the ten-year anniversary charge if a claim is made and the undertakings are given *before* the time of that charge. But in that case a tapered flat rate charge will apply if a chargeable event subsequently occurs.[14]

Exemption from IHT may be claimed for a transfer to a settlement established for the maintenance of an outstanding historic building (and its amenity land and historically associated objects) or land of outstanding scenic, scientific or historic interest provided that the settlement meets certain conditions.[15] The settlement is then also exempt from the ten-year anniversary charge and the proportionate charge but charges may arise if the property ceases to be held on maintenance fund trusts.[16] Relief from higher rates of income tax can also be claimed for the income of the settlement. Capital gains tax may be deferred when heritage property is transferred to and out of the settlement.

B. Relief for business property

As the result of sections 113A and 113B, introduced by the Finance Act 1986, for IHT business property relief to apply, not only are there statutory conditions to

9 S 35.
10 Applicable to deaths prior to 15 March 1975.
11 Covers death during the period 13 March 1975 to 6 April 1976 but only if the transfer was in fact made on death.
12 Sch 6, para 4(4).
13 S 78.
14 S 79.
15 Sch 4, Part I.
16 Sch 4, Parts II and III.

be met at the time the transfer of value is made but also there are statutory conditions to be met at the time the transferor dies should he not survive his gift by seven years. These additional conditions are dealt with at the end of this sub-chapter.

It is to be recognised that section 3A likewise introduced by the Finance Act 1986 and amended by the Finance (No 2) Act 1987, has limited the effect of IHT and therefore of business property relief in respect of lifetime gifts. As sub-chapter B of chapter 5 explains, where there is a PET, which in brief means an absolute gift of property by one individual to another individual or into a trust other than one without an interest in possession, there is no IHT liability on the making of it and that will remain so unless the transferor dies during the following period of seven years. Where the donor dies during that period but survives the making of his gift by three, four, five or six years the IHT liability otherwise to be paid on the resultant chargeable transfer is reduced by 20%, 40%, 60% or 80% respectively.

Sections 103 to 114 deal with IHT relief for business property. Where the whole or part of the value transferred by a transfer of value is attributable to the value of any relevant business property, the whole or that part of the value transferred is treated as reduced by an appropriate percentage.[17]

Relevant business property,[18] subject to the other conditions including period of ownership, together with the appropriate percentage of relief means:

a) property consisting of an unincorporated business or an interest in one, thus including a partner's interest in a partnership (50%);

b) shares or securities of any company which (either by themselves or together with other shares or securities owned by him) gave the transferor control[19] of the company immediately before the transfer (50%);

bb) unquoted shares in a company which do not fall within paragraph (b) above and which immediately before the transfer and throughout the two years immediately preceding the transfer[20] (either by themselves or together with other shares or securities owned by him) gave the transferor control of powers of voting on all questions affecting the company as a whole which if exercised would have yielded more than 25% of the votes capable of being exercised on them (and shares which are 'related property' can be taken into account) (50%);

c) unquoted shares in a company which do not fall within paragraphs (b) or (bb) above (30%);

d) land, buildings, machinery or plant owned by a partner or controlling shareholder and used wholly or mainly in the business of the partnership or company immediately before the transfer, provided that the partnership interest or shareholding would itself, if it were transferred, qualify for business relief[1] (30%);

e) land, buildings, machinery or plant which immediately before the transfer was used wholly or mainly for the purposes of a business carried on by the transferor, was settled property in which he was then beneficially entitled to an interest in possession and was transferred while the business itself was being retained[1] (30%).

---

17 S 104(1).
18 S 105(1).
19 S 269.
20 S 109A.
 1 S 105(6).

'Business', for the foregoing purposes, includes a business carried on in the exercise of a profession or vocation, except one not carried on for gain.[2]

Investment and property dealing organisations and those holding investments, including land which is let, are excluded from the relief:[3] but there are exceptions in the case of market makers and discount houses in the United Kingdom and where property consists of shares in or securities of a company whose whole or main business is being a holding company of one or more companies the business of which is not dealing in securities and the other mentioned items, nor making or holding investments.[4] The relief is *not* confined to manufacturing and industry. It applies to professional assets including goodwill. As the relief applies to business assets generally, and not solely to land, buildings, machinery and plant, it covers stock-in-trade. There is no requirement that the business must be carried on in the United Kingdom.

Property is not 'relevant business property' qualifying for this relief unless:[5]
 a) owned by the transferor throughout the two years immediately preceding the transfer; or
 b) it replaced other property and it, the other property, and any property directly or indirectly replaced by the other property were owned by the transferor for periods which together comprised at least two years falling within the five years immediately preceding the transfer of value. In the latter respect the other property must itself have been suitable for being relevant business property.

In the case of relevant business property which is inherited it is treated as being owned from the date of death.[6] When such property passed to a surviving spouse, the period of ownership of the latter includes that of the deceased spouse.[7]

Nevertheless, there is an exception,[8] to the requirement of the two-year period of ownership, in the case of premature death. Relief will be given when:
 a) the transferor and his or her spouse acquired the relevant business property by a transfer on which relief was, or would have been due; and
 b) either the earlier transfer or the present transfer took place on death.

The relief is not available where the asset is not used wholly or mainly for business during the last two years or is not required at the time of the transfer for future business use.[9] It is also not available when the asset has been used wholly or mainly for the personal benefit of the transferor or of a person connected with him.[10]

As in the case of agricultural property, it is not necessary to elect for this relief to apply. It is mandatory, and accordingly is to be granted by the Revenue whether or not a claim is made. There are, however, provisions for the avoidance of double relief, where there is agricultural property[11] or woodlands.[12]

In the case of an unincorporated business, the value is the net value of the business

2 S 103(3).
3 S 105(3).
4 S 105(4).
5 Ss 106 and 107.
6 S 108(a).
7 S 108(b).
8 S 109.
9 S 112(2).
10 S 112(6).
11 S 114(1).
12 S 114(2).

or the interest in it, being the value of the assets used in the business, including goodwill, less the business liabilities.[13] In the case of the value of shares and securities the normal open market principle, for IHT purposes, applies. Where these are unquoted it is assumed that there is available to a prospective purchaser all the information which a prudent prospective purchaser might reasonably require if he were proposing to purchase from a willing vendor by private treaty and at arm's length.[14]

There are conditions in section 113A covering the case of a chargeable transfer which was initially a PET. Where any part of the value transferred was in fact a PET but then proves to be a chargeable transfer, because the transferor dies during the period of seven years following the making of his gift, business property relief otherwise available does not apply unless first the originally gifted property is owned by the beneficiary of it at the death of the transferor[15] or owned by the beneficiary at the time of the beneficiary's earlier death *and* secondly the beneficiary himself would have obtained business property relief were he to have made a transfer of value of it at the time of the foregoing death but without the requirement, under section 106, of two years' length of ownership on the part of the beneficiary.[16] If these further conditions are satisfied only with respect of part of the originally gifted property, the availability of business relief is proportionate.[17]

Section 113B applies the foregoing provisions of section 113A to replacement property. Replacement property is only to be taken into account if it is acquired by the reinvestment within twelve months of the entire proceeds of the disposal of any part of the originally gifted property and both the disposal and the acquisition are made on arm's length terms.[18]

c. Relief for agricultural property

As the result of sections 124A and 124B, introduced by the Finance Act 1986, for IHT agricultural property relief to apply not only are there statutory conditions to be met at the time the transfer of value is made but also there are statutory conditions to be met at the time the transferor dies should he not survive his gift by seven years. These additional conditions are dealt with at the end of this sub-chapter. They are similar but not the same as those in the case of business property relief, discussed in sub-chapter B.

It is to be recognised that section 3A, likewise introduced by the Finance Act 1986 and amended by the Finance (No 2) Act 1987 has limited the effect of IHT and therefore of agricultural property relief in respect of lifetime gifts. As sub-chapter B of chapter 5 explains, where there is a PET, which in brief means an absolute gift of property by one individual to another individual or into a trust other than one without an interest in possession, there is no IHT liability on the making of it and that will remain so unless the transferor dies during the following period of seven years. Where the donor dies during that period but survives the making of his gift by three, four, five or six years the IHT liability otherwise to be paid

13 S 110.
14 S 168.
15 S 113A(3)(a).
16 S 113A(3)(b).
17 S 113A(5).
18 S 113B(2).

on the resultant chargeable transfer is reduced by 20%, 40%, 60% or 80% respectively.

Sections 115 to 124B deal with IHT relief for agricultural property. Where the whole or part of the value transferred by a transfer of value is attributable to the agricultural value[19] of agricultural property,[20] the whole or that part of the value transferred is treated as reduced by an appropriate percentage.[1]

To enable the relief to apply there must have been a minimum period of ownership or occupation of the agricultural property by the transferor viz:

a) *Occupation* for the purposes of agriculture throughout the period of two years ending with the date of transfer,[2] or

b) *Ownership* by him throughout the period of seven years ending with the date of the transfer *and* that it was throughout that period *occupied* (by him or another) for the purposes of agriculture.[3]

The appropriate percentage of the relief is 50% where the interest of the transferor in the property immediately before the transfer carries the right to vacant possession of the agricultural property or the right to obtain it within the next twelve months.[4] In all other cases the relief is 30%.[5] The latter relief will thus be available in respect of the ownership of agricultural property subject to a tenancy.

In the case of agricultural property which is replaced, briefly the original property and any replacement property must have been occupied by the transferor for agricultural purposes for at least two out of the preceding five years or, in the case of tenanted property, owned for at least seven out of the preceding ten years.[6]

Occupation by a company is treated as occupation by the transferor if the company is controlled[7] by the transferor.[8] The conditions of two-year occupation or seven-year ownership need to be satisfied by the company, *and* the transferor must have owned the shares throughout the same period.[9]

Occupation by a partner should, it would seem, not present any problems as each partner can qualify for the appropriate relief regardless of the size of his interest.

Where a transferor became entitled to agricultural property on the death of another person, his period of ownership (and his period of occupation if he subsequently occupies it) is regarded as beginning on the date of that death.[10] Where the other person was the transferor's spouse, the spouse's period of occupation or ownership can be added to that of the transferor.[11]

Where there has been a transfer under which the transferor did or could have qualified for relief and the transferee makes a subsequent transfer within a two-year period or seven-year period and one or both of the transfers were on death, the two-year period of ownership or seven-year period of occupation is waived. The

19 S 115(3).
20 S 115(2).
 1 S 116(1).
 2 S 117(a).
 3 S 117(b).
 4 S 116(2)(b). There is in fact a second alternative, where the transferor has been beneficially entitled to the interest before 10 March 1981 and the conditions in s 116(3) are satisfied.
 5 S 116(2).
 6 S 118(1), (2).
 7 S 269 defines the circumstances when a person has control of a company.
 8 S 119(1).
 9 S 123(1).
10 S 120(1)(a).
11 S 120(1)(b).

property must have been occupied for agricultural purposes either by the second transferor or by the personal representatives of the first transferor.[12]

Section 16(1) states that the grant of a tenancy of agricultural property in the United Kingdom, the Channel Islands or the Isle of Man for use for agricultural purposes is not a transfer of value by the grantor if he makes it for full consideration in money or money's worth. As a result, it is not necessary in those circumstances to rely on section 10(1) to avoid a charge to IHT, notwithstanding that the grant of the tenancy will inevitably reduce the value of the interest of the grantor, being the freeholder. Nevertheless, the 'associated operations' rule would apply should there be a gift of the reversion within three years[13] or a release in respect of the rent within three years of the grant of the tenancy, or, even outside the period of three years, if the grant was not made for full consideration in money or money's worth. If that rule applies then the full value of the property will be chargeable to IHT with the agricultural relief limited to 30% because of the existence of the tenancy.

It is to be accepted that if a farmer grants a tenancy of his farm to a partnership of which he is a member, while this will reduce the value of the freehold of his farm, for IHT purposes he will qualify for the 30% relief only.

Section 169(1) provides a general restriction in respect of the value of agricultural property which includes cottages occupied by workers employed thereon. No account is to be taken of the fact that the cottages are suitable for residential purposes by persons not so employed.

As in the case of business property relief, it is not necessary to elect for agricultural property relief to apply. It is mandatory, and accordingly is to be granted by the Revenue whether or not a claim is made. Where the conditions for both agricultural property relief and business property relief are satisfied, the former is given.

When there is a loan, for example, on formal mortgage or securing a bank overdraft, charged on agricultural property, the amount will reduce the value of the encumbered property.[14] Accordingly if there is a charge to IHT on agricultural property the value of it for the purposes of agricultural property relief will be correspondingly reduced. An owner should consider charging other property instead, if necessary in priority to any secondary charge over his agricultural property.

There are conditions in section 124A covering the case of a chargeable transfer which was initially a PET. Where any part of the value transferred was in fact a PET but then proves to be a chargeable transfer, because the transferor dies during the period of seven years following the making of his gift, agricultural property relief otherwise available does not apply unless: first, the originally gifted property is owned by the beneficiary throughout the period beginning with the date of the chargeable transfer and ending with the death of the transferor ('the relevant period') and it is not at the time of death subject to a binding contract for sale;[15] *and* secondly (except where the third condition applies) the originally gifted property is agricultural property immediately before the death and has been occupied (by the beneficiary or another) for the purposes of agriculture throughout the relevant period;[16] *and* thirdly where the originally gifted property consists of shares in or securities of

12 S 121(1).
13 Compare s 268(2).
14 S 162(4).
15 S 124A(3)(a).
16 S 124A(3)(b).

Event	IHT payable on	Business relief available	Instalment option available
5. Partnership continues and partnership share falls into deceased's estate but partnership agreement provides obligation for executors to sell and for surviving partners to buy partnership share either at valuation or in accordance with formula.	Value of partnership interest (normally calculated in accordance with valuation or formula).	No.	No.

E. Relief for non-agricultural woodlands

Sections 125 to 130 give IHT relief for non-agricultural woodlands. Where any part of the value of a person's estate *immediately before his death* is attributable to the value of land in the United Kingdom on which trees or underwood are growing but which is not agricultural property,[2] and the stated condition is satisfied, then if the person liable for the IHT so elects, by written notice to the Revenue, within two years of the death or such longer period as may be allowed, the value of the trees or underwood is left out of account.[3] IHT, nevertheless, will be payable on the value of the land itself.

The stated condition is that the deceased was beneficially entitled to the land, or to an interest in possession in it,[4] throughout the five years before his death or became beneficially entitled to it otherwise than for a consideration in money or money's worth.[5] Accordingly the land must not have been bought by the deceased within five years of his death.

Where the value of the trees or underwood has been so left out of account, on the death of a person, IHT becomes chargeable on any disposal, but not between spouses, on the following basis:

a) if the disposal is a sale for full consideration in money or money's worth, on the net proceeds of sale; and

b) in any other case, on the net value, at the time of disposal, of the trees or underwood.

The IHT rates are those that would have been chargeable on the death if that amount so calculated had been included at the time of death and had formed the highest part of the deceased person's estate.[6]

In order to arrive at the net proceeds of sale, expenses are deductible except to the extent that they are allowable for the purpose of income tax.[7] Such expenses are those incurred as follows:

a) in disposing of the trees or underwood;

---

2 Within the meaning of Ch II of Part V.
3 S 125(2).
4 See s 49.
5 S 125(1)(b).
6 S 128.
7 S 130(1)(b).

    b) in replanting, within three years of a disposal or such longer time as the Revenue may allow, to replace the trees or underwood disposed of; and

    c) the expenses incurred in replanting to replace trees or underwood previously disposed of so far as not allowable on the previous disposal.[8] 8 S 130(2).

Where a disposal of trees or underwood takes place which is itself a chargeable transfer, because for example it is a gift, and where deferment was obtained on the immediately preceding death there would be a double charge to IHT. In that event the value of the trees or underwood transferred on the current chargeable transfer will be reduced by the IHT chargeable following from the deferment.[9] In such a case the deferred IHT is payable in one sum but the IHT on the lifetime transfer may, if the taxpayer so elects, be paid at his option by ten equal yearly instalments, of which the first is payable six months after the end of the month in which the transfer is made and payment by instalments does not cease if the trees or underwood are sold later.[10] Instalments are interest-free if paid on time.

The person liable for IHT is the person who is entitled to the proceeds of sale or would be so entitled if the disposal were a sale.[11]

The Finance Act 1986, paragraph 46 of Schedule 19, denies potentially exempt transfer treatment for IHT purposes, under the Inheritance Tax Act 1984, section 3A, to all property comprised in a single transfer any part of which, however small, is woodlands subject to a deferred estate duty charge. By concession, announced by the Inland Revenue on 5 December 1990, the scope of paragraph 46 is thenceforth restricted solely to that part of the value transferred which is attributable to the woodlands which are the subject of the deferred charge.

It will be recognised that as growing trees have an appreciating value, apart from any occasioned by general price rises, it may in some circumstances prove better to pay IHT on death, in the usual way, rather than to elect for deferment. Where a woodland is run as a genuine commercial business, the full value of the business or interest in the business (including standing timber and land) would qualify for the 50% business relief under sections 103 to 114 provided that the relevant conditions are met.

8 S 130(2).
9 S 129.
10 S 229.
11 S 208.

Chapter 5
Inheritance tax on lifetime gifts, availability of potentially exempt transfers and exemptions and property subject to a reservation

A. Introduction and the principles of IHT

During the course of the making of a will, depending on the amount and nature of the testator's assets, it may become evident that the will, though itself an important part of any tax planning arrangements, may also give an opportunity for considering what can be done to mitigate the aggregate amount of the potential IHT liabilities on his death and that of his wife. The amendments to the 1984 Act brought about by the Finance Act 1986 (and the Finance (No 2) Act 1987), particularly in introducing by section 3A[1] potentially exempt transfers ('PETs'), give greater scope than previously for mitigating the impact of IHT, in the case of persons of means and with families. The matter of PETs and the required conditions are described in the next sub-chapter. Subject to the making of PETs which by definition are not initially chargeable transfers, the pattern of the IHT legislation is that lifetime transfers of value by a transferor, unless they are exempt transfers or dispositions of excluded property or dispositions stated not to be transfers of value, and thus are chargeable transfers, give rise to a charge to IHT on a cumulative basis starting with a nil% band for amounts or values of up to £140,000[2] (this figure for the period to 5 April 1992 is subject to annual adjustment as mentioned in the next paragraph), and thereafter the rate is 20% for lifetime chargeable transfers irrespective of the amounts or values over £140,000.[2] Again, subject to the implications of PETs, the calculation of IHT on each additional chargeable transfer commences in the table at the point where the aggregate of the values of earlier chargeable transfers, made during the prior seven years, ended.[3]

By section 8, each 6 April the IHT rate bands, in relation to their respective percentage rates, are increased in line with the increase in the retail prices index over the year leading to the previous December. If the resultant figure is not a multiple of £1,000, it is to be rounded up. This is subject to Parliament's overriding right to determine otherwise.[4] Before each 6 April, the Treasury is required, by statutory instrument, to make an order specifying the amounts in the table in Schedule I, in relation to the respective IHT percentage rates, that are to apply thereafter.[5] The 1991 Order is the Inheritance Tax (Indexation) Order 1991 (SI 1991/735). IHT on a lifetime chargeable transfer, which is immediately liable to a payment of IHT in contrast to a PET, is charged to IHT at one-half of the rates in the table.[6]

---

1 S 3A was inserted into the 1984 Act by FA 1986, Sch 19, para 1.
2 Sch 1 contains the table of rates of IHT. By FA 1988 the IHT rate bands were reduced to two and are now as mentioned in the text.
3 S 7(1)(b).
4 S 8(1).
5 S 8(4).
6 S 7(2).

B. PETs

Under section 3A, for a gift which is not an exempt transfer[7] to qualify as a PET, therefore not initially being a chargeable transfer, it needs to be a gift by an individual, on or after 18 March 1986, to another individual or into an accumulation and maintenance trust or into a disabled trust. As the result of amendments to section 3A by the Finance (No 2) Act 1987, section 96, with effect from 17 March 1987 a gift into a trust under which another individual has a beneficial interest in possession can also qualify as a PET. Likewise, on or after 17 March 1987 there is no immediate lifetime charge to IHT on a disposal or termination of an individual's beneficial interest in trust property, thus also constituting a PET, if on that event another individual became beneficially entitled to the trust property in which the interest subsisted or to an interest in possession in that trust property, or that trust property becomes subject to an accumulation and maintenance trust or trust for the disabled.[8]

A PET also includes a transfer for the benefit of an individual, but not in the case of an accumulation and maintenance trust or a disabled trust, whereby although no property in fact passes direct from the donor to the beneficiary the estate of the beneficiary is increased in value. Accordingly, for example, the discharge by the donor of a debt which is owed by the beneficiary to a third party will constitute a PET. Such provisions equally apply, on or after 17 March 1987, where the transfer increases the value of trust property in which another individual has a beneficial interest in possession or, as a result of a disposal or termination of an individual's beneficial interest in trust property, where another individual's estate is increased.[9]

On the making of the PET there is no IHT liability; nor does its making affect the donor's cumulative total of chargeable transfers. It is assumed that the gift, despite being a transfer of value, will prove to be an exempt transfer. If the donor survives his gift by seven years, its status as an exempt transfer is confirmed. If, however, he dies during that period of seven years, the PET becomes and is therefore treated as being a chargeable transfer. The value transferred, for the purposes of assessing the IHT liability at the death rates at the time of death, is the value of the transfer for IHT purposes when the gift was made. Nevertheless, where the donor survives his gift by three years the amount of the IHT liability (not the value of the gift) is tapered. Thus, if the death occurs between three and four years after the making of the former PET, the percentage reduction of the IHT otherwise to be charged is 20%, between four and five years it is 40%, between five and six years it is 60% and between six and seven years it is 80%.[10]

It is accepted[11] that where the estate of the donor is reduced as the result of the transfer of value by a greater amount than the increase in the estate of the beneficiary the whole gift qualifies as a PET. For example: A owns 51% of the shares in X Ltd. He makes a gift of 2% to B. The PET exemption relates to the reduction in value of A's estate from a 51% holding to 49% which also loses him control of the company and not only to the value of the gifted 2% holding received by B.

---

7 S 3A(1)(b) in fact describes such a transfer as one which, apart from this section, would be a chargeable transfer.

8 S 3A(7).

9 It would also include the case where the individual enjoys an interest in possession in a trust.

10 S 7(4).

11 See, for example, paras 2.12 and 2.13 of IHT 1 issued by the Board of Inland Revenue in January 1991.

As already mentioned, section 96 of the Finance (No 2) Act 1987 amended section 3A to enable a PET to be made, on or after 17 March 1987, by way of such a gift to an interest in possession trust. Section 96 and Schedule 7 to that Act amended the Inheritance Tax Act 1984, in particular by the additions of sections 54A and 54B. The purpose of those amendments is to counter IHT advantages which might otherwise be obtained by channelling transfers to discretionary trusts through short-term interest in possession trusts.

c. Direct and indirect effects of death of donor of a PET

Where the donor of a PET dies during the period of seven years following the making of it there are several direct and indirect effects.

In those circumstances the PET becomes, and is therefore treated as being, a chargeable transfer. The value transferred for the purposes of assessing the IHT liability at the death rates at the time of death is the value of the transfer for IHT purposes when the gift was made, although if the value of the gifted property for IHT purposes has decreased since the date of the transfer relief will in certain circumstances be available unless the property was a wasting asset.[12] Where the donor survived the making of his gift by three years *the amount of IHT charged* is tapered by a reduction of 20%, 40%, 60% or 80% according to whether the donor survived three, four, five or six years. It is to be emphasised that this taper relief cannot affect the cumulative value or total for the purposes of calculating or recalculating the IHT liability on subsequent lifetime chargeable transfers including other former PETs and the transfer deemed to be made immediately before the donor's death.

To calculate the IHT liability on a PET becoming a chargeable transfer as the result of the death of the donor during the period of seven years following its making it is necessary to take into account, for the purposes of arriving at the donor's cumulative total of chargeable transfers including earlier former PETs, the aggregate value of those made during the period of seven years *prior* to the making of the particular PET.

The beneficiary of a PET is primarily liable for the IHT which becomes due because of the death of the donor within the period of seven years following its making. There are circumstances where the personal representatives of the deceased donor can become liable for the IHT payment.

Under sections 199(1) and (2) and 205 the beneficiary and the personal representatives of the donor are each liable for the IHT. Nevertheless by section 204(8)(b) the liability of the personal representatives is limited to the extent that the IHT remains unpaid twelve months after the end of the month in which the death of the donor occurs. When making a PET it is sensible that the donor and the beneficiary should recognise the position, in the interests of everyone. The beneficiary should consider the need to effect seven-year term insurance on the life of the donor at a reducing figure which takes into account the benefit of taper relief. Additionally, as a condition of the making of the PET, the donor may well consider it proper to require a formal deed of covenant and indemnity from the beneficiary for the benefit of his personal representatives although accepting that even so there could remain practical problems of enforcement in the event, for example, of the beneficiary emigrating. The Inland Revenue have confirmed that such an indemnity is not

12 Ss 131 and 132.

regarded as a reservation of a benefit. A precedent of such a deed can be found under 119 on page 261.

In the circumstances of a PET becoming a chargeable transfer, because of the death of the donor during the following seven-year period, the donor's cumulative total needs to be revised upwards for the purposes of calculating or recalculating and lifting the IHT liability on subsequent lifetime chargeable transfers including other former PETs and the transfer deemed to be made immediately before the donor's death. Accordingly, the indirect effect of a PET becoming a chargeable transfer can have serious IHT consequences for other persons, in particular the beneficiaries under the will of the deceased donor, apart from those for the beneficiary of a PET.

It is important therefore that a person considering making a PET should be advised to take into account all the circumstances, including the amount of other transfers during the prior period of seven years, for the purpose of assessing the adverse IHT consequences that would materialise both for his lifetime and testamentary beneficiaries should he die during the subsequent period of seven years.

Apart from any seven-year term insurance effected by the beneficiary of a PET on the life of the donor, the donor should himself consider the effecting of life insurance, but for a fixed figure upon trusts, for the protection of those who are to be the beneficiaries of his estate under his will.

In the case of a PET which becomes a chargeable transfer, the value on which IHT is charged is not to be grossed up. That is because the primary liability for IHT in those circumstances rests with the beneficiary which therefore prevents that happening.[13]

When an interest in possession in settled property comes to an end during the lifetime of the person entitled to it, section 52(1) of the Inheritance Tax Act 1984 states that the value for inheritance tax purposes is '. . . equal to the value of the property in which his interest subsisted.' Until recently this value has been determined as a rateable proportion of the aggregate value of that settled property and other property of a similar kind in the person's estate. The Inland Revenue now take the view that, in these circumstances, settled property in which the interest subsisted should be valued *in isolation* without reference to any similar property.

These statements of the Inland Revenue's position are made without prejudice to the application in an appropriate case of the *Ramsay* principle or the provisions of the Inheritance Tax Act 1984 relating to associated operations. The changes of view will be applied to all new cases and to existing cases where the tax liability has not been settled. *Law Society's Gazette*, May 9, 1990.

D. Property subject to a reservation

In summary, to prevent gifted property from being chargeable to IHT on his death, the donor, apart from surviving his gift by seven years, must ensure that the gift is properly made and is complete and total, without any conditions or continuing benefits irrespective of size for himself whether they are direct or indirect. If, on the donor's death, it transpires on looking back that the gifted property is what is called by the Finance Act 1986, section 102(2), 'property subject to a reservation'

---

13 There is no statutory right of recovery, if the personal representatives discharge the liability, from the beneficiary. This follows from the wording of s 211(3) which limits the right of recovery to chargeable transfers made on death.

it will be regarded, along with anything else, as property to which he was beneficially entitled immediately before his death and accordingly subject to the charge to IHT.[14]

The reservation of benefit rules apply, by the Finance Act 1986, section 102, where, on or after 18 March 1986, an individual disposes of any property by way of gift unless:[15]

    a) the donee bona fide assumes possession and enjoyment of the property at, at the latest, the beginning of 'the relevant period'; *and*

    b) the property is enjoyed to the entire exclusion, or virtually to the entire exclusion, of the donor throughout 'the relevant period'; *and*

    c) the property is enjoyed throughout 'the relevant period' to the entire exclusion, or virtually to the entire exclusion, of any benefit to the donor by contract or otherwise.

'The relevant period' means the period ending on the date of the donor's death and beginning seven years before that date or, if it is later, on the date of the gift.[16] Where *any* of the three requirements is not satisfied in relation to gifted property, it is property subject to a reservation and so liable to IHT on the donor's death irrespective of the length of time since the gift was made.[17] It will be recognised that the three requirements will be examined for IHT purposes looking back from the time of the donor's death.

In determining whether the third requirement is satisfied, the Finance Act 1986, paragraph 6(1)(c) of Schedule 20, provides that a benefit which the donor obtained by virtue of any associated operations (as defined by section 268 of the Inheritance Tax Act 1984) of which the disposal by way of gift is one shall be treated as a benefit to him by contract or otherwise. The definition of associated operations in section 268 which is dealt with in sub-chapter G of this chapter is extremely wide.

Examining the three requirements together, the first requires actual possession and enjoyment by the donee, not simply the right to obtain possession and enjoyment, the second requires entire exclusion of the donor from any benefit of any size arising from the gifted property whether actual or potential not only in law but also in fact and the third requires entire exclusion from any benefit of any size arising as a consequence of the transfer itself, which benefit can therefore be collateral and not arise from the gifted property itself.

The wording of section 102(1) is modelled on estate duty provisions prior to 13 March 1975 when estate duty was replaced by capital transfer tax. The statutory provisions are similar but not identical. Thus, the words 'virtually to the entire exclusion' are new and clearly aimed to protect a donor from IHT consequences, otherwise occasioned because of minor benefits subsequently enjoyed by him from the gifted property such as when he is a guest staying temporarily in a house he previously gifted. Although these new provisions are engrafted on to taxation law with different principles, it is generally accepted, including by the Inland Revenue, that the old estate duty cases will give useful guidance on the way the provisions will operate in practice but accepting a degree of uncertainty and therefore a proper need for care.

In the case of property which is *an interest in land or a chattel,* retention or assumption

---

14 FA 1986, s 102(3).

15 FA 1986, s 102(1) contains two paragraphs only. In fact, para (b) has two limbs to it. Therefore, for easier understanding, (b) has been broken down in the text into (b) and (c).

16 Ibid, s 102(1), at end.

17 Ibid, s 102(3).

by the donor of actual occupation of the land or actual enjoyment of an incorporeal right over the land, or actual possession of the chattel, is disregarded if it is for full consideration in money or money's worth.[18] This may not be an attractive possibility in practice when, for example, a commercial rent is paid by a donor for the subsequent use of his former house. The rent will be paid by him out of income after it has borne income tax and that rent will then be subject to income tax in the hands of the donee. The full consideration test needs to be satisfied at the time of the gift and continue to be satisfied at all times after it. That would require, for example, regular rent reviews.

In the case of property which is *an interest in land*, occupation by the donor of all or part of the land is to be disregarded in determining whether the statutory requirements are infringed where the donee is a relative of the donor or his spouse and:

    i) it results from a change in the circumstances of the donor since the time of the gift, being a change which was unforeseen at the time and was not brought about by the donor to receive the benefit of this provision; and

    ii) it occurs at a time when the donor has become unable to maintain himself through old age, infirmity or otherwise; and

    iii) it represents a reasonable provision by the donee for the maintenance and care of the donor.[19]

Mention has previously been made of the usefulness of the old estate duty cases. From a study of them it is important in relation to any set of facts to ascertain the exact subject matter of any gift in order then to decide whether or not there is in fact property subject to a reservation. To illustrate the possible contrasting results of the present legislation reference is made to two old Australian cases.

In *Munro v Stamp Duties Comr for New South Wales*[20] the deceased owned freehold land. He carried on there, prior to his gift in 1913, a sheep farming business in partnership with his six children. In 1913 he gave the land to his children but the partnership continued. He died in 1929. It was held that what he had given away in 1913 was his interest in the land but subject to the existing prior rights of the partnership. Hence, there was no reservation and no tax or duty liability on his death. The carve out of prior rights was in existence before his gift.

In *Chick v Stamp Duties Comr of New South Wales*[1] there was an absolute gift in 1934 of grazing land, by the deceased to his son. A year later that land was brought into partnership by the son; the partners included the deceased who was to be remunerated as manager. The deceased died many years later, in 1952. It was held that the land was dutiable or taxable. The deceased had given away his land but subsequently enjoyed a benefit over it, it being immaterial that the benefit was received in return for full consideration.

It is helpful to consider a scheme of arrangements illustrating what might be a satisfactory course of action in the case of a house to be gifted. It is assumed that a father wishes to give to his son his house, but to carry on living there without payment. If he was to do exactly that, the house would without doubt be property subject to a reservation. Instead, he first grants a lease of his house property at a nominal rent to himself and to his wife, the term of the lease being a fixed period

18 Ibid, Sch 20, para 6(1)(a).
19 Ibid, Sch 20, para 6(1)(b).
20 [1934] AC 61.
 1 [1958] AC 435, [1958] 2 All ER 623, PC.

of years sufficient to cover the joint expectations of life of the two of them.[2] Subsequently, but not simultaneously, the father makes a gift of his freehold, but subject to the then existing lease, to his son. The view generally taken about such circumstances is that, as the gift to the son is of the reversionary interest in the house, the gift will not constitute a gift with a reservation. Having regard to the landlord and tenant legislation the lease should be for a term of at least seven years but less than 21.[3] It should be a full repairing lease without any terms which in any way would be onerous in due course on the beneficiary, so as to avoid any possibility of the gift being caught by the gift with reservation provisions of the Finance Act 1986, section 102.[4] It is considered advisable that under his will the donor should give the benefit of the lease to someone other than the beneficiary of the freehold reversion. That is because otherwise the Revenue might seek to invoke the associated operations provisions on the grounds that on the donor's death, by the arrangements as a whole, he had made a disposition of the unencumbered freehold by associated operations.[5]

Kildrummy (Jersey) Ltd v IRC[6] is a Scottish stamp duty case decided in the Court of Session (Inner House) with judgment delivered on 30 August 1990. It was held that a lease by persons to nominees of those persons was a nullity. The circumstances surrounding the parties and terms of the lease in that case are not identical with the scheme of arrangements illustrated in the foregoing paragraph. Nevertheless that Scottish case should be kept in mind.[7]

If the scheme of arrangements is adopted it is likely that for capital gains tax purposes unless, the house is a 'second home', under the Capital Gains Tax Act 1979, section 101 on the disposal of private residence will apply. Nevertheless, a future disposal by the beneficiary (being the son in the illustrated scheme of arrangements) may not qualify under section 101.

Paragraphs 2 and 5 of Schedule 20 to the Finance Act 1986 contain provisions embracing the gift with reservation provisions under section 102 to subsequent substitutions and accretions for the original property which was gifted either absolutely or by a settlement.

2 The lease of the property must not be one for life or for a period ascertainable by reference to a death or which is terminable on a date ascertainable by reference to death since, unless the lease is granted for full consideration in money or money's worth, the lease will be regarded as a settlement, with the former tenant enjoying an interest in possession for IHT purposes and the property as settled property; see s 43(3).
3 From *Nichols v IRC* [1975] 2 All ER 120, [1975] STC 278, CA, it is evident that the terms of the lease should not be onerous in due course on the beneficiary in his capacity as landlord. It is necessary to avoid the statutory covenants of the Landlord and Tenant Act 1985, ss 11-17. Under those provisions, where a lease of a dwelling-house is granted for a term of less than seven years there are implied covenants on the part of a lessor, including to keep the structure and exterior in repair. If, in contrast, there is a lease of a house for a term exceeding 21 years at a rent of less than two-thirds the rateable value, under the Leasehold Reform Act 1967, Part 1, the tenant has rights to obtain a 50-year extension of his lease and to buy the freehold. The effect of such rights would materially decrease the value of the freehold reversion gifted to the beneficiary and increase the value of the lease 'retained' by the donor and which will form part of his estate on his death.
4 This emerges from a study of the circumstances in *Nichols v IRC* [1975] 2 All ER 120, [1975] STC 278.
5 See in particular s 268(3).
6 [1990] STC 657.
7 There is an excellent and instructive commentary which also refers to the observations of others on this case in the *Law Society's Gazette* No 26, 10 July 1991, by M Gowar and P Borrie.

Under section 102(4) if at any time before the end of 'the relevant period' (the period ending on the date of the donor's death and beginning seven years before that date or, if it is later, on the date of the gift) any property ceases to be property subject to a reservation, the donor is to be treated as having at that time made a disposition of the property by a disposition which is a PET.

Under section 102(5) the property subject to a reservation provisions do not generally apply where a transfer or gift has the benefit of one of the exemptions under chapter I of part II of the Inheritance Tax Act 1984. Thus, for example, they do not apply where the spouse exemption is applicable. Nevertheless they *do* apply in the cases of transfers or gifts enjoying the benefit of section 19 (annual exemption) and section 21 (normal expenditure out of income).

E. Lifetime transfers immediately chargeable

It follows from the pattern of the IHT legislation that where there is a lifetime transfer of value which is not exempt (see sub-chapters H and I of this chapter) and which is not a PET (see sub-chapter B) it will on its making be a chargeable transfer. It can therefore be said, leaving aside exempt transfers, that when a lifetime transfer does not comply with the strict conditions of section 3A about the making of PETs it will be a chargeable transfer thus giving rise to an immediate liability to IHT.

Other than because a gift does not comply with the precise conditions in section 3A, the gifts which generally *do not* qualify as PETs are those made to a trust without an interest in possession, being a discretionary trust, or to a company or to a non-charitable body such as a members' club.

F. Additional principles of IHT

Sub-chapter A of this chapter dealt with the general principles of IHT and the pattern of the legislation in relation to lifetime transfers. Because of their overriding implications, the next three sub-chapters then dealt with PETs and property subject to a reservation. It is convenient in this sub-chapter to examine the statutory provisions of the Inheritance Tax Act 1984 in relation to lifetime transfers of value generally and also to refer to certain additional principles of IHT.

Section 1 states that IHT shall be charged on the value transferred by a chargeable transfer. Section 2(1) continues by stating that a chargeable transfer is a transfer of value which is made by an individual but is not an exempt transfer. A transfer of value made by a close company is treated, by section 94, as if made by its participators and the provisions that are applicable are in sections 94 to 102. Section 3(1) follows by stating that a transfer of value is a disposition made by a person as the result of which the value of his estate immediately after the disposition is less than it would be but for the disposition and that the amount by which it is less is the value transferred by the transfer.

Thus, in relation to a lifetime transfer which results in a reduction in a person's estate, the plan is not directly to define what is a gift, disposition or transfer, but to give a wide meaning to the term 'transfer of value', then by sections 3(2) and 10, to cut down the meaning so as to make eliminations in relation to excluded property and because of the necessity for gratuitous intent and, finally, by reverting to section 2(1) which defines 'chargeable transfer', to exclude a transfer which is an exempt transfer. As already mentioned, the value transferred by a transfer of value is the amount by which the value of the transferor's estate, immediately after the disposition, is less than it would be but for the disposition, and the amount by which it is less is the value transferred by the transfer. It therefore follows that where a transfer involves an equal exchange of assets for assets or of assets for cash, because of the definition of 'transfer of value' in section 3(1), there can be no liability to IHT, irrespective of the exclusion of commercial arrangements by section 10.

Where there is a gratuitous transfer resulting in a reduction in value, unless for one reason or another it is exempt, the value of it is measured by the reduction in value of the transferor's estate. That reduction in value is not necessarily limited to the value of the gift, since its making may also reduce the value of assets and interests retained by the transferor. For the purpose of assessing the reduction in value, one includes the transferor's liability for IHT on the transfer but not any other tax or duty, such as capital gains tax, resulting from the transfer.[8]

Accordingly, as the transferor is accountable for IHT on a chargeable transfer, if he wishes the beneficiary to receive the gift net of IHT then, for the purpose of calculating the IHT liability, it is necessary to gross up the value of the transfer in order to assess the value which, after deduction of IHT, will be the net value of the transfer. The view may well be taken that when in such circumstances the transferor pays the IHT he is in effect paying two taxes: the IHT on the gift and the IHT on the tax itself. If the beneficiary in fact pays the IHT then the transferor's estate is not reduced by IHT as the result of the transfer and IHT is only paid on the value by which the transfer alone reduces his estate. It is also the case that when the beneficiary and not the transferor pays the IHT, for determining the value transferred by a transfer of value, there is the right to deduct expenses incurred by the transfer.[9] In the case of certain types of assets, there is also the right in those circumstances to pay the IHT by instalments.[10]

In practice, as the result of the introduction of PETs into the IHT legislation by the Finance Act 1986, the principle of grossing up lifetime transfers has lost importance because most gifts will be absolute ones from one individual to another individual and therefore qualify as PETs. Should a PET become a chargeable transfer, because of the death of the transferor within seven years after the making of the gift, there is no grossing up of the value transferred. That is because the primary liability for IHT in those circumstances rests with the beneficiary, which therefore prevents that happening.

Under section 10(1), which is the primary provision which distinguishes between gifts and sales, when there has been a loss in value as the result of the transferor's disposition:

1) A disposition is not a transfer of value if it is shown that it was not intended, and was not made in a transaction intended, to confer any gratuitous benefit[11] on any person and either—
   a) that it was made in a transaction at arm's length between persons not connected with each other,[12] or

8 S 5(4).
9 S 164(b).
10 S 227(1)(b).
11 A gratuitous intent does not necessarily need to be in favour of the particular transferee. It could be associated, under s 268, with past or future transfers and operations; see definition of 'transaction' in s 10(3).
12 S 270.

b) that it was such as might be expected to be made in a transaction at arm's length between persons not connected with each other[12].

Section 10(2) then states that the foregoing does not apply to a sale of unquoted shares or unquoted debentures unless it is shown that the sale was at a price freely negotiated at the time of the sale or at a price such as might be expected to have been freely negotiated at the time of the sale.

Section 3(3) states that where the value of a person's estate is diminished and that of another person's estate, or of settled property in which no interest in possession subsists, is increased by the omission of the first person to exercise a right, he shall be treated as having made a disposition at the time (or latest time) when he could have exercised the right, unless it is shown that the omission was not deliberate. Examples of this could be where there is a failure to increase rent, when it is possible to do so under a lease, and a failure to take up a rights issue of shares which as a result benefits others.

Where during the life of a person his interest in possession comes to an end, thus giving rise to a charge under section 52(1), either immediately because it is not a PET or on his death because he does not survive seven years, it is accepted, including by the Inland Revenue, that in determining the value transferred the settled property is to be valued in isolation without reference to property in the person's free estate.

G. Associated operations and *Furniss v Dawson*[13]

Section 272 extends the definition of 'disposition' to include a disposition effected by associated operations. In view of its importance, section 268 is set out, in full, as follows:

'1) In this Act "associated operations" means, subject to subsection (2) below, any two or more operations[14] of any kind being:
   a) operations which affect the same property, or one of which affects some property and the other or others of which affect property which represents, whether directly or indirectly, that property, or income arising from that property, or any property representing accumulations of any such income; or
   b) any two operations of which one is effected with reference to the other, or with a view to enabling the other to be effected or facilitating its being effected, and any further operation having a like relation to any of those two, and so on;
   whether those operations are effected by the same person or different persons, and whether or not they are simultaneous; and "operation" includes an omission.
2) The granting of a lease for full consideration in money or money's worth shall be taken to be associated with any operation effected more than three

---

13 [1984] AC 474, [1984] STC 153, HL. This case was an extension of *Ramsay Ltd v IRC, Eilbeck v Rawling* [1982] AC 300, [1981] STC 174 and *IRC v Burmah Oil Co Ltd* [1982] STC 30. Nevertheless the principle was limited by three conjoined appeals, *Craven v White, Baylis v Gregory* and *IRC v Bowater Property Developments Ltd* [1988] STC 476, where it was held that the principle of *Furniss v Dawson* did not apply because (inter alia) there was not a pre-ordained series of transactions.
14 The word 'operation' has a wide meaning and is not necessarily confined to dispositions.

years after the grant, and no operation effected on or after 27 March 1974 shall be taken to be associated with an operation effected before that date.

3) Where a transfer of value is made by associated operations carried out at different times it shall be treated as made at the time of the last of them; but where any one or more of the earlier operations also constitute a transfer of value made by the same transferor, the value transferred by the earlier operations shall be treated as reducing the value transferred by all the operations taken together, except to the extent that the transfer constituted by the earlier operations but not that made by all the operations taken together is exempt under section 18 above.'

The foregoing definition of associated operations can be seen to be extremely wide and, save for the two exceptions in sub-section (2), the possible linking of operations[14] seems boundless. It does not follow that where operations are associated there will be an increased charge to IHT. The effect of sub-section (3) is to treat associated operations as if they were all one disposition made at the time of the *last* operation. IHT can then be levied on the value transferred as a result of all the operations taken together. From the combined total of values transferred, there is however to be deducted the value of those transfers in the chain which were transfers of value, including exempt transfers (but not transfers exempted only by reason of the exemption for gifts between spouses). Later in this chapter[15] in the context of arrangements between spouses, official expressions of view will be quoted which may be helpful in advance of case law.

Although the 1984 House of Lords' decision in *Furniss v Dawson*[13] involved considerations of capital gains tax, there seems no reason why it should not equally apply to cases involving IHT mitigation despite the fact that sections 272 and 268 embrace in the wide manner already described 'associated operations' for the purposes of the definition of 'disposition'. The Inland Revenue are of the opinion that the doctrine of *Furniss v Dawson* does apply to IHT despite the anti-avoidance legislation of section 268.

The principle behind the decision is that where a tax avoidance or tax deferment scheme comprises a pre-ordained series of transactions, in which steps have been inserted which have no commercial or business purpose other than the avoidance or deferment of tax, liability to tax is to be determined according to the substance of the scheme as a whole and its end result.

All five Law Lords gave judgment, naturally not in identical terms. In addition Lord Scarman, in his very short judgment, added an observation for the benefit of, principally, the legal profession, by saying that

'the law will develop from case to case . . . What has been established with certainty by the House in *Ramsay*'s case is that the determination of what does, and what does not, constitute unacceptable tax evasion is a subject suited to development by judicial process.'

As a result of *Furniss v Dawson*, it is to be recommended that any scheme devised with the object of mitigating IHT should be conventional and straightforward and should be effected as a whole at the same time. Nevertheless, in order to form a judgment about any set of circumstances the following questions can be put:

1) Is there a pre-ordained scheme of arrangements?

2) Have steps been inserted in that scheme purely to avoid or defer tax?

15 P 58 below.

3) Do those steps have any commercial or business purpose?
4) On the assumption that the answers to the first two of the foregoing questions are 'yes' and to the third 'no', what in fact are the deemed substituted taxable transactions and the taxable result?

H. Spouse exemption

Under section 18 a transfer of value is an exempt transfer to the extent that the value transferred is attributable to property which becomes comprised in the estate of the transferor's spouse, or so far as the value is not so attributable, to the extent that that estate is increased. Accordingly, direct and indirect transfers or gifts for the benefit of the other spouse are exempt. A life interest conferred on the other spouse or, more correctly, the underlying trust capital supporting it, is exempt in the same manner as an absolute gift.[16] There is also freedom from capital gains tax for lifetime gifts between spouses.[17] As the result of the Stamp Duty (Exempt Instruments) Regulations 1987, SI 1987/516 subject to the inclusion of an appropriate certificate, there is no stamp duty whatsoever on gifts, the Finance Act 1985, section 82(1) having abolished the 1% ad valorem stamp duty on any conveyance or transfer operating as a voluntary disposition inter vivos. Nevertheless, where the spouse making the gift or bequest is domiciled in the United Kingdom for IHT purposes and the other spouse is domiciled overseas, IHT exemption is limited to a cumulative total of £55,000.[18] The exemption is not given where the gift or bequest is not immediately in favour of the other spouse or is made dependent on a condition which is not satisfied within twelve months. The exemption is not however excluded only because the gift is dependent on the recipient spouse surviving the other by a specified period.[19]

It is the case that even when the loss to the transferor-spouse is greater than the gain to the other the whole transfer is exempt. This could apply, for example, in the case of the gift of shares in a company resulting not only in the loss to the transferor of such amount of shares but, because of the gift, the loss of strength existing by reason of his shareholding ceasing to be a majority one.

Where a marriage is stable, there is a strong case for the wealthier spouse making gifts to the other to enable each of them to make full use of their IHT nil% bands on their deaths. It is preferable to do so by lifetime gifts, as opposed to equalisation under their wills, since they may die in the wrong order, the materially poorer dying before the wealthier.

I. Regular lifetime exemptions

The real value of the following exemptions, which are available only in the case of lifetime transfers, should not be underestimated. There will be a future saving of IHT at the top rate which would otherwise be payable on the amount of the particular gift or transfer had it not been made.

1) Section 19 exempts gifts other than gifts with a reservation up to an aggregate value of £3,000 during each tax year (6 April to following 5 April) irrespective

---

16 S 49(1).
17 Capital Gains Tax Act 1979, s 44.
18 S 18(2).
19 S 18(3).

of whether or not made out of capital. Any unused part of such annual exemption can be carried forward one year only. For example, if £2,000 has been given and set against this exemption for the year ending 5 April 1990 and £2,000 for the year ending 5 April 1991, the amount available for the year ending 5 April 1992 is £4,000 (not £5,000). This exemption can also be set against the value of any underlying trust capital over which the transferor's life/income interest is relinquished; see section 57(3) to (5) for the terms and conditions applicable.[20] When a PET is made, in the first instance it is left out of account for the purposes of this annual exemption. If, because of the death of the donor within seven years after its making, it proves to be a chargeable transfer, it is taken into account as if in the tax year it was made it was made later than any transfer of value which was not a PET. Nevertheless, if a PET was made in the year before the tax year in which an immediately chargeable transfer was made and if that PET becomes chargeable because of the donor's death, the benefit of the annual exemption for the latter will be given to the PET. If there is more than one PET in any tax year, the annual exemption will be set against the PETs in the order in which the gifts were made.

2) Section 20 exempts gifts which do not exceed £250 to any one person during each tax year (6 April to following 5 April). Any number of these small transfers, not exceeding a total of £250 per person, are exempt. Nevertheless, this exemption is not available to cover part of a larger gift, and is therefore lost completely if more than £250 is transferred to one person, whether by one or more gifts in the same year. It also cannot be used to augment the £3,000 under (1) above. Any such gift needs to be outright as the exemption is not available for a gift into settlement.

3) Section 21 exempts gifts other than gifts with a reservation which represent normal, and thus typical or habitual, expenditure out of the transferor's income, thus in contrast to capital, and which leaves him sufficient income to maintain his usual standard of living. The opening words of section 21(1) 'A transfer of value is an exempt transfer if, or to the extent that, it is shown . . .' shows that it is not all or nothing and that the exemption is available pro tanto, even if it is exceeded, to the extent that the conditions would have been complied with. These conditions are that the transfer of value:
   a) was made as part of the normal expenditure of the transferor; and
   b) taking one year with another it was made out of his income; and
   c) after allowing for all transfers of value forming part of his normal expenditure, the transferor was left with sufficient income to maintain his usual standard of living.

It is thus clear that the gifts must be habitual and regular in relation to the transferor. Normal expenditure means typical or habitual and not necessarily natural or reasonable. Thus it must have been the habit of the transferor to make such kinds of gifts regularly and similarly. In practice three gifts are usually required to establish regularity. Premiums paid under life policies, upon trusts for the benefit of others, are a convenient method of using such exemption, since premiums are paid regularly and are normally of the same amount. It is understood that in the event of the unexpected early death of the transferor who effected the policy, the Revenue will accept the exemption in respect of his payments to date if they are satisfied that

20 For a precedent see 112, p 253 below.

he had a normal expectation of life and intended to continue to discharge the premiums, thereby establishing the necessary pattern of payments. The same would apply in the case of payments under a deed of covenant. The measure of income for the purpose of this exemption is the transferor's net income after tax. Section 21(2) denies exemption to premiums on 'back to back' policies where associated with purchased life annuities. Section 21(3) excludes the capital element of annuity payments from being regarded as income for the purposes of assessing the transferor's income in the case of annuities purchased after 12 November 1974.

4) Section 22, in brief, exempts transfers of values made by gifts in consideration of marriage to the following extents:
   a) £5,000 in the case of a gift from a parent of either party to the marriage;
   b) £2,500 in the case of a gift from one party to the marriage to the other, or from any ancestor other than a parent of either party to the marriage;
   c) £1,000 in any other case.

As in the case of the annual exemption under section 19, this exemption can be set against the value of any underlying trust capital over which the transferor's life/income interest is relinquished; see section 57(3) to (5) for the terms and conditions applicable. The gift must be made 'in consideration of marriage'. This means that it must be made on the occasion of the marriage, it must be conditional on the marriage taking place and it must be made by a person for the purpose of encouraging or facilitating the marriage. It would be useful if there was a suitably worded letter or paper, written prior to the wedding. It is worth remembering that an actual transfer before marriage is not necessary. It is possible to enter into a written undertaking or covenant prior to and 'in consideration of (the) marriage' to make or rather complete the gift subsequently; the benefit of the exemption will be obtained as soon as the gift is 'discharged' which naturally should be done as soon as possible, and must be done during the transferor's lifetime.

The foregoing exemptions under sections 19, 21 and 22 are available in addition to each other. Husband and wife are regarded as separate persons and can each use such exemptions. Thus, a man and his wife could *each* in the particular year a child is getting married apart from using their section 21 exemption make that child exempt gifts totalling £8,000, consisting of £5,000 (marriage gift) and £3,000 (annual exemption). There could also be a further £3,000 if the annual exemption for the previous year has not been used. A point of difficulty arises when, for example, a father and mother wish to give £6,000 to a child of theirs so that each of them can take full advantage of the benefit of their exemptions under section 19, but while the father has funds the mother has not. Can the father first transfer to his wife £3,000, being itself an exempt transfer as between spouses, and then she would make her onward gift to the child? Would the 'associated operations' provisions under section 268 cause both gifts to be treated as the father's, so that only £3,000 of the £6,000 would enjoy the benefit of the exemptions? Mr J Barnett, Chief Secretary to the Treasury stated the following in committee on 13 February 1975:

'It is always possible that a wife with no capital of her own will receive funds from a wealthy husband. It is perfectly reasonable that a wealthy husband will stand ready to share his capital with his wife. That is a legitimate and commendable thing to do. If the wife then chose to make gifts out of the money from her husband, of a sort that fell within the exceptions, there would be no question of the Revenue invoking the associated operations rule to regard her gifts as taxable.'

Despite such statement there must be doubt, and care will be needed even when one is apparently following the view of Mr Barnett.[1] If the prior gift from the husband to the wife is subject to an express or indeed implied condition or undertaking that it is to be passed on to their child, it would seem difficult to contend that the arrangements, taken as a whole, are not associated. It is important that the wife should have true dominion over the gift from her husband, and that it is accepted that she can in fact use it in such manner as she wants. A contemporaneous letter or memorandum from the husband could record that as being the case. Possibly a safer way, if the practical circumstances allow, would be for the wife to make her exempt gift, if necessary by incurring a bank overdraft, and that thereafter it would be open to her husband to place her back in funds. Whatever may be the best procedure, in any particular set of circumstances, a reading of section 268 shows how very far reaching the provisions may be, if based on a literal interpretation.

J. Exemptions available for lifetime and testamentary gifts

Apart from transfers between spouses, the following exemptions apply to both lifetime and testamentary gifts:

Section 23(1) exempts gifts to charities which are established in the United Kingdom.

Section 24(1) exempts gifts to political parties. A political party qualifies for this exemption if two of its members were elected to the House of Commons at the last general election before the gift, or if one of its members was elected and at least 150,000 votes were cast for its candidates.

Section 24A exempts gifts of land to Registered Housing Associations.

Section 25(1), with Schedule 3, exempts gifts to national museums, universities, the National Trust and certain other bodies.

Section 26(1) exempts gifts of national heritage property to a suitable non-profitmaking body, where approved by the Board of Inland Revenue.

There are limitations to the right to the foregoing exemptions in sections 23(2) to (5), 24(3), 24A(3), 25(2) and 26(7) where, for example, the gifts can be terminated by a future event. These limitations are dealt with in sub-chapter E of chapter 6, page 72.

K. Section 11 (dispositions for maintenance of family)

By this section *lifetime* dispositions for the maintenance of a spouse,[2] child or dependent relative of the donor are exempt in the circumstances mentioned. A disposition for the maintenance of a spouse[3] or former spouse[4] is unconditionally exempt. A disposition for the maintenance, education or training of a child of either the donor or his spouse is exempt provided that it is for the child's maintenance etc up to the age

1 The Inland Revenue Press Release dated 8 April 1975 states that s 44 is not seen as affecting the ordinary case where a gift between husband and wife is followed by a gift by the recipient spouse to a third party, unless it was a condition of the first gift that the second should be made. It may, however, be apt to apply in more complex situations where a transfer between husband and wife forms part of a series of associated operations, the effect of which as a whole is merely the means whereby one of them makes a disposition in favour of a third party.

2 See penultimate paragraph of this sub-chapter.

3 S 11(1)(a).

4 See definition of 'marriage' in s 11(6).

of 18 or until, if later, completion of full-time education.[5] Similarly, a disposition made for the maintenance, education or training of a child who is not in the care of either of his parents is exempt. These exemptions are also available for dispositions for stepchildren, adopted children[6] and illegitimate children[7] of the person making the disposition.

A disposition made for a dependent relative of the person making the disposition is exempt to the extent that it makes reasonable provision for the relative's care or maintenance. 'Dependent relative' means any relative of the particular person or his spouse who is unable to maintain himself or herself because of old age or incapacity; it also includes the particular person's mother or mother-in-law, whether or not she is elderly or infirm, unless she is living with her husband.[8] Under section 11(5) a disposition, which in part satisfies such conditions, is to be treated as two separate dispositions.

There is *no* relief under section 11 where a person entitled to a life/income interest in settled property, in effect, releases his interest pro tanto by consenting to the trustees exercising their powers of advancement, under the Trustee Act 1925, section 32, or any other power, for the maintenance, education or training of his child.

In the case of transfers between spouses the normal IHT exemption under section 18 will ordinarily oust the necessity for any exemption under section 11. Nevertheless, section 11 will be important where the spouse making the disposition is domiciled in the United Kingdom for IHT purposes and the other spouse is domiciled elsewhere when in such a case the IHT spouse exemption is limited to a cumulative total of £55,000.

Without section 11(1), a composition sum payment by a parent to commute future school fees of a child would be a transfer of value under section 3(1), thus giving rise to a charge to IHT. The Revenue take the view that in normal circumstances such a payment by a parent, as opposed to a grandparent, has the benefit of the exemption under section 11(1).

L. **Section 12 (dispositions allowable for income tax or conferring retirement benefits)**

A disposition made by a person is not a transfer of value for IHT purposes if it is allowable in computing that person's profits or gains for income tax or corporation tax purposes or would be so allowable if those profits or gains were sufficient. Such exemption also covers contributions to pension and retirement schemes, and to appropriate benefits (including rent-free accommodation), on or after retirement, for employees (or their widows or widowers or dependants after their death).

M. **Sections 14 and 15 (waiver of remuneration and dividends)**

A waiver or repayment of remuneration is not a transfer of value for IHT purposes provided that the remuneration would, apart from the waiver, have been assessed to income tax under Schedule E. But if, as a result of the waiver, the remuneration

---

5 S 11(1)(b) and (2).
6 See definition of 'child' in s 11(6).
7 S 11(4).
8 S 11(6).

will not be treated as a deductible expense by the payer, for income tax or corporation tax, or otherwise brought into charge, this relief does not apply.

A waiver of a dividend is not a transfer of value for IHT purposes if made within twelve months before any right to the dividend has accrued.[9]

N. Receptacle trusts

Assuming the wish on the part of a person to take advantage of his regular annual IHT exemption[10] or of an amount which will absorb all or part of his nil% band[11] or, alternatively, to make PETs,[12] it will be a matter for consideration how best that can be done. The gifts, and any similar ones from the person's spouse, may be comparatively small and regular, when use is made of the annual IHT exemption. They may have a number of children to be benefited. Those children may have a wide range of ages and be of varying characters. Although those who are of age can themselves receive their gifts, even then it may be considered undesirable to break down and divide the amounts, thus running the danger that the gifts will be made in a manner that does not encourage thrift and lacks the benefit of size.

The following possibilities are mentioned for consideration:

1) The donor should take out a policy on his life upon trusts for those whom he wishes to benefit. A trust policy can be a statutory policy, written under the Married Women's Property Act 1882[13] or a non-statutory one where incorporated into the policy are express terms constituting the beneficial trusts with appropriate powers for the trustees. The donor can thereafter make his gifts by discharging the regular premiums as they become due.

2) The donor should make a settlement, upon discretionary trusts, which include power to accumulate income for a period not exceeding 21 years.[14] Provided that the donor's transfer, cumulated with his other non-exempt transfers[15] in the previous seven years, is within the amount of his nil% band there can never be any IHT liability in respect of it. The ten-yearly periodic charge[16] or the proportionate charge when any settled property leaves the settlement[17] or a beneficiary acquires an interest in possession[17] is unlikely to give rise to a liability for IHT. It must, however, be recognised that in the case of a discretionary trust made after a PET which then becomes a chargeable transfer because of the death of the transferor within seven years there will be adverse IHT consequences. Not only will the IHT liability on the making of the discretionary trust need to be recalculated but also the rate of IHT paid on any exit charges prior to the transferor's death or any future ten-yearly periodic or exit charges will be increased. This is because the PET will forever be

---

9 There is a comprehensive article on waiver of dividends by Mr B J Sims in *British Tax Review* (1977) p 28.
10 S 19.
11 £140,000 for year to 5 April 1991.
12 S 3A.
13 S 11 of that Act.
14 See Perpetuities and Accumulations Act 1964, s 13(1)(a) which amended the Law of Property Act 1925, s 164.
15 Thus including PETs which would become chargeable if he does not survive for seven years after making them.
16 S 64.
17 S 65(1)(a).

locked into the cumulation of the discretionary trust. A material disadvantage of such a settlement will be the income tax liabilities, using the 1991/92 tax year rates, of 25% for basic rate tax and of 10% for additional rate tax.[18]

3) The donor should make a PET by constituting a settlement which either confers interests in possession[19] or complies with the accumulation and maintenance trust conditions of section 71. In the latter case, during the time prior to the beneficiary acquiring his interest in possession, there will be the income tax liabilities mentioned in the case of the kind of settlement under (2) above.

4) The donor should make a settlement which confers on the beneficiaries absolute interests in both capital and income, notwithstanding that any are under age.[20] It would follow that a beneficiary on attaining full age at 18 would be entitled to receive his share of the capital, including accumulated income. The trustees, in the meantime, would be enabled to accumulate income under the terms of the Trustee Act 1925, section 31(2) and thus, it would seem,[1] avoid the settlement provisions of the Income and Corporation Taxes Act 1988, section 663(1), notwithstanding that the donor is the parent of the beneficiaries; provided that no income, including any income tax recovered, is paid to or in any way applied for the benefit of a beneficiary while under age. Likewise, there must be no releases of capital, otherwise section 664(2)(b) will apply. The income, subject to the foregoing points, would be the beneficiary's income for tax purposes. The income tax and capital gains tax advantages of such a settlement are material. The beneficiary despite being under age, like an adult, would have his own personal allowance for income tax purposes, amounting to £3,295 in the tax year 1991/92, thereby giving rise to the possibility of annual reclaim of the basic rate tax of 25%, the 10% additional rate of income tax not being applicable.[18] So far as concerns capital gains tax, disposals by the trustees will be treated as disposals by the beneficiary who is under age with the annual exemption for the first £5,500[2] of gains, in contrast to the lesser exemption for trustees generally. In the event of the death of the beneficiary the settled capital, including accumulated income, will pass with his estate and being under age its distribution will depend on the intestacy provisions applicable to himself. The intestacy rules would cause the settled capital to revert to the parents of the beneficiary but that result could be changed by a deed executed under the terms of section 142. There will be a charge to IHT under section 4(1), but, dependent on his other assets and interests, IHT is likely to be minimal.

In the case of the policy and settlements described above it may well be envisaged that the trust capital, being built up free of IHT, could be used towards funding the IHT liability arising on the death of the donor or the subsequent death of his wife. In fact he may well regard this as the most satisfactory reason for using his IHT exemptions and making such a settlement. The beneficiaries of the settlement

---

18 ICTA 1988, s 686.
19 For the definition of that expression see *Pearson v IRC* [1981] AC 753, [1980] STC 318, HL. The Court of Appeal decision of *Re Delamere's Settlement Trusts, Kenny v Cunningham-Reid* [1984] 1 All ER 584, [1984] 1 WLR 813 supports the conclusion that where any accumulated and capitalised income is the absolute and indefeasible property of a beneficiary who is under age that applies also for income tax purposes.
20 For a precedent see 114, p 255 below.
1 This reflects the views of the Inland Revenue.
2 This being the figure for the tax year 1991/92.

may not be identical to those persons benefiting under the will of the donor (and his wife), but very often they will be similar. The assets under the settlement, and in any event the policy money on maturity, may well be more easily realisable than the assets under the will which it may be desired, because of their nature, to retain intact within the family. Towards that end, it could well assist any family's overall position if the trustees of the settlement were able to buy assets from the executors, so placing the latter in funds towards meeting their IHT liability. As in those circumstances there may be one or more persons who are both trustees of the settlement and executors under the will, there should be a clause, mirrored in both the settlement and will, which would enable such persons to 'trade' with themselves and not be precluded from doing so only on the ground that there could be a conflict of duty.[3]

o. Lifetime nil% band discretionary trusts

As appears from sub-chapter E a gift to a trust without an interest in possession, being a discretionary trust, does not qualify as a PET, under section 3A, and accordingly is a transfer immediately chargeable to IHT as a chargeable transfer. A gift to a discretionary trust of an amount which, subject to the cumulation of earlier chargeable transfers during the prior seven years, does not exceed the IHT nil% band, being £140,000 for the tax year 1991/92, has the same effect as a PET because no IHT is paid when the trust is made. Because of the property subject to a reservation rules, see sub-chapter D, the transferor should not be included within the class of discretionary beneficiaries. For IHT purposes there is no objection to the settlor's spouse being included, although that would mean that anti-avoidance provisions would apply for income tax purposes under the Income and Corporation Taxes Act 1988, Part XV, and for capital gains tax purposes under the Finance Act 1988, section 109 and Schedule 10. Those sets of anti-avoidance provisions do not apply where instead the discretionary beneficiary included within the class is the settlor's widow or widower.

Because the transfer is a chargeable transfer for IHT purposes hold-over relief, subject to an election being made, is available for capital gains tax purposes; see the Capital Gains Tax Act 1979, section 147A(2)(a) and sub-chapter S of this chapter. For the same reasons it is available when settled capital leaves the discretionary trust.

p. Life assurance

The taxation and other technicalities of life assurance are detailed and complex and the variety of policies available and their terms change. It will be necessary to make enquiries about the available policies and their terms, whether direct from life offices or through the services of brokers. With considerations of IHT in mind a trust policy will often be required. Such a trust policy can be a statutory policy written for the benefit of dependants under the Married Women's Property Act 1882, section 11, or a non-statutory one, where incorporated into the policy are special terms setting out the beneficial trusts with appropriate powers for the trustees. Whatever

3 See Form 88, p 224 below.

assistance is sought, the ultimate responsibility for the advice must inevitably rest with the solicitor.

The following are two kinds of policies, in respect of the payment of the premiums, of which advantage can be taken of the IHT exemptions for normal expenditure out of income (section 21) and annual transfers not exceeding £3,000 whether or not out of capital (section 19).

a) A whole life policy, with trusts which either confer interests in possession or comply with the conditions of section 71 to provide a cash sum which can, if so decided at the time, go towards the IHT liability on death in similar manner to that indicated at the end of N, above. The assumption behind such a policy could be that the surviving spouse is adequately provided for already or under the deceased's will and the IHT liability contemplated would be in respect of that portion of the deceased's assets gifted to non-exempt beneficiaries, such as the children.

b) A whole life and last survivor policy (on the lives of both husband and wife), with like trusts as those for the whole life policy, to provide a cash sum on the second death. In the case of such a policy there may be doubt whether it is a qualifying policy and accordingly whether the premiums would attract income tax relief. There are three main points to note. First, that whatever happens there is a potential premium paying period of ten years, discounting the possibility that the persons whose lives are insured may both die within that period. Secondly, that if the annual premium is at some time to be reduced, such as on the first death, each subsequent premium thereafter payable is not less than one-half of each paid previously. Thirdly, that if such premium reduction is arranged it does not come into operation until the end of the sixth year from the effecting of the policy whether or not one of the persons insured has died in the meantime.

Q. Gift of chattels

Chattels, such as paintings, furniture and jewellery, are suitable assets with which a person can take tax advantage of his £3,000 annual exemption under section 19. That is the case provided that he no longer requires their use, because otherwise the retention of any gifted chattels would result in their being property subject to a reservation for the purposes of the Finance Act 1986, section 102, the provisions of which *do* apply to section 19 transfers.[4] The donor must make sure when making such a gift to comply with the legal formalities to enable it to be complete and effective in law.

Accordingly, he should adopt either of the following methods:

a) By physical delivery and handing to the beneficiary articles or some token item, representing the whole, accompanied by words which convey the unequivocal meaning that an absolute gift, in contrast, for example, to the right to use and enjoy, is intended.[5] It is helpful for a witness to be present who is either a solicitor or who has been properly briefed, and that the person should as soon as possible thereafter swear a declaration or make a signed

4 See omission of mention of section 19, in FA 1986, s 102(5).
5 See for example *Re Cole* [1964] Ch 175, [1963] 3 All ER 433, CA, *Re Kirkland* [1964] 108 Sol Jo 197, CA.

statement recording what he saw and heard, including the fact that the gift was an absolute one and therefore without conditions or reservations.[6] As a matter of expediency it may well assist if any such declaration or statement has been pre-prepared and used by the donor and the beneficiary so that they do and say what is required of them to comply with the strict formalities for such a gift.

b) By execution of a deed.[7] This method in the past could give rise to an unwelcome stamp duty liability. That is not now the case; see sub-chapter S of this chapter. Accordingly, it may in future be the most convenient of the two methods.

For considerations of capital gains tax on a gift of chattels reference should be made to sub-chapter S below.

R. Gift of reversionary interest

Section 47 defines a reversion as 'a future interest under a settlement, whether it is vested or contingent . . .'. Under section 48 a reversionary interest is excluded property but with exceptions. It will not, in particular, be excluded property if the reversion has been acquired for money or money's worth or if the settlor or his or her spouse is or has been beneficially entitled to the reversion. To state the obvious, once the reversionary interest has ceased to be one, by becoming vested in possession, any future disposition by the beneficiary can have IHT repercussions based on his own IHT position. Stemming from the pre-1974 estate duty days, when it was very usual for a person under his will to give his spouse a life interest in settled property, it may be very advantageous for the already wealthy child of a marriage during the life of his surviving parent to give away his reversionary interest, before it falls into possession, and thereby lessen his own potential IHT liability. A gift of a reversionary interest could be an absolute one or a gift in settlement.

The gift and assignment will not result in a charge to capital gains tax because of the exemption in the Capital Gains Tax Act 1979, section 58(1), unless the assignor acquired his interest for a consideration in money or money's worth or unless the Finance Act 1981, section 88, applies (disposals of interests in non-resident settlements).

S. Capital gains tax on gifts

A gift is a disposal[8] for capital gains tax (CGT) purposes. The main CGT implications in relation to gifts are as follows:

1) As from 6 April 1990 the chargeable gains of husband and wife are calculated separately with each entitled to their own annual exemption, the amount of which see 5) below.

2) The Finance Act 1982, sections 86 to 88, introduced an indexation allowance on the disposal of assets after 5 April 1982. The Finance Act 1985, section 68, made improvements to that allowance for disposals after 5 April 1985. Generally, items of allowable expenditure are index-linked so that the chargeable gain on disposal is intended to represent real profits.

---

6 For a precedent see 117, p 259 below.
7 For a precedent see 118, p 260 below.
8 Capital Gains Tax Act 1979, s 1(1).

3) The Finance Act 1988, section 96, introduced re-basing for assets owned on 31 March 1982 and disposed of after 5 April 1988 whereby in calculating the chargeable gain of assets held on 31 March 1982 they are deemed to have been sold by the taxpayer and immediately reacquired by him at market value on that date. Accordingly that part of any earlier capital gain was removed.

4) Chattel exemption.[9] A gain accruing on a disposal of an asset[10] which is tangible movable property is not a chargeable gain if the (amount or) value (of the consideration for the disposal) does not exceed £6,000.

5) Annual exemption, which is index-linked, is, in the tax year 1991/92, for the first £5,500 of chargeable gains.[11] Generally, trustees of a trust have half the annual exemption available to an individual.

6) Hold-over relief for gifts including gifts into settlement. Under the Finance Act 1980, section 79, as extended by the Finance Act 1981, section 78, subject to the appropriate claim for relief being made, where there was a disposal otherwise than under a bargain at arm's length to an individual resident or ordinarily resident in the United Kingdom, and thus a gift, the amount of the chargeable gain was held over, the transferor's chargeable gain on disposal and the transferee's 'consideration' being reduced by an amount equal to the held-over gain. Section 79 was further extended by the Finance Act 1982, section 82, to property coming out of settlement. By the Finance Act 1989, section 124, for disposals on or after 14 March 1989, section 79 ceased to have effect. Hold-over relief is now only available for the following, in the cases of (a) to (b) by the Capital Gains Tax Act 1979, section 126 and Schedule 4, and in the cases of (f) to (i) by a new section 147A of that Act:

a) gifts by individuals of assets used for the purpose of a trade, profession or vocation by the donor, his family company or member of a trading group of which the holding company is the donor's family company;

b) disposals by trustees, otherwise than under bargains at arm's length, of assets used for the purposes of a trade, profession or vocation carried on by the trustees or by a beneficiary who had an interest in possession in the settled property immediately before the disposal;

c) gifts by both individuals and trustees of unquoted shares in trading companies and holding companies of trading groups, provided that such shares are not dealt in on the Unlisted Securities Market;

d) gifts of shares in quoted or USM trading companies and holding companies of trading groups, where the person making the disposal is
 i) an individual, provided that the company is his family company; or
 ii) a body of trustees who control not less than 25% of the voting rights exercisable by the shareholders of the company in general meeting;

e) gifts of agricultural land and buildings by both individuals and trustees which attract 30% or 50% agricultural property relief for IHT purposes (or which would attract such relief if the disposal were a chargeable transfer, instead of being an exempt or potentially exempt transfer);

f) gifts of any form of chargeable asset by both individuals and trustees which

---

9 Ibid, s 128.

10 Although each article is normally considered as a separate unit, s 128(4) can group together a set of articles.

11 Ibid, s 5. The figure is subject to indexation each 6 April.

are chargeable transfers for IHT purposes and which are not potentially exempt transfers;

g) gifts of any form of chargeable asset by the trustees of accumulation and maintenance settlements in circumstances where the Inheritance Tax Act 1984, section 71(4), prevents a charge to IHT arising (for example, when a beneficiary of an accumulation and maintenance trust becomes beneficially entitled to all or part of the settled property on or before attaining the age of 25 years);

h) gifts of heritage property to heritage maintenance funds and for public benefit; and

i) gifts to political parties.

Section 147A takes priority over section 126; see section 126(2)(d).

The result is that the making of a lifetime gift, unless of assets which are exempt from CGT or where hold-over relief as explained above is available, gives rise to a charge and liability to CGT under the Capital Gains Tax Act 1979, section 4. By the Finance Act 1988, section 98, CGT is levied at the appropriate income tax rate. It is computed, in the case of an individual, by adding the chargeable gains, after deduction of his annual exemption, to his taxable income for the tax year, thus subjecting the gains to his appropriate income tax rate. Accordingly, depending upon the taxpayer's income for the year and the amount of the chargeable gains, the rate of charge will be 25% or 40%.

It will be appreciated that the lifetime bounty of a transferor or donor would cause the worst of both sets of tax circumstances should he, having made a gift and disposal which did not enjoy the benefit of hold-over relief for CGT purposes, not survive the subsequent seven years with the result that his gift, which at the time of making was a potentially exempt transfer, becomes retroactively a chargeable transfer for IHT purposes, with a liability to be discharged. If that person had not made his gift, for CGT purposes there would have been no capital gain liability in respect of the particular assets on his death. Under the Capital Gains Tax Act 1979, section 49(1)(a), there is a deemed acquisition of the assets of the deceased person, at their value on death, by his personal representatives. Nevertheless, by section 49(1)(b) there is no disposal by the deceased person and thus no CGT liability. For IHT purposes if, for example, the spouse exemption applied, there would also be no IHT liability on the death.

T. Stamp duty on gifts

The Finance Act 1985, section 82(1), abolished the 1% ad valorem stamp duty on any conveyance or transfer operating as a voluntary disposition inter vivos, thus on lifetime gifts. Nevertheless, voluntary dispositions remained liable to 50p fixed duty under the heading 'Conveyance or Transfer of any kind'. The necessity for adjudication continued.

The combined provisions of sections 82(9) and 87 enabled regulations to be made to exempt voluntary dispositions from the liability to 50p fixed duty. The Treasury exercised their powers under section 87(2) to make regulations by the Stamp Duty (Exempt Instruments) Regulations 1987, SI 1987/516 which came into force on 1 May 1987. Under those regulations, from that date, *subject to a written certificate,* among other documents covered, the conveyance or transfer of property operating as a voluntary disposition inter vivos for no consideration in money or money's worth is exempt from 50p fixed duty and no longer requires adjudication. The regulations specify the requirements about the certificate. Having regard to those requirements it is suggested that any such document should include the necessary certificate within its terms.

The Finance Act 1991, sections 110 to 117, provides for the abolition of stamp duty on dealings in property other than land with effect from abolition day, the date to be appointed for the ending of stamp duty on share transactions.

u. Future bankruptcy of donor of gift

Regard needs to be had to the Insolvency Act 1986, section 339 et seq, which governs the position where a person is adjudged bankrupt and he has previously entered into a transaction with someone at an undervalue, including a gift.

If a gift is made within two years before the presentation of the bankruptcy petition, it can be impeached by the trustee in bankruptcy irrespective of the solvency of the donor at the time it was made.

If the gift is made within five years before the presentation of the bankruptcy petition it can likewise be impeached where the donor was insolvent at the time it was made or became insolvent because of it. Should the gift have been made to an 'associate', which expression includes a spouse, it is presumed that the donor was insolvent at the time of the gift unless the contrary is shown.

Chapter 6
Inheritance tax considerations in drafting wills

A. General principles

The way in which a will is drafted can materially affect the IHT liability arising on a testator's death in respect of his assets. The most common example is the use or not of the exemption as between spouses.[1] The spouse exemption can also be used to delay, until the second death, the need for sales by executors to meet IHT. This could be of practical importance where sales of certain assets may, at the time of the first death, be difficult or inconvenient. In advising clients it is necessary to keep a sense of proportion. If the testator has few assets, there is no IHT problem. If the testator wishes to benefit one person only, there is also no problem. Nevertheless, when that person happens to be the testator's mistress, and there is no matrimonial impediment, it should tactfully be pointed out to him that neither she nor his estate will qualify for any IHT exemption. Given the circumstances of a person with some capital, the making of a will itself is a tax planning exercise whether or not it leads to any other action.

Accordingly, apart from the more personal reasons for making one, a person's will is a tax planning exercise in itself, particularly when the testator has a husband or wife and the spouse exemption is thus available. In these circumstances, subject always to keeping in mind the needs of the surviving spouse, the aims should be to avoid any payment of IHT on the first death, to make full use of the nil% band at that time and to facilitate subsequent opportunities for tax mitigation. To enable use to be made of the nil% band, each spouse requires assets of sufficient value to cover it. An examination of the respective assets of the husband and wife should be made[2] and, for that purpose, account should be taken only of those assets which are owned by each, which may thus include a tenancy-in-common in the matrimonial home but not a joint tenancy which may therefore need to be changed by a simple notice to a tenancy-in-common; see form 115, page 256. In addition, regard should be paid to likely financial expectations in the future which would increase their assets. Regard should also be had to the current ages and health of the testator and his wife and therefore any material discrepancy in their likley expectations of life.[3]

There is sometimes a tendency to decry the surviving spouse receiving a life interest, as opposed to an absolute one, on the grounds that, for IHT purposes, the effect is the same.[4] It is nevertheless suggested that the possibility of a life interest, with the existence of suitable powers for the trustees over capital, should not be lightly discarded. The decision will be based on personal reasons and not fiscal ones, but

1 S 18.
2 See Form 9, p 156 below, for assets questionnaire.
3 See K of this chapter, p 82 below, for life expectancy table.
4 S 49(1).

a husband might well wish to give his wife a life interest only so that she may have the benefit of the financial guidance and wisdom of considerate trustees of whom she could, if desired, be one. They may also have differing views, even if only of degree, about the eventual destination of their assets. Such wills, in these days of people living longer and widows and widowers marrying again, will also safeguard the future inheritance of their children, come what may.

There are tax benefits generally which encourage the surviving spouse being limited to a life interest and which are dealt with in chapter 8.

B. Use of dwellinghouse or other settled property by a beneficiary

Where, under the trusts of a will, the trustees, pursuant to a direction or in exercise of their powers permit the person who enjoys the life/income interest to occupy a dwellinghouse which is an asset of the residuary estate there are no IHT consequences. Both before and after occupation the life tenant enjoyed an interest in possession in the totality of whatever comprised the settled property.

What is considered in this sub-chapter are the IHT effects, whether the life tenant is the surviving spouse or a non-exempt person, of occupation of the dwellinghouse being granted to another beneficiary, with the result that the life tenant effectively loses, whether or not permanently, his or her interest in that part of the settled property; and also the IHT effects when the right of occupation eventually ends. If the circumstances are such that the person, granted occupation, is regarded for IHT purposes as enjoying an interest in possession in the dwellinghouse, that will terminate the interest in possession of the life tenant therein, and subsequently result in a termination of the interest in possession of the occupier of the dwellinghouse when his own right of occupation ceases.[5]

Although Inland Revenue Statement of Practice, SP 10/79 is principally directed to circumstances where there is a settlement without an interest in possession, and occupation is granted to a beneficiary, it also gives guidance in its last paragraph on the view of the Inland Revenue in relation to the IHT effects on the granting of rights of occupation and seemingly also on the making of loans on non-commercial terms and intended to be permanent rather than short term and temporary.

The Statement of Practice reads as follows:

'Many wills and settlements contain a clause empowering the trustees to permit a beneficiary to occupy a dwellinghouse which forms part of the trust property on such terms as they think fit. The Inland Revenue do not regard the existence of such a power as excluding any interest in possession in the property.

Where there is no interest in possession in the property in question the Inland Revenue do not regard the exercise of the power as creating one if the effect is merely to allow non-exclusive occupation, or to create a contractual tenancy for full consideration. The Inland Revenue also take the view that no interest in possession arises on the creation of a lease for a term or a periodic tenancy for less than full consideration, though this will normally give rise to a charge for tax under paragraph 6(3) of Schedule 5 to the Finance Act 1975.[6] On the other hand, if the power is drawn in terms wide enough to cover the creation of an exclusive or joint right of residence, albeit revocable, for a definite or indefinite

5 S 52(1).
6 Now s 65.

period, and is exercised with the intention of providing a particular beneficiary with a permanent home, the Inland Revenue will normally regard the exercise of the power as creating an interest in possession. And if the trustees in exercise of their powers grant a lease for life for less than full consideration, this will also be regarded as creating an interest in possession in view of paragraph 1(3) and 3(6) of Schedule 5.[7]

A similar view will be taken where the power is exercised over property in which another beneficiary had an interest in possession up to the time of the exercise.'

Clear principles emerge from the study of SP 10/79. An analysis of any set of circumstances needs to be directed towards what the trustees intend to do or have in fact done. If, for example, the facts point to the grant by trustees of a settlement without an interest in possession of a right of exclusive occupation or in comparable circumstances a loan, of other kinds of goods, with *any* degree of permanence for the benefit of the particular beneficiary, then that would point to the beneficiary becoming entitled to an interest in possession for IHT purposes and a charge under section 65(1)(a). There would also be a charge on death as the result of the combined effect of sections 4(1) and 49(1). The cesser of occupation or enjoyment during the particular beneficiary's lifetime, subject to the detailed provisions of section 3A, will constitute a PET, in respect of which see the first paragraph of sub-chapter B of chapter 5, page 46 above.

c. Incidence of IHT

Under section 211(1), where personal representatives are liable for IHT on their deceased's free estate, so far as it is attributable to the value of property, both real and personal, in the United Kingdom which vests in them and was not immediately before the death comprised in a settlement that IHT liability is treated as a general testamentary and administration expense of the estate and thus, by the Administration of Estates Act 1925, section 33(2), and its First Schedule, is payable out of the general residuary estate.

Section 211(2) states that the foregoing provisions are subject to any contrary intention shown by the deceased in his will. It is recommended that in the case of all testamentary legacies of any kind, whether of realty or personalty, to non-exempt beneficiaries, the testator should state either that the gift is to be 'free of inheritance tax' or, in contrast, include words such as 'this gift shall bear its own share of any inheritance tax (and all other like taxes and duties) payable on or by reason of my death'. Section 211(1) does not apply to joint property. Joint property does not vest in the testator's personal representatives although it is part of his estate on death for IHT purposes and they are accountable for IHT in respect of it, but with the right to be repaid, under section 211(3), by the person in whom the property vests. There may be a case in any event for severing the joint tenancy so that thereafter each of the then tenants in common can express their wishes in their wills both about the destination of their respective interests and the burden of IHT.[8]

Care should be taken about altering the burden of IHT on assets that have the

---

7 Now ss 43(3) and 50(6).
8 Ch 7 is on the matrimonial home and considers these circumstances.

benefit of conditional exemption under section 30 etc (relief for works of art, historic buildings etc)[9] since if the liability arising on any future sales has effectively been placed by the terms of the will on the residuary estate, rather than the owner at the time, the personal representatives would, seemingly, need to retain an indeterminate fund for an indefinite period. The same factors should be taken into account in the case of woodlands[10] which have the benefit of relief under section 125 etc. Sections 207 and 208 should be noted in those respects.

D. IHT when payable by instalments

Reference should be made to sub-chapter L of Chapter 3.[11]

E. Exceptions when spouse and other transfers not exempt

This sub-chapter covers circumstances which can deny IHT exemption, in relation to both testamentary and lifetime gifts, in respect of transfers otherwise exempt, to spouses (section 18), charities (section 23), political parties (section 24), registered housing associations (section 24A), for national purposes etc (section 25) and for public benefit (section 26).

The six sets of exemptions do not apply if the testamentary or other gift takes effect on the termination after the transfer of value of any interest or period.[12] Thus, exemption from IHT is denied if the gift does not take effect immediately which would be the case if there was an intermediate interest, such as a prior life interest. Nevertheless, the exemption in the case of a spouse is not lost only because it is subject to a condition as to a survival period to be satisfied within twelve months.[13] The six-month period under section 92(1) needs also to be taken into account; see next sub-chapter F.

The six sets of exemptions, likewise, do not apply if the testamentary or other gift depends on a condition which is not satisfied within twelve months after the transfer.[12] By section 56(1) they also do not apply in relation to property which is given in consideration of the transfer of a reversionary interest if, by virtue of section 55(1), that interest does not form part of the estate of the person acquiring it.

The five sets of exemptions under sections 23 to 26 – section 23 (charities), section 24 (political parties), section 24A (registered housing associations), section 25 (national purposes etc) and section 26 (public benefit) – do not apply if:

  a) the gift is defeasible after twelve months or has been defeated within such period; or
  b) the gifted property is an interest in other property and that interest is less

9 See A of ch 4, p 31 above.
10 See E of ch 4, p 43 above.
11 P 25 above.
12 Ss 18(3), 23(2), 24(3), 24A(3), 25(2) and 26(7).
13 S 18(3)(b).

than the donor's or it is given for a limited period; any question whether any interest is less than the donor's must be decided as at a time twelve months after the transfer; or

c) the gifted property is an interest in possession in settled property and the settlement does not come to an end in relation to the settled property on the making of the transfer; or

d) the gifted property is land or a building and is given subject to an interest reserved or created by the donor which entitles him, his spouse or a person connected with him to possession of, or to occupy, the whole or any part of the land or building rent-free or at a rent less than might be expected to be obtained in a transaction at arm's length between persons not connected[14] with each other; or

e) the gifted property is not land or a building and is given subject to an interest reserved or created by the donor other than:

   i) an interest created by him for full consideration in money or money's worth; or

   ii) an interest which does not substantially affect the enjoyment of the property by the person or body to whom it is given; or

f) the gifted property or any part of it may become applicable for purposes other than charitable purposes or those of a body mentioned in sections 24, 25 or 26 or, where it is land, of a body mentioned in section 24A.

Where a person or body acquires a reversionary interest in settled property for a consideration in money or money's worth after 15 April 1976 section 18 (spouse exemption) does not apply in relation to the property when it becomes the property of that person or body on the termination of the interest on which the reversionary interest is expectant.[15] The exemptions under sections 23 to 26 do not apply if immediately before the time when the property becomes the property of the exempt body it is comprised in a settlement and at or before that time an interest under the settlement is or has been acquired for a consideration in money or money's worth after 11 April 1978 by that or another exempt body, but there shall be disregarded any acquisition from a charity, political party or body within sections 23 to 25.[16]

F. Section 92, survivorship clauses[17]

Where under the terms of a will (or otherwise) gifted property is subject to a condition of survival for a specified period of not more than six months, for IHT purposes whether the primary beneficiary so survives or not, the resultant gift is to be treated as taking effect from the time of death.

G. Sections 36 to 42, allocation of IHT exemptions

The above sections determine, where there is a transfer of value which is not wholly

14 S 270.
15 S 56(2).
16 S 56(3), (4).
17 Reference can also usefully be made to the note under Form 94, p 229 below.

exempt, particularly in the case of a deceased's estate taken as a whole, to what extent that transfer of value is exempt and the allocation of the relief from IHT.

As a preliminary matter, notice should be taken of section 41 which makes it clear that, *notwithstanding the terms of any disposition*, none of the IHT liability is to fall on or be attributable to any specific gift or any gift of the residuary estate to the extent that they are exempt transfers for IHT purposes.

Under section 4(1) the deemed transfer of value of a person's estate immediately before their death is for IHT purposes regarded as a single transfer of the whole. It may be taxable in full, exempt as a whole or partly taxable and partly exempt. Sections 36 to 42 only apply where the estate is partly taxable and partly exempt. Accordingly, if the beneficiaries are all exempt *or* all non-exempt those sections have no application.

A will is likely to be drafted in a manner that it can reasonably be anticipated that the value of the estate will be sufficient to meet the administration expenses and the non-residuary legacies, without regard to any IHT payable. If this does not prove to be the case, it will be necessary to abate the non-residuary legacies, according to the normal rules, before considering the IHT position: section 37(1).

Also, if, following the death, having dealt with the 'attribution of value to specific gifts' (see below), it is found that the residuary estate is of minus value, then the value of the specific gifts must be abated to produce a residuary estate of nil value. Abatement is to be in accordance with the will or according to the normal rules of law: section 37(2).

Specific gifts are gifts other than gifts of residue (section 42(1)).

The first task, in any event, is to calculate 'the attribution of value to specific gifts' (thereby also ascertaining 'the attribution of value to residuary gifts') *when* there are specific gifts (a) which are not to exempt beneficiaries or are to exempt beneficiaries outside the limits up to which their gifts are exempt (e.g. gifts exceeding £55,000 to a non-domiciled United Kingdom spouse from one who is) and (b) which do not bear their own IHT: section 38(1).

(a) Under section 38(3), where the *only* non-exempt (chargeable) gifts under the will, as a whole, are specific gifts, not bearing their own IHT, the gifts are aggregated and grossed up at the rate of IHT which would be appropriate if they alone were chargeable. A grossing up table is contained in C of the Appendix, p 275 below. If there have been chargeable lifetime transfers, during the seven year period prior to the death, the starting point of net transfers in the table must first be determined in the manner summarised in the note under that grossing up table. The foregoing calculation, under section 38(3), in accordance with section 39 also decides the value to be attributed to the residuary estate and thus enables the IHT calculation to be made.

(b) Under section 38(4) and (5) where the specific gifts, not bearing their own IHT, are not the only gifts which are chargeable, because for example part of the residuary estate is also non-exempt, it is necessary to start with the calculation under (a) above but to continue it with an *additional* grossing up calculation. The double set of calculations is illustrated by Example 2 in this sub-chapter.

When sections 36 to 42 apply, it is convenient to summarise the sequence to be applied in the following diagrammatic form:

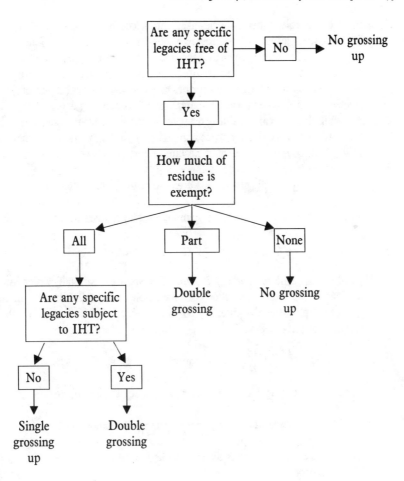

The following two examples using the IHT rates for the period from 6 April 1991 will assist.

Example 1
Estate £600,000.
Legacy of £200,000 free of IHT to son.
Residue to testator's spouse.
No lifetime chargeable transfers to be taken into account.
  a) The £200,000 legacy when grossed up on its own amounts to £240,000. This figure of £240,000, because the legacy is the only non-exempt gift and bears its own IHT, is its attribution of value.
  b) Accordingly, because the residuary estate is left to an exempt person the IHT liability on the estate amounts to £40,000.
  c) Thus, of the £600,000 the son receives £200,000, the Revenue for IHT £40,000 and the spouse £360,000 (but less administration expenses).

Example 2
Estate £600,000.
Legacy of £100,000 free of IHT to son.
Residue equally between spouse and daughter.

No lifetime chargeable transfers to be taken into account.
a) The £200,000 legacy, when grossed up on its own, amounts to £240,000.
b) The residue is therefore worth £360,000. Half of this figure, £180,000, being the part attributable to the spouse, is exempt, so that for the purposes of *this* stage of the calculation there is established a total chargeable part of £240,000 (the son) and £180,000 (the daughter), which comes to £420,000.
c) Accordingly, one can establish the percentage grossing-up rate, referrable to the son's £200,000 legacy, based on what would have been the amount of IHT (£112,000) on an unexempt estate of £420,000.

$$\left(\frac{£112,000}{£420,000} \times 100\right) \text{ is equivalent to a rate of } 26.67\%$$

d) At this rate of 26.67% the son's £200,000 legacy grosses up to

$$£272,740 \left(\frac{100}{100-26.67\ (=73.33)} \times £100,000\right)$$

e) On that basis, the residue is £327,260. The spouse's one-half, which amounts to £163,630 is exempt so that the chargeable part of the estate will be the £272,740, plus the daughter's £163,630 making £436,370, on which IHT amounts to £118,548.

$$\frac{£118,548}{£436,370} \times 100 \text{ is equivalent to a rate of } 27.17\%$$

f) At this rate of 27.17% the son's £200,000 legacy grosses-up to

$$£274,612 \left(\frac{100}{100-27.17\ (=72.83)} \times £200,000\right)$$

g) Thus the £600,000 estate is distributed as follows:

The total estate		£600,000
Son's legacy	£200,000	
IHT on £274,612 at 27.17%	£ 74,612	
		£274,612
		£325,388
Division of residue:		
Spouse's exempt share		£162,694
Daughter's share	£118,490	
IHT on £162,694 at 27.17%	£ 44,204	£162,694
		£325,388
Overall summary of division of estate:		
Son		£200,000
Spouse		£162,694
Daughter		£118,490
IHT £74,612 + £44,204		£118,816
		£600,000

The Inheritance Tax Act 1984, section 40, directs that 'where gifts taking effect on a transfer of value take effect separately out of different funds' – for example where on a death there are gifts out of the free estate and out of settlements – then

Sell → Convert those

investments while still non-non-remits

∴ non-domiciled.

Walk in Love.

The theme of Walk in Love (primary 5) is living in the christian community.
Most lessons concentrate on moral education.
The teaching on the Mass has to fit into that context.

Unit 3:4 is entitled 'At Mass we celebrate.' It revises and expands p 3.
We help pupils to describe the signs of celebration at mass.
We familiarise pupils with the parts of the mass.

Unit 3:5 'At Mass we are united in love'.
Sharing meals; the early Roman community at mass.
The Lord Jesus is with us at mass. He gives us the Bread of Life.
Prayer service focusing on Communion; a class mass.

Theologically
We link together the celebration of mass today
with the self-giving of Jesus on earth especially on Calvary
and with his Last Supper when he asked us to follow his example
and told us he would be with us as we 'remember' his words and actions.

At Mass Jesus offers himself to the Father.
We offer to the Father, in thanksgiving, the love and obedience of Jesus.
We unite ourselves with his offering.
Jesus is present to help us to love his Father and to love each other.

Note how Jesus 'redeems' us by being with

Passover - Last Supper - Jesus' teaching about the Bread of Life.

Unit 5.2. We remember Jesus' love for us.
Good Friday, the historical occasion;
Pupils make crucifixes as reminders of Jesus' suffering and of his love.

Unit 5:3. We celebrate the resurrection of Jesus.
Easter celebrations; the Emmaus story; prayer service.

Unit 5:4. We celebrate the presence of the risen Jesus in the sacraments.
Celebrations.
People who love us want to be with us on special occasions.
The risen Jesus wants to be with us in the sacraments.

These lessons are not directly concerned with the Mass.
They fill in the background and help the pupils understand
the historical origins of the Mass.
They will come to see the Mass as a celebration of the presence of the
risen Jesus.

Donald —

If Reardon & Donnell.

in Hong Kong. There are considerable tax advantages.

<u>1st</u>

If he has <u>lost</u> his Residency in the U.K but is domiciled outside the U.K there are still advantages though less than if both Reardon & Donnell

each fund is to be considered separately for the purpose of the allocation of exemptions under chapter III, including the grossing-up of the gifts. The rate of tax used by the Capital Taxes Office to gross-up separate gifts out of different funds has until recently been the rate applicable to the total value of *all* property chargeable on the testator's death. The Inland Revenue now accepts that the rate of tax to be used for grossing-up should be found by looking at each fund separately and n isolation.

Where a person died before 18 March 1986 owning property which attracted business property relief or agricultural property relief, it was possible under the terms of the will, including as the result of a variation under section 142, by a major cash legacy to a surviving spouse but with the residuary estate comprising such kind of property passing to non-exempt beneficiaries, to achieve surprising and dramatic mitigation of the total IHT liability. Section 39A, inserted by section 105 of the Finance Act 1986, changed the position with respect to transfers, including on death, made on or after 18 March 1986.

For such future transfers, in attributing the value transferred (as reduced by business property relief or agricultural property relief) to specific gifts and residuary gifts, the following rules now apply:

a) the starting point is the value transferred reduced by relief;

b) specific gifts of relievable property are to be taken at their value as reduced by the relief;

c) gifts other than specific gifts of relievable property (where the estate includes relievable property and is partly exempt), are to be reduced by multiplying them by the appropriation fraction–

$$\frac{\text{the value of the estate after relief}}{\text{the value of the estate before relief}}$$

save that where the estate includes specific gifts of relievable property and other relievable property, the specific gifts of relievable property, at their reduced and unreduced values respectively, are omitted from both the numerator and the denominator;

d) for grossing up purposes the reduced values are appropriate.

There are two examples illustrating the effects of section 39A in paragraph 9.29 of the booklet IHT I issued by the Board of Inland Revenue in January 1991. In summary, to take maximum advantage of business property relief or agricultural property relief it is necessary to bequeath the relevant property specifically to non-exempt beneficiaries. Whether that is a practicable possibility depends on the particular set of circumstances.

H. The nil% band

Each person on death has the benefit of a nil% band under the IHT table in Schedule I, to the extent that it has not been absorbed by the value of lifetime chargeable transfers made by him during the preceding seven years. For the year to 5 April 1991 the nil% band runs from £0 to £140,000.[18] If a deceased testator, as the following combined examples show, not having made any chargeable transfers during the seven years preceding his death, leaves all his assets to his spouse, and thus does not take advantage of his nil% band, a material IHT advantage will have been disregarded. The interests of the surviving spouse must, depending on the figures and

18 This figure is subject to indexation each 6 April, see p 16 above.

circumstances, inevitably take priority over any advantage in mitigating the IHT liability.

Example 1

    a) Testator's assets are worth £300,000. There have been no chargeable transfers during the preceding seven years which would affect his nil% band. He gives everything to his wife, who has assets worth £100,000. She dies worth £400,000.

    b) There is no IHT liability on the testator's death because of the spouse exemption. Based on current IHT rates there will be an IHT liability of £104,000 on the wife's death.

Example 2

    a) Testator's assets are worth £300,000. There have been no chargeable transfers during the preceding seven years which would affect his nil% band. He gives £140,000 to his children and the balance to his wife, who has assets worth £100,000. She dies worth £260,000.

    b) There is no IHT liability on the testator's death because of the nil% band and the spouse exemption. Based on current IHT rates there will be an IHT liability of £48,000 on the wife's death.

Accordingly, if circumstances allow, a will to conform with Example 2, as opposed to Example 1, would result in a saving in IHT of £56,000.

Desirable though that saving of £56,000 may be the financial circumstances may well not allow for the testator to make his will in a form in keeping with Example 2. The testator's primary aim will no doubt be to safeguard his wife financially and therefore the mitigation of IHT and increasing the benefits to go following the death of the survivor, to their children or other beneficiaries, must take second place. The financial circumstances which militate against that means of saving IHT may include the fact that a substantial part of the value of the joint assets of the testator and his wife is the matrimonial home. Therefore the assets available to provide an investment income for the wife may be comparatively small and will only be sufficient if she enjoys the benefit of the husband's assets as a whole in addition to her own.

Nevertheless, instead of making his will in a form in keeping with Example 2, it would be possible for the testator to bequeath a settled legacy of £140,000[19] on discretionary trusts, therefore without a 'qualifying interest in possession',[20] under which nevertheless the wife is to be regarded as the primary beneficiary. Subject thereto the wife, as before, is to be entitled to the testator's residuary estate. The intention would be that ultimately the settled legacy would be distributed to the children or other beneficiaries following the death of the wife.

Example 3

    a) Testator's assets are worth £300,000. There have been no lifetime chargeable transfers to be taken into account which would affect his nil% band. He settles £140,000 upon discretionary trusts. The wife is entitled to his residuary estate of £160,000. She dies worth £260,000.

    b) i) There is no IHT liability on testator's death because of the nil% band and the spouse exemption. Based on current IHT rates there will be an IHT liability of £48,000 on the spouse's death.

19 This figure is subject to indexation each 6 April, see p 16 above.
20 S 59(1).

 ii) On the assumption that the capital value of the discretionary trust either did not exceed £140,000 or that it increased in value broadly in line with the changes in the retail price index there will be no, or at most little, IHT liability as the result of the periodic charge every ten years[1] or when the settled capital leaves the discretionary trust[2] following the death of the wife as the result of the trustees exercising their powers of distribution in whatever manner may be considered appropriate.

While the IHT saving by adopting such a scheme is material there will be during their currency the expense of administering the discretionary trust and the need to discharge the additional rate tax liability of 10%[3] under the Income and Corporation Taxes Act 1988, section 686, although as the result of receiving any income, the wife in due course may be able to recover the tax, dependent on her tax circumstances. So far as concerns capital gains tax, although there will be a deemed disposal, under the Capital Gains Tax Act 1979, section 54(1), subject to an election being made, hold-over relief will be available under the Capital Gains Tax Act 1979, section 147A(2)(a), when the settled capital leaves the trust.

A point to be emphasised is that, when there is such a nil% band discretionary trust, other non-exempt trusts within the same will must be avoided as they would be classed as related settlements under section 62 and as the result of the surrounding sections that would adversely affect any such scheme to save IHT. It is possible to avoid settlements being related by a testator during his lifetime constituting lifetime trusts with a nominal sum and for him to give a legacy under his will to the trustees of those trusts. The lifetime trusts, despite the addition to them, and the testamentary trusts will not be related settlements for the purposes of section 62 because they will not have commenced on the same day. It is likewise possible after the death of the testator to have a deed under section 142(1), whereby, for example, an absolute beneficiary varies the testator's will in such manner that assets he has inherited are directed to be held upon the trusts of two newly constituted groups, with different dates, for separate branches of his family. Those settlements commencing on separate days are not related to each other within the terms of section 62(1).

1. Section 143 ('precatory trusts')

Section 143 provides that where a testator expresses a wish that property (therefore not necessarily chattels) bequeathed[4] by his will should be transferred by the legatee to other persons, *and* the legatee transfers any of the property in accordance with that wish within the period of two years after the testator's death, the effect is to treat the gift not as a transfer of value by the legatee himself but as if made by the deceased under his will for IHT purposes. It is important to recognise that not only does there need to be an actual expression of wish by the deceased but its terms must be certain, with available evidence in support. Accordingly, although the wishes of the testator need not necessarily be in writing, it is advisable that they should be.

1 S 64.
2 S 65(1)(a).
3 This is the percentage for 1991/92.
4 This word suggests that this provision is limited to personalty.

It will be recognised that this sub-section is of very practical help in the case of articles such as jewellery, pictures and furniture, and will avoid the necessity of a testator listing his detailed wishes in his will with the consequent need to make changes, by further will or codicil, should he, thereafter, need to change those wishes.

Form 31, page 177 below, and the succeeding Form 32 illustrate first the kind of clause which can be inserted in the testator's will and secondly the note or memorandum in which he can record his wishes, to be updated and amended as and when desired. The clause in the will should make clear what is to happen to the rest of his personal effects, possibly the major part, not covered by his note or memorandum.

J. Death in service benefits under approved pension scheme

On the death in service and therefore before retirement of an employee who is a member of an approved pension scheme constituted by his employer, it is usual for a lump sum death benefit to be payable. The cash sum can, typically, be equal to four times what is described as the employee's pensionable salary. It can therefore be large.

The pension trustees will receive the cash sum from the insurance company concerned to be held by them upon the trusts expressed in the Pension Rules. Those trusts will usually be of a discretionary nature whereby the pension trustees are required to pay the lump sum death benefit to one or more of the deceased employee's dependants or to his personal representatives as they in their discretion decide. Included among the dependants will naturally be the employee's widow.

Although the ultimate decision about the manner of distribution will rest with the pension trustees, employees are invariably invited to express their own wishes on a standard form, which wishes will doubtless be adhered to in the absence of unusual circumstances.

As mentioned in sub-chapter O of chapter 3, no liability to IHT arises in respect of benefits payable on a person's death where the pension trustees make a discretionary payment of a lump sum. That will be the case irrespective of the manner in which the pension trustees in accordance with the exercise of their discretion make the distribution, whether to the surviving spouse or to other persons.

It will be appreciated that although a distribution of the cash sum to the employee's widow will be free of IHT, the lump sum or what represents it to the extent that it is retained will on her death form part of her assets. Accordingly, it will then suffer IHT as part of her estate.

In contrast, it would be possible for all or part of the distribution to be made to the employee's children. That possibility may not be a practical one because of the financial needs of the widow herself.

In the circumstances envisaged, the following set of arrangements can save a substantial amount of IHT for the benefit of the children or ultimate inheritors, yet at the same time safeguard the financial needs of the widow:

   a) On the particular form expressing his wishes the employee requests the pension trustees to pay the lump sum benefit to his executors. It could be considered sensible if he was to mention in the form with whom his will is lodged, particularly if it is with his solicitors who are thus aware of the circumstances.
   b) In his will the employee expressly anticipates the possibility of his executors receiving money from the trustees of his pension scheme which he will describe

by name. He then declares that the money should be held upon the trusts and with and subject to the powers and provisions which he thereafter sets out in his will. Those trusts will be discretionary. Nevertheless in the course of those provisions he will expressly declare but without imposing or creating any binding trust or legal obligation upon them that his executors and trustees should regard his wife as the primary discretionary beneficiary of the income of the invested cash. He can also state that capital as and when needed by her should be made available.

Undoubtedly the foregoing arrangements can result in a substantial mitigation of the IHT liability when contrasted with the position that would apply on the death of the widow had she herself received the lump sum benefit. Nevertheless, the IHT position following the executors receiving it is not a straightforward one. The position would appear to be as follows:

a) It will generally be governed by Chapter III of Part III of the 1984 Act.

b) Under section 58(1) once the lump sum is paid away by the pension trustees it will cease to be protected by paragraph (d) of that sub-section, in relation to section 151, and will become 'relevant property' and accordingly subject to the IHT regime of settlements without interests in possession, thus for discretionary trusts.

c) Because of section 81 which deals with property moving between settlements the settled property representing the lump sum is deemed to continue to remain in the first settlement which comprises the trusts of the pension scheme itself. Until the death of the employee section 58(1)(d) applies but in any event the settled property will have no value.

d) When it comes to applying the IHT charges under section 64, at a ten-year anniversary, or under section 65, charges at other times including when the capital is distributed by the executors and trustees to their beneficiaries, it would appear that the settlement is treated as having commenced when the employee joined the pension scheme for the purposes of sections 60 and 61. That would seem to be so having regard to the definition of 'settlor' in section 44 whether the pension scheme is a contributory one or a non-contributory one.

e) In the case of a charge under section 65 on a capital distribution before the following ten-year anniversary, it would at first sight appear that, for the purposes of section 69, the rate between ten-year anniversaries, that rate being controlled by the value on the immediately previous ten-year anniversary, is nil because the employee was living at that time, when no value can be placed on the settled property. Nevertheless, because of section 69(2)(b) the settled property representing the lump sum will be regarded as if the settled property had been 'relevant property' for the purposes of section 58 at the date of the prior ten-year anniversary and the value attributed to it because of section 69(3) being its value when it became relevant property, that is following the employee's death.

f) In the case of the charge under section 64, when that ten-year anniversary occurs which is the next one after the death of the employee, the rate will be determined by section 66 in the ordinary way.

Despite the complexity of the foregoing statutory provisions, as has been mentioned such a scheme of arrangements can result in a substantial mitigation of IHT bearing in mind that the rates on discretionary trust capital can never at any time exceed

6%, being 30% of half the highest rate in the table in Schedule I to the 1984 Act, which is 40%.

K. Life expectancy tables

For male lives

Age	Life expectancy	Age	Life expectancy
18	56.438 years	51	25.165 years
19	55.494	52	24.298
		53	23.443
20	54.545	54	22.599
21	53.593		
22	52.638	55	21.767
23	51.680	56	20.948
24	50.719	57	20.142
		58	19.351
25	49.755	59	18.573
26	48.789		
27	47.822	60	17.811
28	46.853	61	17.065
29	45.883	62	16.334
		63	15.620
30	44.912	64	14.923
31	43.941		
32	42.970	65	14.243
33	42.000	66	13.582
34	41.031	67	12.938
		68	12.313
35	40.063	69	11.707
36	39.097		
37	38.133	70	11.119
38	37.172	71	10.551
39	36.214	72	10.003
		73	9.474
40	35.260	74	8.964
41	34.310		
42	33.365	75	8.474
43	32.425	76	8.004
44	31.491	77	7.553
		78	7.121
45	30.564	79	6.708
46	29.643		
47	28.730	80	6.315
48	27.826	81	5.940
49	26.929	82	5.583
		83	5.244
50	26.042	84	4.923

Age	Life expectancy	Age	Life expectancy
85	4.618 years	89	3.562 years
86	4.331		
87	4.059	90	3.336
88	3.803		

For female lives

As above, as in the case of males, but with the following increases of years according to age.

Age	Increase of years
Under 61	4
61 to 70	3
71 to 80	2
81 and over	1

NOTE

These tables are reproduced from *CTT News* of January 1979, p 58. The most uncertain factors in tax planning, including on the making of wills, are the date of death of the client and the date of death of his or her principal beneficiaries or beneficiary usually in the person of the spouse. Any calculation of life expectancy can of course be distorted by a history of ill health apart from death as a result of accidents and the effects of injuries. Conversely, and more happily, a person whose parents live for many years is likely to do the same. Nevertheless, these tables can be useful for the purpose of giving, with suitable tact, examples by way of illustration for testators, apart from enabling the draftsman to form a view.

Chapter 7
Matrimonial home in relation to will drafting

There is a strong and respectable body of opinion, from professional advisers and individual clients, that the matrimonial home is too important and personal an asset to be the subject of any IHT mitigation scheme. That is understandable. Nevertheless, this chapter demonstrates how the drafting of the will in relation to the matrimonial home can mitigate future IHT liability where the circumstances are appropriate.

It may well be the case that when the assets of the testator and his wife are examined that, apart from investments from which the survivor will need the income, the main asset is the matrimonial home. It may thus form a large proportion of the value of their joint assets. Hence, the limiting factor and the importance of the matrimonial home and the possible disproportionately large value of it in relation to the husband's and wife's assets as a whole.

The IHT incentive to move towards the equalisation of the assets of husband and wife has reduced since 15 March 1988. Before that date there were a series of progressive IHT rate bands. Because there is now only the one positive rate of 40% over the upper limit of the nil% band, that means that any necessary move towards equalisation need only result in the less wealthy of two spouses having sufficient assets also to enjoy the nil% IHT band. Thereafter everything suffers IHT on death at 40%.

If the matrimonial home is in the name of the husband then, unless there are reasons to the contrary, there is a good case for the husband assigning, say, a half interest in it to his wife or executing a declaration of trust to the same effect to enable her to have sufficient assets to cover her nil% IHT band on her death. On the making of such a gift, there will be no IHT liability,[1] no capital gains tax liability[2] and no stamp duty liability.[3]

Although each case needs to be considered on its separate merits it is suggested that, generally, when house property is bought in the names of husband and wife jointly their beneficial rights should be as tenants in common, whether or not in equal shares. And likewise, if their property is held by them as joint tenants beneficially, the joint tenancy should be severed, by notice,[4] and thus changed into a tenancy in common, inevitably in equal shares.

The reason for the foregoing is, in the first instance, practical. By section 184 of the Law of Property Act 1925, where two (or more) persons have died in circumstances rendering it uncertain which of them survived the other(s), such deaths

---

1 S 18.
2 Capital Gains Tax Act 1979, s 44.
3 Finance Act 1985, s 82(1), which abolished 1% ad valorem stamp duty, and the Stamp Duty (Exempt Instruments) Regulations 1987, SI 1987/516.
4 Precedent 115, p 256 below.

shall . . . for all purposes affecting the title to property, be presumed to have occurred in order of seniority, and accordingly the younger shall be deemed to have survived the elder. The point about to be made applies equally where there is a joint calamity and it is known whether the younger survived the elder or vice versa. In the case of a joint tenancy the interest of the first to die, whether in fact known or in the sequence presumed by section 184, would pass automatically by survivorship to the (presumed) survivor, and thus to the survivor's estate, and devolve in accordance with the terms of the latter's will or intestacy provisions. Accordingly, for example, where they have no children, the beneficiaries could be the parents of the presumed survivor, to the total exclusion of the parents of the other.

If the property is held by them as tenants in common, then each of them will be able, under their respective wills, either as a specific legacy or as part of their residuary estates, to give their interest in the property to the other, but subject to a condition of survivorship by a stipulated period, of say, three months; and each can then state who are the substitutional beneficiaries should that not happen.

For the purposes of IHT on death, section 4(2) states that where it cannot be known which of two or more persons who have died survived the other (or others) they shall be assumed to have died at the same instant. This does not cover the position where in fact it is known which of two deceased persons survived the other although IHT quick succession relief under section 141 would be available.

Although practical considerations, affecting the surviving spouse in relation to the matrimonial home, should always be foremost in contrast to considerations of IHT, where there is a tenancy in common it is possible to save IHT on the spouse's death by the testator bequeathing all or part of his interest in the property to, say, their children and so to take practical advantage of his IHT nil% band. The surviving spouse, by reason of her interest, would be able to continue to occupy the property, without payment,[5] and the testator, in order further to safeguard the existing rights of the survivor, could stipulate, in making his testamentary gift to the children, that the trust for sale over the property should not be enforced without the survivor's personal consent in writing.[6] It would equally be possible for a husband and wife, indeed when making themselves tenants in common, to enter into a deed safeguarding the position of the survivor.[7]

A fundamental matter, in the latter circumstances, which needs to be anticipated and considered is what would be the position of the surviving spouse, being already the owner of a half interest in the house, requiring a substantial proportion, possibly more than her one-half of the total proceeds of sale, to finance the acquisition of another home. Is it desirable that other members of the family should be entitled to the other one-half of the proceeds and therefore that she might need to be beholden to them for their co-operation and bounty? Is it, therefore, possible to overcome this necessity by the testator bequeathing his one-half share upon discretionary trusts? If so, under those trusts should the widow be one of the discretionary beneficiaries?

Although, as already mentioned, the surviving spouse, by reason of her interest, would be enabled to continue to occupy the property, without payment,[7] care on the part of the will trustees will be required when exercising their powers. In that

5 See, for example, *Bull v Bull* [1955] 1 QB 234 at 237, CA and *Williams & Glyn's Bank Ltd v Boland* [1980] 2 All ER 408 at 414 g–h, HL.

6 See, for example, the proviso and declaration at the end of (b) of the investment powers in Form 80, p 218 below.

7 Precedent 115, p 256 below.

respect Inland Revenue Statement of Practice, SP 10/79 should be studied. It reads as follows:

'Many wills and settlements contain a clause empowering the trustees to permit a beneficiary to occupy a dwelling-house which forms part of the trust property on such terms as they think fit. The Inland Revenue do not regard the existence of such a power as excluding any interest in possession in the property.

Where there is no interest in possession in the property in question the Inland Revenue do not regard the exercise of the power as creating one if the effect is merely to allow non-exclusive occupation, or to create a contractual tenancy for full consideration. The Inland Revenue also take the view that no interest in possession arises on the creation of a lease for a term or a periodic tenancy for less than full consideration, though this will normally give rise to a charge for tax under section 65.[8] On the other hand, if the power is drawn in terms wide enough to cover the creation of an exclusive or joint right of residence, albeit revocable, for a definite or indefinite period, and is exercised with the intention of providing a particular beneficiary with a permanent home, the Inland Revenue will normally regard the exercise of the power as creating an interest in possession. And if the trustees in exercise of their powers grant a lease for life for less than full consideration, this will also be regarded as creating an interest in possession in view of sections 43(3) and 50(6).[9]

A similar view will be taken where the power is exercised over property in which another beneficiary had an interest in possession up to the time of the exercise.'

If the husband bequeaths his one-half share of the matrimonial home upon trusts under which the widow is a discretionary beneficiary, there is a case for the Capital Taxes Office to contend, having regard to the practical result, that she has an interest in possession. And, if that was correct, then the testator's former share in the matrimonial home will be subject to IHT on the widow's death and the scheme thereby will fail.

If, in contrast, the widow is not a discretionary beneficiary then the trustees of that discretionary trust, in exercise of their fiduciary powers, would be unable in the future to use the half share of the proceeds of sale towards a substitute home for the widow because to do so would be in breach of trust.

Thus, to have a successful IHT testamentary scheme using the matrimonial home does not depend solely on whether the testator's share is bequeathed direct to the children or is subjected to discretionary trusts under which the widow is not a beneficiary even though in either case it is stipulated that the trust for sale over the property cannot be enforced without the survivor's personal consent in writing.

The result is unsatisfactory because in both cases it is not possible to make sure that the particular part of the proceeds of sale can be used towards a future substitute home for the widow. An alternative, but more modest possibility, is therefore proposed.

It is fair to assume that any substitute house will be of less value than the original matrimonial home. Accordingly, the testator and his adviser could well form a judgment about what percentage of the sale proceeds of his share the widow may sufficiently need, in addition to her own share, for her subsequent purchase.

If that is done then the testator should gift or settle his own share as to X% for his wife and as to Y% either to the children or otherwise upon discretionary

8 The statement refers to para 6(3) of Sch 5 to the Finance Act 1975.
9 The statement refers to paras 1(3) and 3(6) respectively of Sch 5 above.

trusts for the benefit of his family other than his wife, in the latter respect in relation to his present house with the stipulation that the trust for sale over the property should not be enforced without the survivor's personal consent in writing.[10]

It is the case that joint interests in property together owned by a husband and wife, whether in equal shares or otherwise, are subject to valuation for IHT purposes as appropriate portions of the value of the related property taken in the aggregate.[11]The result is that no discount in valuation on account of the divided ownership is allowed even where the husband and wife in fact own their undivided shares in the property as tenants in common. Nevertheless, in the circumstances discussed, on the death of the survivor his or her share in the property will no longer be related property for the purposes of valuation, with the possibility of a discount of around 15%.[12] The valuation of an undivided share in property which is not related property and where the relationship of tenants in common exists was examined by the Land Tribunal in *Wight and Moss v IRC*[13]which case can usefully be studied. The suggested 15% discount is based on the existence only of a joint ownership. If there are contractual provisions which affect the rights of the joint owners or the particular one, it can be suggested that the share to be valued should receive a greater discount than 15%. And that would also apply if that share is under one-half of the whole on the analogy of the valuation of a minority shareholding in a company where there is a controlling shareholder.

Whatever testamentary dispositions are made the future capital gains tax consequences need consideration. The exemption for a gain on the disposal of an individual's private residence under the Capital Gains Tax Act 1979, section 101, extended by section 104 to the residence of a beneficiary who is entitled to occupy it by the terms of a settlement or under a discretion exercised by the trustees, does not extend to the proportion of the ownership of others who are not in occupation.

---

10 See, for example, the proviso and declaration at the end of (b) of the investment powers in Form 64.
11 S 161 contains the related property provisions. See also p 22 above.
12 See *Dymond's Capital Taxes* 23.520.
13 (1982) 264 Estates Gazette 935.

Chapter 8
Considerations in framing the trusts of the residuary estate

A. Introduction

Provided that the assets, both present and future, are likely to be of sufficient substance to warrant testamentary drafting to mitigate future tax liabilities, particularly IHT, and provided also that the family and other circumstances generally warrant it the scheme of residuary trusts under sub-chapter C is recommended. Nevertheless, it is helpful first to examine what until recently has been the customary choice of drafting absolute trusts, with straight gifts or life interest trusts over a testator's residuary estate.

B. Absolute trusts and life interest trusts

There is sometimes a tendency to assume that because of the spouse exemption for IHT purposes it is simple and best for the testator under his will to give his residuary estate absolutely to his spouse, if she survives him. Apart from the fact that the spouse exemption equally applies when the surviving spouse's interest is limited to a life interest,[1] it is nevertheless suggested that the possibility of a life interest, with the existence of suitable powers for the trustees over capital, should not be lightly discarded. The decision will be based on personal reasons and not fiscal ones, but a husband might well wish to limit his wife to a life interest if only so that she may have the benefit of the financial guidance and wisdom of considerate trustees of whom she could, if desired, be one. They may also have differing views, even if only of degree, about the eventual destination of their assets. Such wills, in these days of people living longer and widows and widowers marrying again, will also safeguard the future inheritance of their children, come what may. It is also the case that, for capital gains tax purposes, where there is a life interest trust the rate of tax on disposals is equivalent to the basic rate of income tax, at present 25%,[2] whereas, in contrast, where the wife's interest is an absolute one, it may be equivalent to a rate of tax at the higher rate, at present 40%.[3] By having such arrangements it will be open to the remaindermen, usually in these circumstances the children, to 'give away' all or part of their interests, while in reversion, at a time when they themselves may have prospered. Any such gift would normally be a 'non-event' in relation to themselves for IHT purposes. Generally, under section 48, a reversionary interest is excluded property. A gift of a reversionary interest could, in contrast to an absolute one, be a gift in settlement, such as by the making

1 Ss 18 and 49(1).
2 FA 1988, s 98(1).
3 Ibid, s 98(2).

of an accumulation and maintenance trust complying with the conditions for relief under section 71. For capital gains tax purposes, although under the Capital Gains Tax Act 1979, section 19, a reversionary interest is capable of being an asset the disposal of which gives rise to a chargeable gain, under section 58 normally no chargeable gain accrues on the disposal of an interest under a settlement, including the reversion to an annuity or life interest by the person for whose benefit the interest was created by the settlement.

c. Overriding power of appointment with underlying life interest trust for widow and/or discretionary trust[4]

It is not difficult to envisage cases where the testator's future wishes, circumstances and assets, and thus the interests of his potential beneficiaries, are uncertain so as to make it helpful to delay the effective making of 'his' testamentary dispositions until after his death. This would also enable those dispositions to be executed in as an effective IHT manner as the financial and other circumstances allow. It will be readily accepted that many testators will not welcome the proposal that their executors and trustees, even within the confines of their expressed class of beneficiaries, should be able, in effect, to 'make' their wills after their deaths. To enable such testamentary provisions to be acceptable, great care is required in the choice of executors and trustees, so that any such testator will have reason to feel confident about their ability to make proper judgment. Also, at the same time as the testator makes his will, he should, both in fairness to himself and his executors and trustees, make a memorandum of guidance which, though not legally binding, would be treated with the seriousness that it undoubtedly would deserve. Accordingly, one should be made by the testator, no doubt with help from his will draftsman, to be altered and updated thereafter, as and when necessary.

Provided that the assets, both present and future, are in fact of sufficient substance to warrant testamentary drafting to mitigate future tax liabilities, particularly IHT, and provided also that the family and other circumstances generally warrant it, the following scheme of residuary trusts is recommended:

a) An overriding power of appointment exercisable by the executors and trustees, during a defined period not exceeding the usually adopted perpetuity period of eighty years, among a reasonably wide class which typically includes the widow, the children and remoter issue and any person who is or has been a spouse of any child or remoter issue. The terms of the power enables absolute appointments for those to be benefited and also appointments whereby trusts can be constituted including those of a discretionary or protective nature. There should be specific provision whereby any appointment can be made by the executors and trustees prior to the obtaining of probate or the completion of the administration of the estate.

b) The underlying trusts apply in default of and until and subject to any appointment by the executors or trustees and are as follows:[4]

i) if the wife survives the testator by three months she is to receive the income during her life;

ii) subject to that, including where the wife does not so survive or dies during a period not exceeding two years after the death of the testator, the executors

---

4 A will of this kind is contained under 1 on p 127.

and trustees, during *that* period, are to pay or apply the income of the residuary estate as they decide to or for the benefit of, say, the children and remoter issue. Alternatively or additionally the executors and trustees can have power to accumulate income;

iii) subject to i) and ii) the residuary trusts continue in typical form for the children, or issue of any deceased child.

The IHT and other tax consequences according to whether, following the death of the testator, the underlying trust over income is as under b) i) for the wife or is as under b) ii) held under discretionary trusts during the period not excluding two years from the death, are examined in turn.

Where the wife survives and is thus entitled to the income there is no IHT liability on the death of the testator because of the spouse exemption subject to the special circumstances about overseas domicile in sub-section (2) of section 18.[5]

If thereafter during the lifetime of the wife, the executors or trustees – of whom the wife might be one – exercise their overriding power of appointment away from the wife in such manner as to extinguish any part of her income/life interest, she will be treated as having made a potentially exempt transfer and on her death, provided that she survives the appointment by seven years, the capital so appointed will also not be liable to IHT.[6]

It is the case that, despite the wife being treated as having made a potentially exempt transfer, the gifts with reservation provisions of the Finance Act 1986, section 102, do not apply in contrast to the position had the wife herself made a potentially exempt transfer by releasing all or part of the trust capital from which she is entitled to the income.

Where the gifts with reservation provisions of section 102 do in fact bite, gifted property is subject to IHT on the donor's death, irrespective of the number of years since the gift was made. Section 102 will apply where possession or enjoyment of the gifted property is not bona fide assumed by the donee at or before the beginning of 'the relevant period'. That period means the period of seven years before the donor's death. It will also apply where at any time in the relevant period that gifted property is not enjoyed to the entire exclusion, or virtually to the entire exclusion, of the donor and of any benefit to him by contract or otherwise.[7]

Thus, there can be gifts with reservation resulting in 'property subject to a reservation' when, for example, either the donor retains some benefit as the result of the arrangements by which he makes the gift, or he enjoys thereafter at any time during the seven years before his death some benefit from the gifted property or as the result of his gift.[7]

The opening words of section 102 are crucial. Section 102 is to apply where on or after 18 March 1986 an individual disposes of any property by way of gift.

It is convenient to assume for the purposes of illustration that the trustees of whom the wife is one exercise their power of appointment over that part of the trust capital which represents the matrimonial home in favour of an adult child of the marriage in such manner that the child becomes absolutely entitled to it. There could be sound family reasons for that course of action such as to persuade a daughter to move into the matrimonial home where her mother continues to live in order to look after her.

---

5 The spouse exemption applies in conjunction with s 49(1) for that result.
6 S 3A, in particular sub-s (7).
7 Ch 5, sub-ch D, p 48 is on the subject of property subject to a reservation.

The wife will be treated as having made a potentially exempt transfer.[8] The gifted property, being the matrimonial home, will not be subject to IHT if she survives the exercise of the power of appointment by seven years. Because of the opening words of section 102 the gifts with reservation provisions do not apply. Those words make it plain that section 102 only applies where an individual has made a gift of property. It is not possible to impute to the testator's wife a gift by her albeit that by the exercise by the trustees of their power of appointment she is deprived of all or part of her life/income interest in the trust capital and thus will be treated as having made a potentially exempt transfer.

For capital gains tax purposes, where the wife has a life interest, the rate of tax on disposals by the trustees is 25%[2] in contrast to the possible rate of 40%[3] where the wife is entitled absolutely. Such a trust cannot be regarded as one where the settlor or his spouse has an interest and thus with their possible higher rate of tax. That is because for the purposes of the Finance Act 1988, section 109 and Schedule 10, 'spouse' does not include a widow or widower. The trustees will, however, have an annual exemption for gains of up to £2,750, in contrast to £5,500 for the surviving wife for chargeable gains in the case of disposals of assets of her own.[9]

Where an appointment by the trustees extinguishes any part of the income/life interest of the wife but constitutes continuing trusts there will not be a charge to capital gains tax as a result. But where that appointment confers absolute interests or, unusually, trusts under what is construed as a different settlement, there will be a charge to capital gains tax in respect of the particular assets under the Capital Gains Tax Act 1979, section 54(1) which applies 'when a person becomes absolutely entitled to any settled property as against the trustee . . .'. Hold-over relief is only available in limited circumstances.[10] Nevertheless, to return to the illustration of the trustees exercising their power of appointment over that part of the trust capital which represents the matrimonial home, almost certainly the relief under the Capital Gains Tax Act 1979, section 101 will apply because section 104 extends that relief to cases where, during the period of ownership of the trustee, the dwelling-house has been the only or main residence of a person entitled to occupy it under the terms of the settlement, being in this case the surviving wife.

Where the wife, in the circumstances under consideration, does not survive the testator or dies within the period of three months after the testator's death (section 92 in fact enables a six month period to be specified) advantage can be taken of section 144. That is because the income of the residuary estate would then be held upon discretionary trusts.

The terms of section 144 are as follows:

'(1) This section applies where property comprised in a person's estate immediately before his death is settled by his will and, within the period of two years after his death and before any interest in possession has subsisted in the property, there occurs

    a) an event on which tax would (apart from this section) be chargeable under any provision, other than section 64 or 79 of Chapter III of Part III of this Act, or

    b) an event on which tax would be so chargeable but for section 75 or 76 above or paragraph 16(1) of Schedule 4 to this Act.

---

8 S 52 and s 3A (see sub-s (7)).

9 CGTA 1979, s 5 and Sch 6. CGT (Annual Exempt Amount) Order, SI 1991/736.

10 See ch 5, sub-chapter S, p 65.

(2) Where this section applies by virtue of an event within paragraph (a) of sub-section (1) above, tax shall not be charged under the provision in question on that event; and in every case in which this section applies in relation to an event, this Act shall have effect as if the will had provided that on the testator's death the property should be held as it is held after the event.'

In summary, section 144 provides that so long as property settled by a will is held on trusts lacking an interest in possession, because they contain discretionary trusts or a power to accumulate income or both, any termination of those trusts within the period of two years will not result in an IHT 'exit' charge which normally applies when settled property ceases to be comprised in such kind of trusts. Instead, as appears from section 144(2), the will is treated as if the testator had effected the resultant variation.

It would seem to be the case that any termination of the non-interest in possession trusts within the period of two years after the death should not as a matter of principle take place within the first three months of that period. Section 144 only applies when there occurs an event on which tax would otherwise be chargeable. If property ceases to be subject to such trusts within three months after the death, because of section 65(4) it would not be subject to IHT and therefore the 'reading-back' provisions of section 144 would not apply and, accordingly, the original liability to IHT will not be affected. In the case of the circumstances under discussion the principle is unlikely to have relevance because the assumption is that the wife is dead. The matter is relevant where an appointment is to be made for an exempt beneficiary, such as the surviving spouse or charity, in which event the IHT spouse exemption will apply retrospectively.

The terms of the overriding power of appointment could in fact be limited to be exercisable only during a two year period after the testator's death, thus reflecting the terms of section 144. Nevertheless, it is recommended[11] that there should be no such limitation although the executors and trustees in advance of the expiry of the two year period should consider whether or not to exercise their overriding power within that period and, if so, in what manner.

If in fact the power is exercised during the two year period after the testator's death whereby a distribution of capital is made which because of section 144 does not result in an IHT 'exit' charge, hold-over relief for capital gains tax purposes is not available. That is because the circumstances for relief under the Capital Gains Tax Act, section 147A(2)(a), only apply when the disposal is a chargeable transfer for IHT purposes.

Where executors and trustees exercise or do not exercise their testamentary overriding power of appointment, the capital gains tax position is not straightforward, because, apart from each case depending on its own facts, in certain respects differing legal views are held. The following remarks are therefore of a tentative nature:

a) Where executors and trustees hold such a power, it is probably the case, despite some previous doubts to the contrary, that the power can be exercised by them, as executors, during and not only after the end of the period of administration, particularly when the will gives specific authority.

b) The time of completion of the administration of a deceased person's estate and, therefore, the end of the administration, is one of fact. It is when the

---

11 That is because a termination of the existing discretionary trust could result in a charge to CGT under CGTA 1979, s 54(1), depending on the terms of the underlying trusts and the beneficiaries of them.

personal representatives have paid or satisfied all the debts, IHT and other taxes payable specifically by the executors, funeral and administration expenses and pecuniary legacies, and thus the net residuary estate is ascertained. Executors, in relation to all assets of the estate other than land, then become trustees of the assets they retain for the persons beneficially interested in the estate. In the case of land, because of *Re King's Will Trusts*,[12] a written assent under the Administration of Estates Act 1925, section 36, is needed to change the capacity in which the executors hold land to that of trustees. Nevertheless, executors may assent in respect of particular assets of the estate while the administration is incomplete and thus may constitute themselves as trustees of some assets while continuing to hold others as executors. There are no formal requirements for an assent in respect of assets other than land. Any act which shows that executors no longer require the asset for the purpose of the administration is sufficient.

c) So long as executors, as such, hold property during the period of administration, it is not regarded as settled property covered by the Capital Gains Tax Act 1979, sections 51 to 58, sections 47 to 50 being applicable.

d) If, during the period of administration, executors exercise their power of appointment in a manner that constitutes continuing trusts, in contrast to interests of an absolute nature or to a completely separate settlement, there is *not* a disposal for CGT purposes.

e) If, during the period of administration, executors exercise their power of appointment over specific assets in favour of a beneficiary who thus becomes absolutely entitled to those assets, there is not a liability for capital gains tax because he acquires those assets as 'legatee', as defined by the Capital Gains Tax Act 1979, section 47(2), under the protection of section 49(4).

f) If, during the period of administration, executors exercise their power of appointment over unspecified assets, such as in respect of all or a share of the deceased's residuary estate, the beneficiary becomes owner of a chose in action, being the right to compel administration of the deceased's estate. It may be the case that where there is an appointment of the residuary estate as a whole for a single beneficiary, the beneficiary likewise acquires this entitlement under the protection of section 49(4).

g) Where, as under e) or f), section 49(4) applies, its paragraph (b) provides that the beneficiary is to be treated as if the personal representatives' acquisition of each asset had been his acquisition of it and therefore at the same deemed cost being, under section 49(1)(a), the market value at the deceased's death. Under section 153, where on the death of a person IHT is chargeable on the value of his estate immediately before his death and the value of an asset forming part of his estate has been ascertained for that purpose, that value is taken to be the market value at the deceased's death for the purposes of capital gains tax.

h) If, at the end of the period of administration, executors and trustees in their capacity as trustees, continue to hold assets upon the trusts that apply there is not a charge to capital gains tax as they acquire those assets as 'legatee' within the definition of section 47(2) under the protection of section 49(4). If, thereafter, they exercise the overriding power of appointment it will be

---

12 [1964] Ch 542, [1964] 1 All ER 833.

exercised over settled property. If, as a result, a person becomes absolutely entitled there will be a deemed disposal and a charge to capital gains tax under section 54(1), with a limited possibility of hold-over relief subject to a joint election by the trustees and the beneficiary. A deemed disposal of qualifying assets may be held over under the Capital Gains Tax Act 1979, section 126, as may a qualifying disposal under section 147A of that Act.

For the purposes of income tax, until the power of appointment is exercised the trusts over the income are discretionary. Nevertheless, the charge to additional rate tax normally payable on discretionary trust income does not apply to personal representatives.[13] Accordingly, a beneficiary who receives income from the deceased's executors is liable to income tax on the amount grossed up at basic rate tax only.[14]

After the end of the administration period or when the overriding power of appointment has been exercised, discretionary trust income suffers tax at the basic rate and the additional rate.[13]

If the exercise of the power of appointment constitutes continuing trusts, the settlor for income tax purposes is the deceased testator. Therefore, in contrast to a variation made under section 142 for the benefit of a minor unmarried child the appointment does not fall foul of the Income and Corporation Taxes Act 1988 sections 663–670 (settlements on children).

The deed exercising the power of appointment does not attract stamp duty and no certificate is required.

D. Interests of the children

Regarding the potential interests of the children of a testator and his wife it is convenient to consider the position when all or some of them are under age. He will wish to make them his beneficiaries, subject to whatever may be the prior entitlements of his widow. The testator will be advised to take into account the circumstances of the children being immediately entitled or becoming entitled as the result, for example, of a joint calamity or, if his wife has a life interest, as the result of her dying while some or all the children are under age. It is likely in those circumstances that the testator will wish the entitlement of a child to capital to be deferred until a greater age than eighteen, thus the interests of the child need to be made contingent on that greater age.

From the point of view of income tax that result is not usually satisfactory. The income from each child's share of capital, while he is under age, will be taxable in the hands of the trustees at the combined rate of 35%, being the basic rate tax of 25% plus additional rate tax of 10%.[15] To the extent that income is not used for the child's benefit it will be accumulated and capitalised in accordance with the Trustee Act 1925 section 31(2). The income so accumulated and capitalised will thus be the remaining 65% only. To achieve a saving of income tax on the whole of the income, or at least on that part where the rate of tax in the hands of a child would be less than 35%, advantage can be taken of wording in the following terms:

'The Trustee Act 1925 section 31 (or any statutory modification or re-enactment

---

13 TA 1988, s 686(6).
14 Ibid, s 695.
15 Ibid, s 686.

of it) shall not apply to the foregoing trusts and accordingly the income of the contingent share of the Trust Fund of each beneficiary as it arises shall belong to the beneficiary absolutely. And thereafter during any period when the beneficiary is under the age of eighteen years my Trustees may pay or apply the whole or any part or parts of that income (whether or not it has been invested in accordance with their power under Clause   of this Will) to or for the benefit of the beneficiary in such manner as my Trustees shall think fit.'[16]

It must be accepted that the child on attaining eighteen will be entitled to the balance of any accrued income remaining. The wording has the following income tax effects:

a) there will be no charge on the trustees to additional rate tax.[17]

b) the income will belong to the child whether it is accumulated or used for his benefit, so that repayment claims can be made annually if he has otherwise unused personal reliefs or a rate of tax below the rate of 25% on income received by the trustees.

For IHT purposes, the child has an interest in possession having a present right to present income; see *Pearson v IRC*.[18] Accordingly, the child's trust will be a fixed interest one and will not therefore be an accumulation and maintenance trust complying with the conditions of section 71.

It follows that, in the event of the child's premature death before becoming entitled personally to receive either income or capital, there will be a charge to IHT.[19] In those circumstances any accrued income remaining, but not the trust capital itself, will devolve according to the intestacy provisions applicable to him. The trust capital will devolve according to the residuary trusts of the will which will no doubt provide substitutional trusts in the event of the child's death before attaining his vested interest in capital.

If the child's entitlement is contingent on attaining a stated age, with no immediate entitlement to income, it is important to comply with the accumulation and maintenance trust conditions of section 71. If that is done, while the settled property will be 'relevant property' being settled property in which no qualifying interest subsists, there will be no ten-year anniversary charge and no proportionate charge when the beneficiary becomes entitled to his share of the settled property or acquires an interest in possession in it. There will also be no charge to IHT on the premature death of the beneficiary. The essential conditions of section 71 are contained in sub-sections (1) and (2), which are set out in full as follows:

'1) Subject to sub-section (2) below, this section applies to settled property if—

a) one or more persons (in this section referred to as beneficiaries) will, on or before attaining a specified age not exceeding twenty-five, become beneficially entitled to it or to an interest in possession in it, and

b) no interest in possession subsists in it and the income from it is to be accumulated so far as not applied for the maintenance, education or benefit of a beneficiary.

2) This section does not apply to settled property unless either—

a) not more than twenty-five years have elapsed since the commencement of the settlement or, if was later, since the time (or latest time) when the

16 See also the note to form 61, p 202 below.
17 TA 1988, s 686(2)(b).
18 [1981] AC 753.
19 Ss 49(1) and 4(1).

conditions contained in paragraphs (a) and (b) of sub-section (i) above became satisfied with respect to the property, or

b) all the persons who are or have been beneficiaries are or were either

   i) grandchildren of a common grandparent, or

   ii) children, widows or widowers of such grandchildren who were themselves beneficiaries but died before the time when, had they survived, they would have become entitled as mentioned in sub-section (1)(a) above.'

On the assumption that the residuary trusts, so far as children or remoter issue of the testator are concerned, are in conventional form, comply with the rule against perpetuities and contain no express, as opposed to statutory, power to accumulate income, the beneficiaries must inevitably obtain an interest in possession – entitlement to income, as of right, being sufficient – to comply with the twenty-five years requirement under sub-section 2(a) above. Nevertheless, the presence of an overriding power of appointment as described in C above breaches the conditions of section 71 because it cannot be said that each child *will*, on or before attaining a specified age not exceeding twenty-five, become beneficially entitled to his share of the trust capital or to an interest in possession in it.

For capital gains tax purposes, on a beneficiary becoming absolutely entitled to capital there is a charge to capital gains tax under the Capital Gains Tax Act 1979, section 54(1), with hold-over relief available in limited circumstances only. In the case of a trust complying with the IHT conditions of section 71, as an accumulation and maintenance trust, hold-over relief is available for capital gains tax purposes. It does not, however, apply when the beneficiary already has an interest in possession and later obtains the capital. That is because section 71(4) ceases to apply when the interest in possession comes into being.

Chapter 9
Post-death variations and disclaimers

A. Introduction

By a Press Release dated 14 March 1989 issued by the Inland Revenue, immediately following the Chancellor of the Exchequer's Budget Statement, it was announced that the circumstances in which redistribution of the estates of deceaseds by beneficiaries using instruments of variation would be restricted. It was proposed that in the case of deaths on or after the Royal Assent to the Finance Bill, which proved to be 27 July 1989, rearrangements of estates would be effective for IHT purposes only if made by:
   a) disclaimer of benefits under wills, intestacies or Scottish legal rights; or
   b) court orders making adequate provision for the deceased's dependants; or
   c) written variations by the beneficiaries themselves making adequate provision for the deceased's dependants which could be ordered by the court.

On its publication on 13 April 1989 it was noted from the Finance Bill that its clause 167 would not only repeal section 142 (variations and disclaimers within two years after the particular death) but also section 143 (precatory trusts) and section 144 (freedom from IHT on distributions within two years from discretionary trusts). Nevertheless, there would be a substituted section 142 giving continuing effect to the use of disclaimers and also effect to the other circumstances in the Press Release dated 14 March 1989. As a result of strong representations, on 20 June 1989 Mr Norman Lamont in the Standing Committee of the Finance Bill announced that the proposals as a whole would be dropped. Nevertheless, he said that the matter would be kept under review with the object of a more targeted, specific measure to counter abuse. Nothing yet has happened.

This chapter needs to be read with the foregoing threat in mind. Because post-death disclaimers were intended to have continuing validity it is therefore useful to include in wills provisions which would increase their range of use following the death of a testator.[1]

Although at first sight it might appear that the terms of section 142, for IHT purposes, and of the Capital Gains Tax Act 1979, section 49(6) et seq, for capital gains tax purposes, in respect of post-death variations and alterations have no direct bearing on the way in which a testator should be advised and his will drafted, the indirect bearing and impact are immense. The will draftsman will be very conscious of those statutory provisions, particularly section 142, just as will be the probate practitioner following a death.

This chapter comments on those provisions. It is typically the case that a beneficiary wishes to relinquish all or part of his entitlement on the particular death without receiving any counter benefit from the deceased's assets in return. Nevertheless,

1 See a) of sub-chapter D, p 101 below.

section 142 can be applicable to more complex variations where the dispositions of a deceased's will are to be treated as varied by, for example, a life tenant releasing his life interest in part of the capital of the deceased's residuary estate and, in return, the remaindermen, whose interest in that part of the capital is thereby accelerated, releasing their reversionary interests in the other part of the capital thereby enabling that other part to go to the life tenant absolutely.

B. Variations, IHT effects

Section 17(a) provides that a variation or disclaimer to which section 142(1) applies is not a transfer of value. Section 142(1) reads as follows:

'Where within the period of two years after a person's death—

a) any of the dispositions (whether effected by will, under the law relating to intestacy or otherwise) of the property comprised in his estate immediately before his death are varied, or

b) the benefit conferred by any of those dispositions is disclaimed,

by an instrument in writing made by the persons or any of the persons who benefit or would benefit under the dispositions, this Act shall apply as if the variation had been effected by the deceased or, as the case may be, the disclaimed benefit had never been conferred.'

The effect is to enable the beneficiaries concerned, within two years after a deceased's death, to vary the dispositions of his will, with IHT or any other factors in mind, in such manner that, in relation to IHT, it will be treated as if made by the testator in its amended form. Thus, for example, the terms of a will leaving everything to the surviving spouse could be varied by that spouse in such manner as to introduce legacies in favour of the children to take advantage of the deceased testator's nil% band for IHT purposes, assuming that in practice assets or cash can be made available surplus to any possible future needs of the surviving spouse.

From an examination of the wording of section 142, the following points are noted:

a) Its application is subject to compliance with the detailed provisions of the section, in particular sub-section (2) which requires in the case of a variation, *in contrast to a disclaimer*, written notice of election to be given to the Inland Revenue within six months after the date of the instrument (or such longer time as the Board may allow) *by all persons* making the instrument and also by the personal representatives where the variation results in additional IHT becoming payable. The latter will be the case where some property originally bequeathed to an exempt person, in particular the surviving spouse, is redirected for the benefit of unexempt persons. The personal representatives may decline to join in that election if, and only if, they do not hold sufficient assets to discharge the additional IHT payable; and it is the case that the obtaining of an IHT clearance certificate will not prevent the collection of any additional IHT payable as the result of the variation or disclaimer. It is suggested that the personal representatives should be parties to the instrument so that they are expressly placed on notice about it in respect of the administration of the deceased's estate. If an election is not made, the variation is treated in the normal way as a transfer of value by the beneficiaries making the dispositions for the benefit of others. Equally, if an election is not made under the Capital Gains Tax Act 1979, section 49(7), the variation is a disposal for capital gains tax purposes.

b) The variation (or disclaimer) must be made within two years. A variation can be made even in respect of assets which the redirecting beneficiary has accepted or from which, in the meantime, he has derived benefit. Assets can be redirected in favour of anybody whether or not a member of 'the family' or whether or not an existing beneficiary.

c) Completion of the administration of the estate or distribution of the assets in accordance with the original dispositions does not preclude a variation within the two year period.

d) 'Any of the dispositions (whether effected by will, under the law relating to intestacy *or otherwise*) of the property comprised in his estate immediately before [the] death' of the deceased can be varied. Accordingly, that property would include property of which he was a joint tenant or tenant-in-common and property which he himself had settled under his will. Nevertheless, the wording is not wide enough to include settled property in which prior to his death the deceased had a beneficial interest in possession. The property comprised in a person's estate includes excluded property (defined in sections 6 and 48) but not settled property as mentioned or property under the Finance Act 1986 section 102, being 'property subject to a reservation'.

e) Any instrument in writing is sufficient, even an exchange of letters. Nevertheless, variations are matters of importance and must have legal effect and be formally recorded. Therefore, variation by deed is recommended. This should help make certain that the title in the redirected assets passes in a legally applicable manner to the new beneficiaries.

f) For section 142(1) to apply there must, under section 142(3), be no consideration in money or money's worth, but this does not preclude consideration consisting of the making of another variation or disclaimer in respect of the same set of dispositions. An agreement to pay a disposing beneficiary's legal expenses or to be reimbursed income tax liabilities or to have mortgage or other liabilities discharged will be within the exclusion of section 142(3) and therefore preclude the application of section 142(1).

g) The 'reservation of benefit' provisions under the Finance Act 1986 section 102 and Schedule 20 do not apply to the terms of a variation such as when the redirecting beneficiary constitutes discretionary trusts under which he is a discretionary object, because under section 142(1) it is the deceased who is deemed to have made those trusts.

h) The IHT rates that apply are those applicable at the deceased's death, not those applicable at the time of the variation or disclaimer. In the event of a significant increase in the value of the estate during the course of its administration and there being a surviving spouse it is possible to 'redraft' a deceased's will in such manner as to achieve a substantial mitigation for the benefit of, say, the children.

In 1984 and 1985 the Inland Revenue refused to grant tax relief for variations in wording and form which previously they had accepted. The outcome was a statement published in the *Law Society's Gazette* of 22 May 1985 at p 1454 disclosing the considered views of the Inland Revenue following the obtaining of further legal advice. The statement included two matters not already mentioned above and which should be noted:

i) The instrument must clearly indicate the dispositions that are the subject of it and vary their destination as laid down by the deceased's will, or under the law relating to intestate estates, or otherwise.

ii) The notice of election must refer to the appropriate statutory provisions.

The statement also refers to multiple variations:

'There have been some cases in which a number of instruments of variation have been executed in relation to the same will or intestacy. The Revenue emphasise that these cases must be considered on their precise facts but in broad terms their views will be as follows:

  i) an election which is validly made is irrevocable;

  ii) an instrument will not fall within section 142 if it *further* redirects any item or any part of an item that has *already* been redirected under an earlier instrument; and

  iii) to avoid any uncertainty, variations covering a number of items should ideally be made in one instrument.

Although multiple variations should therefore be avoided when not essential, the Revenue recognise that they are not as such prohibited by section 142. For example, a widow left all her husband's estate and who makes a small gift to her children soon after death is not thereby precluded from making considered provision for those children out of the remainder by a further variation involving the relocation of different property towards the end of the two year period.'

The decision in *Russell v IRC*[2] should be noted. When an individual has made a deed varying a disposition made by a deceased person it is not possible, under section 142(1), to make a further deed in respect of the same assets. This confirms the views of the Inland Revenue under ii) above.

The Inland Revenue accepts that the personal representatives of a beneficiary who has also died within the two year period from the first death can make a variation or disclaimer under section 142(1) in respect of the original estate. This is of particular importance, in not infrequent circumstances, when the survivor of two spouses dies not long after and within two years of the death of the other. Thus, where a husband leaves a large estate to his wife who dies shortly after him, her personal representatives could be asked to vary the deceased's husband's will so as to leave part of his estate to the children direct. That would avoid the bunching effect of IHT on the second death by spreading the two estates in a manner which will reduce the aggregate IHT liability on the two estates taken overall. Likewise, it is possible by variation to increase the estate of a dead beneficiary. Thus, where a husband died leaving his estate to his children and the wife dies shortly afterwards similarly leaving her estate, which is less substantial than his, to the children, the aggregate IHT liability could be reduced by the children varying their father's will so that a large part of his estate went initially to their deceased mother's estate. For this to be possible, the beneficiary whose estate is to be increased must have been alive when the person whose estate is to be varied or disclaimed died. Accordingly, there is a strong case despite section 142(1) for husbands and wives to move towards greater equalisation of their assets, to enable each to make full use of their nil% band on their death, where they are united in regarding their financial positions as a whole because they may die in the wrong order, the materially poorer dying before the wealthier.

It has been reported that the Inland Revenue were seeking to apply the principles of *Ramsay v IRC*[3] to variations of the estates of deceased persons where the destination

2 [1988] STC 195.
3 [1982] AC 300.

of the estates remains the same despite the particular variation and therefore the deed results in no change in the beneficial ownership of the assets. The Controller of the Capital Taxes Office having investigated the position has said that he has not found any case in practice where a 'double death' variation has been disallowed and so far as he is aware there has been no change in the practice of accepting them as valid variations.

c. Variations, IHT effects of the Finance Act 1986

This Act introduced PETs (potentially exempt transfers) and property subject to a reservation and those matters will be taken in turn in the context of variations.

There will be cases where a deceased testator by his will has divided his substantial estate between his widow on the one hand and his adult children on the other. That part given to the widow will be exempt and that part given to the children will be subject to a liability to IHT. By a deed of variation to comply with section 142 it would be possible for the children to assign their interests to the wife, being their mother. If that happened the whole of the deceased testator's estate would thereupon become exempt with no liability for IHT. Thereafter, it would, for example, be open to the widow herself to make gifts to her children or to an accumulation and maintenance trust, which complies with the conditions of section 71, for the benefit of their children's children. Any such gifts will qualify as potentially exempt transfers. On their making, there will be no IHT liability. If the widow survives her gift by seven years they will be free of IHT on her death.

In sub-chapter H of chapter 6[4] there is an example of the terms of the will of a deceased leaving everything to his surviving spouse being re-drafted in such manner as to introduce legacies in favour of the children to take advantage of his nil% band for IHT purposes. Where the financial circumstances of a husband and wife do not allow for the will of that husband to include such legacies for their children it would be possible for the husband to bequeath a settled legacy on discretionary trusts under which nevertheless the wife is to be regarded as the primary beneficiary. Where, for example, the surviving wife is absolutely entitled, it would be open to her to vary her husband's will by introducing a settled legacy equal in value to the amount available of his nil% band to be held on discretionary trusts under which she is the primary beneficiary. The settled property on her death will not be property subject to a reservation. This is because the wording at the end of section 142(1) makes clear that the legislation applies *as if the variation had been effected by the deceased*; therefore, the resulting gift is not to be treated as one by the redirecting beneficiary for the purposes of 'the property subject to a reservation' provisions of the Finance Act 1986, section 102.

d. Disclaimers, IHT effects

Much of what has been written earlier in this chapter, in relation to variations, equally applies to disclaimers. It is, therefore, convenient to mention the following differences:

    a) As a matter of English, in contrast to Scottish, legal construction a single

---

4 P 77 above.

undivided testamentary gift cannot be disclaimed in part. Difficult questions of construction may arise in determining whether one or two independent gifts have been made. Nevertheless, being a matter of legal construction it would be possible for a will in express terms to enable beneficiaries being of full age to disclaim any part or a fraction or a percentage of their entitlements. The decision in *Guthrie v Walrond*[5] and the confirmation of the Capital Taxes Office are referred to in the exchange of correspondence in *Tolley's Practical Tax*, 28 June 1989, page 102. It would also appear to be the case that those terms of such a will could stipulate what should be the destination of any disclaimed gift such as to the children of the disclaiming beneficiary.

b) As a matter of law, it is not open to a beneficiary to disclaim a gift under a will following his having derived benefit and thus having accepted it.[6]

c) Section 142(2), providing for a notice of election in respect of a variation, does *not* apply to a disclaimer. Therefore it is not as flexible in relation to its IHT consequences.

d) Section 93 enables a person who becomes entitled to an interest in settled property, whether or not following a death, to disclaim his interest. Provided that it is not made for a consideration in money or money's worth, the IHT consequences apply as if he had not become entitled to that interest. There is no time limit but equally such a person would need to disclaim in full and before having derived any benefit or in any way accepted his interest.

E. Variations and disclaimers, capital gains tax effects

There are very similar provisions and advantages under the Capital Gains Tax Act 1979, section 49(6)–(10) to those contained in section 142. Accordingly, the variation or disclaimer, made within the two year period, will not constitute a disposal for capital gains tax purposes and section 49 generally, which covers the capital gains tax position on death, is to apply as if the variation had been effected by the deceased or the disclaimed benefit had never been conferred. This is subject to sub-section (7) which requires, in the case of a variation, written notice of election to be given to the Inland Revenue within six months after the date of the instrument by the person(s) making it, or such longer time as the Board may allow.

When the variation of a will constitutes a settlement by a beneficiary of property comprised in the deceased's estate it would appear that he and not the deceased testator is regarded as 'the settlor'. The Inland Revenue are of the opinion that under the Finance Act 1988, Schedule 10, chargeable gains accruing to the trust are regarded as accruing to him, therefore at 40% if he is a higher rate taxpayer. The settlor's annual exemption of £5,500 is available if not otherwise used. The settlor has a right of recovery from the trustees for the CGT he pays. Despite the opinion of the Inland Revenue, a Special Commissioner has decided that it is the deceased who is 'the settlor'. It is understood that an appeal is to be heard in the High Court towards the end of 1991.

It is possible that a written notice of election might be given for IHT purposes but not for capital gains tax purposes, and vice versa. Thus there could be cases when it would be beneficial for an election to be made for IHT purposes only.

5 [1883] 22 Ch D 573.
6 See form 76, p 214 below.

Chapter 10
Domicile, inheritance tax and double taxation relief

A. General principles of domicile[1]

Under English law, the law of domicile connects a person to a particular legal system and thereby governs those transactions which affect him most closely in a personal sense, such as marriage, divorce, legitimacy, capacity to contract and succession to property. Domicile is also the connecting factor for the purposes of IHT.

The English courts decide, according to English law based on the evidence, what is a person's domicile. They could hold that a person is domiciled in a particular country or state when the courts of that country or state would reach a different decision. A person's domicile is related to a distinct legal jurisdiction such as England and Wales, Scotland or a state within the USA but not to the United Kingdom or the USA as a whole.

Although a person may have more than one nationality or no nationality at all, that person must always have a domicile and only one operative domicile at any one time, for the purposes of English law.

A person's domicile is often attributed to their permanent or natural home, but it can best be defined as the place with which a person has the closest personal connections and where they intend ultimately to live and die. The person may be away from it for very substantial periods of time but intend ultimately to return.

In attempting to ascertain a person's domicile the courts may well consider the whole history of their life, and while no single fact is in itself decisive, even small incidents may be relevant.

As so much can turn on a person's domicile of origin, including for the purposes of IHT, any examination of the circumstances, for the purpose of forming a view, can go back many years to those surrounding the parents and their domiciles of origin. A person's domicile of origin is fixed at the time of birth and is the same as that of the person upon whom they are legally dependent. Thus:
   a) A legitimate child born in wedlock to a living father acquires the same domicile of origin as the domicile of their father at that time, not necessarily the father's domicile of origin.
   b) An illegitimate child acquires the then same domicile of their mother.
   c) A legitimate child born after their father's death acquires the domicile of their mother.

---

1 The Law Commission, No 168, and the Scottish Law Commission, No 107 (HMSO, Cmnd 200) in September 1987 jointly published their proposals for retaining the concept of domicile while recommending substantial changes to some of its component rules. No changes have been announced.

The place of birth is immaterial except that it may be assumed to be the domicile of origin in the absence of knowledge about the parents.

The domicile of origin is very important. Although it may be supplanted by the acquisition of a domicile of choice it is never wholly lost albeit that it may at any time be in abeyance. It will always revive and be treated as the operative domicile of a person if at any time they have no other domicile. Thus:

'A' had a domicile of origin in France. When of full age he acquired a domicile of choice in England. Subsequently, he abandoned his English domicile and sailed for Ireland where he intended to settle. During the voyage his French domicile of origin revived, because he had abandoned a domicile of choice without simultaneously acquiring another.

The domicile of origin is also important in that it is much harder to displace than a domicile of choice. Thus:

In *Winans v A-G*[2] the court had to determine whether the deceased, an American subject, had lost his American domicile of origin in favour of an English domicile of choice. Winans was a member of his father's engineering business and assisted in the supply of naval and military equipment to Russia, where he lived during the Crimean War. For reasons of health, he was obliged to live in England from 1860 to 1897, the year of his death, apart from short periods spent elsewhere. The court found, after an examination ranging over almost all his life, that his interests remained almost entirely American and anti-British. It was held that he had never lost his domicile of origin.

A domicile of choice is acquired by taking up residence in the country of choice with the intention, either at the commencement or during the time of residence, of living there permanently. The two factors must both be present; actual residence accompanied by the intention, which is a question of fact, to live there permanently.[3]

Although the requirement of residence does not necessitate a person having to live in the same house, or indeed in the same place within a country for an indefinite time, it does involve habitual presence within the country in some kind of accommodation which could be described as that person's home. Length of residence is not in itself essential for the acquisition of a domicile of choice, though it is important from the point of view of evidence. Therefore, although residence itself cannot constitute domicile, the longer the residence the stronger becomes its value as evidence of the intention to live permanently in a country. The presence of an intention to remain permanently in a country is one of fact which therefore depends on evidence.

The acquisition of a domicile of choice presupposes a freedom of choice about where a person will live. Where that freedom is removed or restricted difficult questions of ascertainment of domicile may arise. It is necessary to distinguish the intention to reside permanently in a country from the motive which inspires the intention. The fact that a person may go abroad to avoid creditors does not prevent them from acquiring a domicile of choice; the reasons for going abroad may establish the necessary intention to reside there permanently. In contrast, a prisoner who

---

2 [1904] AC 287.
3 *Udny v Udny* (1869) LR I SC & Div 441, HL (Sc). That decision was referred to in *Plummer v IRC* [1988] 1 All ER 97, [1988] 1 WLR 292, where it was held that a taxpayer having a domicile of origin in England and Wales and maintaining a residence there could only acquire a domicile of choice in a new country if the residence established in that country was his chief residence.

in days gone by was transported for life did not automatically change domicile since there was an absence of the necessary intention.

The question of freedom of choice arises frequently in the case of invalids who are advised to make their home in some other country for reasons of health. In such cases, it is a question of weighing the pressure of necessity upon the mind of the individual concerned. If the evidence discloses the alternatives of a change of air or an untimely death, the acquisition of a new domicile of choice may not necessarily arise.

Where a person is posted abroad to carry out official or other duties, there would be no presumption of a change of domicile.

Just as a domicile of choice requires for its acquisition both actual residence and the necessary intention to reside permanently, the domicile of choice can only be lost when *both* those factors cease to exist. A person therefore having acquired a domicile of choice, no subsequent change of mind or doubts arising out of the wisdom of doing so can, by themselves, affect their acquired domicile of choice. Thus:

Re Raffenel[4] Madam Raffenel, the widow of a French Naval Officer was before her marriage a British subject having a domicile of origin in England. On her marriage she automatically acquired the domicile of her husband[5] but when he died she decided to settle in England with her children. She embarked at Calais on a cross-channel steamer, with the intention of leaving France for good, but before the ship sailed she was taken ill and spent several months in Calais where she died. The court held that her domicile at the date of her death was French since there had in fact been no abandonment of residence even though the element of intention to leave France was present. It seems clear that had Madame Raffenel been able to sail beyond French territorial waters her domicile of origin, being English, would have been revived on the complete abandonment of her French domicile, even before she had set foot in England.

Until 1 January 1974, when the Domicile and Matrimonial Proceedings Act 1973 took effect, a woman on marriage acquired her husband's then domicile, and, during the subsistence of the marriage, her domicile followed his irrespective of the practical circumstances affecting each of them. In the event of their living apart, in different countries, this could produce unusual effects. By the 1973 Act the domicile of a married woman is fixed by reference to the same factors and circumstances as apply in the case of anyone else capable of having an independent domicile.[6] Nevertheless a married woman, who on 31 December 1973 had her husband's domicile, by dependence as under the law then prevailing, is to be treated as retaining that domicile (as a domicile of choice, if it is not also her domicile of origin) until it is changed thereafter by acquisition or revival of a different domicile.[7] *IRC v Duchess of Portland*[8] establishes, that, in the foregoing circumstances, a married woman who is thus treated as retaining her husband's domicile, as a domicile of choice, does not cease to hold that domicile until it has been abandoned under the general law of domicile in the same way as the abandonment of an actual domicile of choice. Therefore, a woman

4 (1863) 3 Sw & Tr 49.
5 Until 1 January 1974, when the Domicile and Matrimonial Proceedings Act 1973 took effect, in English law the rule was absolute that the domicile of a married woman was the same as, and changed with, the domicile of her husband.
6 Domicile and Matrimonial Proceedings Act 1973, s 1(1).
7 Ibid, s 1(2).
8 [1982] Ch 314, [1982] 1 All ER 784.

married before 1974 wishing to revive her overseas domicile of origin has not only to have an intention to cease living permanently in England but also to take up residence permanently in another country.

A child first becomes capable of acquiring an independent domicile when he attains the age of 16 or marries under that age.[9] In the case of the latter alternative, though under English law it is only on attaining the age of 16 that the capacity to marry is acquired, there are some foreign countries which permit earlier marriage. Until the time when the child gains the right to acquire an independent domicile, a child's domicile may be changed by the act of the person upon whom he is legally dependent. Thus, the domicile of a legitimate child follows that of his father but this is subject to section 4 of the Domicile and Matrimonial Proceedings Act 1973, which deals with the position where the parents are alive but living apart.

The necessary weight of proof and evidence, involving the intention required to establish a domicile of choice with the simultaneous intention of abandoning a domicile of origin, are difficult matters to assess in practice. The burden of proof lies with the party who asserts the change. There has been judicial tendency to accept the importance of a person's domicile of origin and to attach less significance to his residence however long in another country and the likelihood of acquiring a domicile of choice there. The Court of Appeal case of *IRC v Bullock*,[10] is instructive:

The taxpayer who was born in 1910 had a domicile of origin in Nova Scotia and was educated there. He came to England in 1932 to join the RAF. In 1946 he married an Englishwoman who was younger than himself. He retired from the RAF in 1959. Two years later, after his retirement from civilian employment, a house was bought in Dorset by his wife. In deference to his wife, who disliked Canada, he decided to remain in England, hoping that she might change her mind. Should she predecease him he intended to return to live in Canada. In 1966 he made a will, subject to Nova Scotia law, under which he appointed a Nova Scotia Corporation as his executor. It contained a declaration that it should be read, construed and take effect in accordance with the law of Nova Scotia. All his assets including those he had inherited on the death of his father in 1961, and which had enabled him to retire, had remained in Canada. He retained his Canadian Passport and never considered obtaining a United Kingdom one. His will contained a declaration in the following terms:

'I hereby declare that my domicile is and continues to be the Province of Nova Scotia, Dominion of Canada, where I was born and brought up, to which Province I intend to return and remain permanently upon my wife's death.'

He never voted in local or Parliamentary elections as he regarded himself exclusively as a Canadian citizen. Buckley LJ said that the acquisition of a domicile of choice in England depended on whether the taxpayer's residence here was clothed with the necessary intention on his part to make it his permanent home. The test to be applied was whether it had been shown that the taxpayer intended to make his new home in this country until the end of his days unless something happened to make him change his mind. The Commissioners had found that the taxpayer had in mind an event on the happening of which he would return to Canada. Brightman J (whose earlier decision was overruled) had been impressed by the fact that the matrimonial home was permanently established in England. However,

9 Domicile and Matrimonial Proceedings Act 1973, s 3(1).
10 [1976] 3 All ER 353, [1976] STC 409, CA.

where, as in this case, there was a not unreal possibility of the taxpayer surviving his wife and of his returning to his domicile of origin, rather than a vague hope or aspiration, it had not been established that he had acquired a domicile of choice in England.

IRC v Bullock can be contrasted against the facts of and decision in the case of *Re Furse, Furse v IRC*[11] where the deceased, whose domicile of origin was in Rhode Island, had lived in England for many years. He intended to remain in England until he was unable to continue an active physical life here, when he would go to the USA. Those intentions were vague and did not limit clearly his intended period of residence here. It was held that he had died domiciled in England.

B. Domicile and IHT

Section 6(1) of the Inheritance Tax Act 1984 states that property situated outside the United Kingdom is excluded property (and therefore not taken into account for IHT purposes) if the person beneficially entitled to it is an individual domiciled outside the United Kingdom.[12] Accordingly, prima facie, all assets in the United Kingdom are within the potential IHT net in relation to lifetime gifts or gifts on death, irrespective of the domicile of the owner. Likewise, if a person is domiciled in the United Kingdom, his assets world-wide, as well as in the United Kingdom, are potentially liable to IHT.

For the purposes of IHT only, the Inheritance Tax Act 1984, section 267(1), *extends* the circumstances in which a person can be deemed to be domiciled within the United Kingdom. Thus, for IHT purposes, a person although not domiciled here under the general law, at the relevant time, can be treated as being so domiciled.

Section 267(1) states that a person not (under the general law) domiciled in the United Kingdom at 'the relevant time' shall be treated as domiciled here at that time if:

a) he was domiciled in the United Kingdom within the three years immediately preceding 'the relevant time'. (Thus, a person does not lose his United Kingdom domicile, for IHT purposes, until three years after they have lost it in accordance with the general rules); or

b) he was resident (for income tax purposes) in the United Kingdom in not less than seventeen of the twenty years of assessment ending with the year of assessment in which 'the relevant time' falls.[13] Section 267(4) provides that the question whether a person was resident in the United Kingdom in any tax year shall be determined as for the purposes of income tax, but without regard to any dwelling-house available here for his use.

These deemed domicile rules do not affect a deceased's domicile on death if a death duties double taxation agreement concluded before 1975 continues to apply.[14]

It is important to recognise that it is necessary to apply both the tests about deemed domicile for IHT purposes under section 267(1). Thus, a United Kingdom

11 [1980] 3 All ER 838, [1980] STC 596.

12 On the death of a person domiciled and resident outside the United Kingdom no IHT will be chargeable on money deposited at a United Kingdom Bank where the account is not denominated in sterling: s 157.

13 For example, the kind of circumstances in *IRC v Bullock* [1976] 3 All ER 353, [1976] STC 409, CA; see p 106 above.

14 S 267(2) and s 158(6).

domiciliary emigrating from this country, having been resident here for many years will not necessarily lose his deemed United Kingdom domicile after three years absence.

As follows from the opening paragraph of this sub-chapter, an individual who is domiciled abroad who makes a settlement of overseas assets is making a settlement of excluded property for the purposes of section 6(1). If for example that person is included as a beneficiary the gifts with reservation rules in the Finance Act 1986, section 102, can never apply to the settled property even though he may subsequently become domiciled in the United Kingdom.

c. Domicile and settled property

Section 49(1) states that a person beneficially entitled to an interest in possession in settled property shall be treated as beneficially entitled to the property in which the interest subsists; and it follows that this applies to any possible IHT charge including on death under section 4(1). However, the effect of section 48(3) is that settled property is excluded property and not subject to IHT when:

a) the assets are situated abroad; and

b) the settlor was domiciled abroad under general law when the settlement was made.

This would apply to a testator, as at the time of his death. This is the case notwithstanding that the beneficiaries, including a deceased person beneficially entitled to an interest in possession, are domiciled and resident here. Hence, where the assets are abroad, the critical importance of the settlor's domicile at the time the settlement is made or of the testator's domicile at the time of his death when the settlement is constituted by his will. The deemed domicile rules, under section 267(1), do not apply for determining the domicile of a settlor of a settlement made before 10 December 1974.

The foregoing rules do not apply to a reversionary interest in settled property. Nevertheless, if the reversionary property itself is situated outside the United Kingdom, it is excluded property if the person beneficially entitled to it is domiciled outside the United Kingdom. The domicile of the transferor determines whether a reversionary interest is outside the territorial scope of IHT.[15] A reversionary interest which is within that territorial scope may, however, be excluded from charge to IHT because it is excluded property under section 48.

d. Section 6(2) (Government securities free of IHT while in foreign ownership)

Under section 6(2), where securities have been issued by the Treasury subject to a condition authorised by the Finance (No 2) Act 1931, section 22 (or the Finance (No 2) Act 1915, section 47) for exemption from taxation so long as the securities are in the beneficial ownership of persons neither domiciled nor ordinarily resident in the United Kingdom the securities are excluded property for IHT purposes. If such securities are settled property, they are not excluded property unless:[16]

15 S 48(3)(b).
16 S 48(4).

a) the individual beneficiary entitled to an interest in possession in them is neither domiciled nor ordinarily resident in the United Kingdom; or

b) if no such interest in possession so subsists, all past, present and future potential beneficiaries are neither so domiciled nor so resident.

For the foregoing purposes, the extended definition of domicile, under section 267, does not apply.[17]

E. Double taxation relief

Double taxation conventions may have an effect on what would otherwise be the situs of property and the domicile of a person for IHT purposes and can also override the extended definition of domicile, under section 267.

Section 158(1) provides that Orders in Council may be made giving effect to agreements providing relief from IHT or for determining the place where any property is to be treated as situated for the purposes of IHT. Of the existing agreements, some were concluded before 1975, during the time of estate duty, and some concluded after. The former have different rules to eliminate double taxation.

Those concluded before 1975 are with France, Italy, Switzerland, India and Pakistan. Negotiations are in progress on new updated agreements with France, Italy and Switzerland. Those concluded after 1975 are with the Republic of Ireland, South Africa, USA, the Netherlands and Sweden.

In brief, the agreements provide that the country in which the transferor was domiciled (for the purposes of the particular agreement) can tax all property wherever situated, whereas the other country may tax only specified categories of property such as immovable property situated in its territory. In most cases, where such a provision does not eliminate double taxation, there are rules for determining which country is to give credit for the other's tax. Where, exceptionally, the relief given by an agreement would be less than that afforded by unilateral relief, dealt with in the next subchapter, the benefit of unilateral relief is given.

F. Unilateral relief

Section 159 grants relief from IHT where there is not a double taxation arrangement in force. Sub-section (1) provides that where in an 'overseas territory' any amount of tax imposed by reason of any disposition or other event is attributable to the value of any property, then, if that tax is of a character similar to that of IHT or is chargeable on or by reference to death or gifts inter vivos *and* IHT chargeable by reference to the same disposition or other event is also attributable to the value of that property, a credit is to be allowed in respect of the amount of 'overseas tax' against the IHT chargeable in accordance with the succeeding sub-sections (2) to (7).[18]

---

17 S 267(2).

18 The detailed provisions are complex. Useful examples are contained in Inland Revenue booklet IHT I para 13.2.

Chapter 11
Inheritance (Provision for Family and Dependants) Act 1975 in relation to testators

While every normal adult has testamentary freedom, that freedom is not without constraint. In particular, the provisions of the Inheritance (Provision for Family and Dependants) Act 1975 need to be borne in mind. What would be reasonable financial provision in the case of a person who would be in a position, following his death, to claim on a testator's estate needs consideration and judgment by him and his solicitor. Accordingly, it is important for them first to identify those persons particularly outside the testator's family who could be successful applicants and secondly to form a view about the result of any application. A potential applicant might, for example, fall within section 1(1)(e) because she or he was being maintained by the deceased immediately before the deceased's death. In such potential circumstances there may be a case for the testator making a written statement, to be kept with his will, containing his reasons for not making testamentary provision or for not exceeding the amount he makes.[1] There may also be a case for the testator to write to the person concerned making clear that reliance should not be placed on any continuing financial provision in the event of his death. It is also apparent from *Re Leach*[2] that adult children may succeed in such applications in more situations than had previously been thought to be the case. The position of a former spouse who has not remarried, as an applicant covered by section 1(1)(b), where there has not been a matrimonial order under section 15 disentitling an application, will need particular consideration.

A substantial body of case law has built up and, therefore, in relation to the 1975 Act, specialist writing should be consulted.[3]

The 1975 Act provides a comprehensive code whereby the court can make orders in respect of a deceased person's estate for the benefit of the spouse, former spouse, child, child of the family or dependant of that person. It applies in respect of deaths occurring on or after 1 April 1976. It is limited to cases where the deceased died domiciled in England and Wales. An application cannot, except with the permission of the court, be made after the end of the period of six months from the date on which representation with respect to the estate of the deceased is first taken out. The potential claimants are:

a) The wife or husband of the deceased.[4]

b) A former wife or former husband of the deceased, who has not remarried.

---

1 See the observations of Megarry V-C in *Re Beaumont, Martin v Midland Bank Trust Co Ltd* [1980] Ch 444 at 458 F-G [1980] 1 All ER 266 at p 276.
2 [1986] Ch 226, [1985] 2 All ER 754 CA.
3 Division H of *Butterworths Wills, Probate and Administration Service* is recommended.
4 This includes a judicially separated spouse.

c) A child of the deceased.[5] This, in contrast to the previous law, is regardless of the child's age and without proof of infirmity or disability.

d) Any person (not being a child of the deceased) who, in the case of any marriage to which the deceased was at any time a party, was treated by the deceased as a child of the family in relation to that marriage.

e) Any person (not being included in the foregoing other categories) who *immediately* before the death of the deceased was being maintained,[6] either wholly or partly, by the deceased. A person is to be treated as being so maintained by the deceased if the deceased, otherwise than for full valuable consideration, was making a substantial contribution in money or money's worth towards the reasonable needs of that person. A co-habitee of the deceased does not have a claim in that capacity.

Any person, within the foregoing categories, is entitled to apply to the court for an order under section 2 on the ground that the disposition of the deceased's estate effected by his will or the law relating to intestacy, or the combination of his will and that law, is not such as to make reasonable financial provision for the applicant. The test is therefore objective, with the relevant circumstances to be taken into account as at the time of death. In the case of the surviving spouse (except where there was a decree of judicial separation operating) she is no longer to be limited to bare maintenance or breadline subsistence. It is provided that the measure of such reasonable financial provision is the financial provision which it would be reasonable in all the circumstances of the case for the spouse to receive, whether or not that provision is required for the spouse's maintenance. In the case of anyone within the other categories of applicants, the measure is such financial provision as it would be reasonable in all the circumstances of the case for the applicant to receive for maintenance.

The following is a summary of the matters which the court is required to take into account in assessing whether reasonable financial provision has been made, and in what manner it shall exercise its powers.

In the case of the surviving spouse being the applicant:

1) The financial resources, including earning capacity, and financial needs, including financial obligations and responsibilities, which the applicant, any other applicant and any beneficiary have or are likely to have in the foreseeable future.

2) Any obligations and responsibilities of the deceased towards any applicant and beneficiary.

3) The size and nature of the net estate of the deceased.

4) Any physical or mental disability of any applicant or beneficiary.

5) Any other matter, including the conduct of the applicant or any other person, which the court considers relevant.

6) The age of the applicant and the duration of the marriage.

7) The contribution made by the applicant to the welfare of the deceased's family, including any contribution made by looking after the home or caring for the family.

8) The provision which the applicant might reasonably have expected to receive

---

5 A child includes an illegitimate child and a child en ventre sa mère at time of death of deceased.
6 The expression 'being maintained' is discussed in Division H[3] J[10] of *Butterworths Wills, Probate and Administration Service.*

if on the day on which the deceased died the marriage had, instead, been terminated by divorce.

In the case of an application by a former spouse who has not remarried, all the foregoing matters except number 8.

In the case of an application by a child of the deceased, the matters numbered 1 to 5 and also the manner in which the applicant was being or might expect to be educated or trained.

In the case of an application by a person treated as a child of the family, the same matters as apply to a child and in addition (a) whether the deceased had assumed any responsibility for his maintenance and, if so, to the extent to which and on the basis upon which the deceased assumed that responsibility and to the length of time for which the deceased discharged that responsibility; (b) whether in assuming and discharging that responsibility the deceased did so knowing that the applicant was not his child; and (c) the liability of any other person to maintain the applicant.

In the case of an application by a person being maintained by the deceased, the matters numbered 1 to 5 and the extent to which and the basis upon which the deceased assumed responsibility for the maintenance of the applicant and to the length of time for which the deceased discharged that responsibility.

Under section 15(1),[7] on granting a decree of divorce or nullity of marriage or judicial separation or at any time thereafter, the court may on the application of either party to the marriage, order that the other party to the marriage shall not on the death of the applicant be entitled to apply for an order under section 2.[8] Irrespective of section 15(1), the Court of Appeal, in *Re Fullard, Fullard v King*,[9] has stated that the situations in which it will be appropriate for a former spouse of a deceased, who has not remarried, to make an application will be comparatively few, such as where periodical payments are ended by the death, or capital is then unlocked under an insurance policy.

Section 21 states that in any proceedings under the 1975 Act a statement made by the deceased, whether orally or in a document or otherwise, shall be admissible under the Civil Evidence Act 1968, section 2, as evidence of any fact stated therein. When appropriate, a testator should consider the making of a written statement, to be placed alongside his will, and, in making it, he should have regard, so far as possible, to the matters which the court is required to take into account for the purpose of assessing reasonable financial provision.

The court can make orders out of the deceased's estate for periodical payments, lump sum payments, the transfer of property and the settlement of property. It can also order the variation of ante-nuptial and post-nuptial settlements.

The net estate[10] of the deceased which is available for such orders is:
a) all property of which the deceased had power to dispose by his will (otherwise than by virtue of a special power of appointment) less the amount of his funeral, testamentary and administration expenses, debts and liabilities, including any inheritance tax payable out of his estate on his death;
b) any property in respect of which the deceased held a general power of

---

7 As amended by the Matrimonial and Family Proceedings Act 1984 s 8.
8 S 15A(2) and (3) extends the power of the court to marriages which have been dissolved or annulled overseas or where its parties have been legally separated and the other party dies while the legal separation is in force.
9 [1982] Ch 42, [1981] 2 All ER 796, CA.
10 S 25(1).

appointment (not being a power exercisable by will) which has not been exercised;

c) any sum of money or other property which is treated as part of the net estate by section 8(1) or (2) of the 1975 Act, (that is property covered by nomination or comprised in a donatio mortis causa, less IHT payable in respect thereof, by nominee or recipient);

d) any property which is treated as part of the net estate by section 9 (that is the deceased's severable share in any property [including a chose in action] of which he was a beneficial joint tenant). Such property is only included if the court specifically so orders, and an order cannot be made unless the availability of the deceased's share will facilitate the making of financial provision for the applicant. Even then, the property will be included only to the extent that the court considers just in the circumstances. An order cannot be made unless it has been applied for, strictly, within the six-month period from the date of the grant of representation (and regard shall be had to any IHT payable in respect of the severable share); and

e) any sum of money or other property which is, by reason of a disposition or contract made by the deceased, ordered to be made available under section 10 or section 11.

Section 10 applies to certain dispositions by the deceased, within six years before his death, and section 11 to contracts by which the deceased agreed to leave property by will or agreed that property would be transferred out of his estate: such sections do not apply to dispositions or contracts made before 1 April 1976.

To make an order under section 10 or section 11 the court must be satisfied:

i) That the deceased made the disposition or the contract with the intention of defeating an application for financial provision. Intention is to be satisfied on a balance of probabilities that the deceased wished to prevent an order or reduce the extent of an order. This need not have been his sole intention. Where no valuable consideration was given or promised, and valuable consideration does not include marriage or a promise of marriage, it shall, in the case of a contract only, be presumed that the deceased wished to defeat an application for financial provision.

ii) That the donee or the person, in whose favour the contract was made, did not give full consideration.

iii) That an order under the particular section would facilitate the making of financial provision for the applicant.

In considering an application under section 10 or section 11 the court is to have regard to the circumstances in which the disposition or contract was made, in the case only of section 10 any valuable consideration given therefor, the relationship (if any) of the donee to the deceased, the conduct and financial resources of the donee and all other circumstances of the case.

The provisions of the 1975 Act do not extend to and cannot therefore interfere with the exercise of the powers of trustees of a pension scheme under which they can make payments for the deceased's dependants even though such trustees may act on wishes expressed by the deceased.

By sub-section (1) of section 146 of the Inheritance Tax Act 1984, property comprised in an order made under section 2 of the 1975 Act is treated for IHT purposes as having devolved on death. By sub-section (8), the foregoing provision extends to a court order that stays or dismisses proceedings under the 1975 Act on terms referred to in the order, to the extent that those terms could have been included in a court order under sections 2 or 10 of that Act. This takes account of the common practice for consent orders to be made by reference to the 1975 Act, though not strictly *under* the Act, being orders by agreement between all the interested parties. Section 146 also provides for adjustment and repayment of IHT where an order is made under section 10 requiring any person to provide money or property by reason of a disposition made by the deceased which was itself a chargeable transfer.

Chapter 12

Testamentary matters concerning children

A. Introduction

The purpose of this chapter, as its title indicates, is to cover matters concerning children which are of importance in relation to the drafting of wills. There will be dealt with in turn, guardianship and the property rights of adopted children, illegitimate children and legitimated children.

According to the ordinary use of English, a person en ventre sa mère is as yet unborn. It is therefore worth mentioning, as a preliminary and general point, that it has long been established that where a will contains a gift to a person 'living' at a particular time then, in the absence of indication to the contrary, the requirement will be satisfied if that person is en ventre sa mère at such time.[1]

B. Guardianship

Part I of the Children Act 1989, which came into force on 14 October 1991, made important changes to the law of guardianship.

Sections 5 and 6 deal with the matter of guardians. A parent has a right to appoint a guardian of a child to act on his death only if he has parental responsibility[2] for that child. By section 2(1) and (2), where a child's parents were married to one another at the time of his birth,[3] each has parental responsibility, otherwise the mother has it but the father does not unless he acquires it under the Act, section 4. Acquisition is either by court order or by a parental responsibility agreement between the parents. Section 4(2) envisages, in respect of such an agreement, a form prescribed by regulations made by the Lord Chancellor.[4]

A parent has a right to appoint a guardian[5] to act on his death only if he has parental responsibility[2] for the child. When the appointment of a guardian takes effect, the guardian himself acquires parental authority.[2] If, on the appointing parent's death, there is no surviving parent who has parental authority[2] for the child, the appointment takes effect on that death. But if there is a surviving parent who does

---

1 *Theobald on Wills* (14th edn) pp 378–379.
2 Defined in s 3(1) as meaning 'all the rights, duties, powers, responsibilities and authority which by law a parent of a child has in relation to the child and his property'.
3 This phrase is interpreted according to the Family Law Reform Act 1987, s 1, under which
   (a) the reference to the time of the child's birth includes any time during the period beginning with the insemination from which the birth results or (if none) his conception and ending with his birth, and
   (b) his parents are treated as being married at the time of his birth if he is treated as legitimate or is legitimated or adopted.
4 Parental Responsibility Agreement Regulations 1991, SI 91/1478, prescribe the form for and manner of recording of such agreements.
5 More than one guardian may be appointed which is effectively confirmed by s 6(1).

have parental authority[2] the appointment does not take effect until there is no such parent, normally when the surviving parent dies.

Section 5(4) enables a guardian to appoint a successor in the event of his own death.

Under section 5(5) it is possible, as an alternative to making the appointment by will, to make an 'informal' appointment which is dated and signed by the person making it or at the direction of that person, in his presence and in the presence of two witnesses who each attest the signature.

Section 6 contains provisions about revocation of an earlier appointment, the disclaiming of an appointment and the power of the court to terminate an appointment of a guardian.

c. Property rights of adopted children

The position is governed by Part IV of the Adoption Act 1976. It applies to any adoption order made by a court in the United Kingdom, the Isle of Man, or the Channel Islands and to certain foreign adoptions. It provides that when construing the will of a testator who dies after 31 December 1975:

a) an adopted child is to be treated as the legitimate child of the married couple who adopt it or if the adoption is by one person as the legitimate child of that one person (but not as a child of any actual marriage of that person); and

b) an adopted child is to be treated as if it were not the child of any person other than the adopting parent(s).

It does not matter whether the adoption order is made before or after the testator's death. Thus, if a testator gives property to his son for life and subject thereto the capital to his son's children, being his grandchildren, a child adopted by the testator's son, whether before or after the testator's death, will be entitled to benefit, in the absence of any contrary intention.

Section 42 contains rules of construction, subject to any contrary intention, in relation to post-31 December 1975 instruments, including the wills and codicils of persons who die after such date.

Where a disposition depends on the date of birth of a child, it is to be construed as follows:

a) as if he had been born on the date of adoption;

b) where two or more children are adopted on the same date, seniority is to be based on the order of their actual births; but

c) such rules do not affect any reference to the age of a child.

The following examples, with the aid of common will wording, illustrate the effect of the law:

1) 'For such of them the child or children of my son X as shall be living at my death who attain the age of 21 years or marry under that age if more than one in equal shares'. A child of X adopted before the testator's death qualifies as a beneficiary but a child adopted afterwards does not, even though the child may have been alive at the testator's death.

2) 'For my son X on attaining the age of 30 years provided that if he dies in my lifetime or having survived me shall fail to attain the age of 30 years leaving a child or children living at the death of the survivor of myself and himself who attain the age of 21 years or marry under that age such child

or children shall take in his place if more than one in equal shares'. If X having survived the testator adopts a child following the testator's death, but dies before attaining the age of 30 years such adopted child qualifies as a beneficiary.

3) 'For the eldest child of X living at my death'. It is necessary, here, to count the seniority in age of an adopted child from the date of his adoption when compared with other children of X.

4) In the case of example 1, a child adopted prior to the testator's death would be entitled on actually attaining 21 (or marrying), and not 21 years after his adoption.

5) 'For that child of my son X who first attains the age of 21 years'. It would seem that an adopted child would be considered on the basis of his actual age.

D. Property rights of illegitimate children

The intention behind the Family Law Reform Act 1987 is to remove, so far as possible, the legal disadvantages of being, or being related to, an illegitimate person.

Section 1(1) lays down a general principle of construction, which generally applies including to all instruments made on or after 4 April 1988, which states that

'. . . references (however expressed) to any relationships between two persons shall, unless the contrary intention appears, be construed without regard to whether or not the father and mother of either of them, or the father or mother of any person through whom the relationship is deduced, have or had been married to each other at any time.'

Section 19 expressly applies the principle of construction to dispositions by a will or codicil made on or after 4 April 1988. Sub-section (7) of that section adds that such a disposition is not to be treated as made on or after that date by reason only that this will or codicil is confirmed by a codicil made on or after that date.

Accordingly *in the absence of any contrary intention* for the purposes of legal construction, an illegitimate person and those who trace their relationship through such a person are regarded in the same way as if they are legitimate.

E. Property rights of legitimated children

The position is governed by the Legitimacy Act 1976. Legitimation includes (a) legitimation under the Legitimacy Act 1926, section 1 or the Legitimacy Act 1976, section 2 (legitimation by subsequent marriage of parents if father at the date of marriage is domiciled in England and Wales) and (b) legitimation within section 8 of the 1926 Act or section 3 of the 1976 Act (legitimation by extraneous law).

The following rules of construction apply to the interpretation of instruments, including wills and codicils made on or after 1 January 1976, subject always to any contrary indication. In the case of wills and codicils the death of the testator is the date on which they are to be regarded as made.

A legitimated person, and any other person including for example his own children, are entitled to take any interest as if the legitimated person had been born legitimate.

Where a disposition depends on the date of birth of a child it is to be construed as follows:

a) as if he had been born on the date of legitimation;

b) where two or more children are legitimated on the same date, seniority is to be based on the order of their actual births;

c) but, such rules do not affect any reference to the age of a child.

Examples of phrases in wills on which the foregoing can operate are set out in section 5(5) of the 1976 Act.

Section 6(3) sets out a useful example, as well as thereby indicating the effect on dispositions depending on date of birth, when an illegitimate child is legitimated or adopted by one of his natural parents.

a) A testator dies in 1976 bequeathing a legacy to his eldest grandchild living at a specified time,

b) his daughter has an illegitimate child in 1977 who is the first grandchild,

c) his married son has a child in 1978,

d) subsequently the illegimate child is legitimated.

In all the foregoing cases the daughter's child remains the eldest grandchild of the testator throughout.

be treated as sufficient in point of form and expression. Deletions, by crossing out, should be initialled, although if they are not, the application to register will not be rejected for that reason alone. An instrument amended by the use of correcting fluid cannot, it is understood, be accepted as an enduring power unless the amendments are authenticated.[11]

In the case of execution by blind or physically handicapped donors, not surprisingly it is considered that additional words of attestation explaining the method and circumstances of execution would not constitute a material difference to the form or to the manner of its execution. In fact, it is to be recommended that the attestation clause should also record that the prescribed explanatory information has been read to and understood by the donor. An instrument executed by someone else acting under the direction and on behalf of a physically handicapped donor would be accepted for registration, but preferably should be attested by two witnesses.[12]

Whether or not strictly necessary, it is desirable where there is to be as attorney a solicitor or trust corporation that there should be included within the terms of the enduring power express authority for paying for the services of the attorney.[13]

A power of attorney cannot be an enduring power unless the attorney is a trust corporation or an individual.[14] To be an enduring power in respect of himself, the attorney must not be under age and must not be a bankrupt, at the time when he executes it.[14] If an attorney under an enduring power of attorney subsequently becomes bankrupt, his authority is terminated.[15]

The Act enables the donor to confer general, that is unrestricted, authority on the attorney or to limit the power to specific matters or specified property.[16] The donor may make the power subject to conditions or restrictions.[17] The donor might provide, for example, that certain transactions, such as a sale of the family home, is not to take place without the written consent of someone else, such as his wife. As previously mentioned, he could provide that the attorney is to have no authority unless and until he has reason to believe that the donor is, or is becoming, mentally incapable.

Section 2(8) states that a power of attorney under section 25 of the Trustee Act 1925 (power to delegate trusts etc by power of attorney) cannot be an enduring power. Nevertheless, section 3(3) provides that, subject to any conditions or restrictions contained in the instrument, an attorney under an enduring power, whether general or limited, may (without obtaining any consent) execute or exercise all or any of the trusts, powers or discretions vested in the donor as trustee and may (without the concurrence of any other person) give a valid receipt for capital or other money paid. Section 3(3) was, in fact, inserted in the 1985 Act to enable the attorney of

---

11 See *Law Society's Gazette* (26 November 1986).

12 See *Law Society's Gazette* (28 October 1987) at 3083-4.

13 In an opinion given in 1958 (1 *Law Society's Digest*, 4th cum supp, p 96) the Law Society expressed the view that if a client gives his solicitor a power of attorney which does not mention remuneration, the solicitor can charge not only for his professional services in drawing up the power, but also for his non-professional services in acting as attorney under it. See the remarks in *Butterworths Wills, Probate and Administration Service*, [191] to [195]. The official view confirms that an attorney who is, for example, a solicitor or accountant can charge for his professional services, subject to any restrictions or conditions which the donor chooses to include in the power of attorney.

14 S 2(7).

15 S 2(10).

16 S 3(1) and (2).

17 S 3(2).

a donor who is a joint tenant of a jointly-owned property to deal with it and so overcome the technical conveyancing difficulties illustrated in *Walia v Michael Naughton Ltd.*[18] In that case one of three legal co-owners of land had made a general power of attorney, under the Powers of Attorney Act 1971, section 10, in favour of one of the others who had executed a transfer of it on his own behalf and also, as attorney, on behalf of the donor co-owner. It was held that the transfer did not confer a good title on the transferee because a general power of attorney, in contrast to one under the Trustee Act 1925, section 25, did not empower the attorney to execute on behalf of the donor a transfer of property of which the donor was himself a trustee.

A donor can appoint more than one attorney, and thus several. The Act stipulates that an instrument which appoints more than one person to be an attorney cannot create an enduring power unless the attorneys are appointed to act jointly or jointly and severally.[19] The Act also stipulates that a power of attorney which gives the attorney a right to appoint a substitute or successor cannot be an enduring power.[20]

Where joint or joint and several attorneys are appointed, a failure, as respects any one attorney, to comply with the requirements for the creation of an enduring power, does not prevent the instrument from being valid in respect of any other attorney.[1] Also, until mental incapacity on the part of the donor intervenes, the enduring power *can*[2] be effective as an ordinary power of attorney in respect of the particular attorney who has not so complied.

It is sensible that an enduring power of attorney should not be granted to one person alone or to more than one but with joint powers only. That is because the death or bankruptcy of an attorney in either of those circumstances would effectively end its authority possibly at a time when the donor is mentally incapable and therefore unable to grant a further enduring power of attorney. Accordingly, the need for the appointment of more than one attorney who can act jointly and severally is important.

c. Registration

The duty to apply for registration of the enduring power arises when the attorney has reason to believe that the donor is or is becoming mentally incapable.[3] That duty requires making an application in the prescribed form, as soon as practicable, to the Court of Protection for registration of the enduring power of attorney.[4] Nevertheless, the Act requires, except in certain limited circumstances, prior formal notice of the intention of the attorney to apply for registration to be given to the donor and certain categories of the donor's relatives, and to any other attorney before application to the Court of Protection is made.[5] The detailed requirements about that duty to give notice are contained in Part I of Schedule I to the Act. Part

---

18 [1985] 1 WLR 1115.
19 S 11(1).
20 S 2(9).
 1 S 11(4).
 2 That is, of course, subject to any specific conditions or restrictions that the donor may have specified in the instrument.
 3 S 4.
 4 S 4(2) and (4).
 5 S 4(3).

II of that Schedule covers the contents of the notices and the form of them is Form EPI in Schedule I to the Court of Protection (Enduring Powers of Attorney) Rules 1986, SI 1986/127.[6]

D. Position immediately prior to registration

A consequence of the attorney believing that the donor is, or is becoming, mentally incapable is that his authority and powers under the enduring power are suspended until it is registered by the Court of Protection. Accordingly he cannot, for the time being, act generally on behalf of the donor. Nevertheless, as soon as the application for registration has been made, the attorney has power first to maintain the donor or prevent loss to his estate and secondly to maintain himself or other persons in so far as section 3(4) permits him to do so.[7]

When the enduring power has been registered the attorney possesses full authority to act under the enduring power of attorney.

E. Special rights available under an enduring power

Without prejudice to his authority under section 3(4), but subject to any conditions or restrictions contained in the enduring power, whether general or limited, the attorney may (without obtaining any consent) dispose of the property of the donor by way of gift to the following limited extents. First, he may make gifts of a seasonal nature or at a time, or on an anniversary, of a birth or marriage, to persons (including himself) who are related to or connected with the donor. Secondly, he may make gifts to any charity to whom the donor made or might be expected to make gifts. Nevertheless there is a proviso, in both cases, that the value of each such gift is not unreasonable having regard to all the circumstances and in particular the size of the donor's estate.[8]

The Court of Protection has power to authorise the attorney to act beyond his statutory powers so as to benefit himself or persons other than the donor.[9] Thus, apparently, the court could entertain an application to authorise the making of substantial gifts which have the object of mitigating the potential liability for IHT on the donor's death.

F. Effect of registration

The effect of registration of the enduring power is that[10]—
   a) the donor is prohibited from revoking it unless and until the Court confirms the revocation, which could happen if the donor recovers his mental capacity;
   b) the attorney is prohibited from disclaiming the enduring power unless and until he has first given notice to the Court; and

---

6 SI 1986/127 has been amended by the Court of Protection (Enduring Powers of Attorney) (Amendment) Rules 1990, SI 1990/864, which increases the fees payable in respect of applications for registration of an enduring power of attorney and applications to search the register.
7 S 1(2).
8 S 3(5).
9 S 8(2)(e).
10 S 7(1).

c) the donor is prohibited from extending or restricting the scope of his enduring power.

G. Conclusion

For the reasons given at the beginning of this chapter there is a strong case for recommending the granting by persons in good health of enduring powers of attorney, whether or not subject to conditions or restrictions. Nevertheless, it will be the case that for many people the concept of a power of attorney, particularly an enduring power, is not easy to grasp. For a memorandum of explanation see Form 120, page 262 below.

Part II. Complete Will Precedents, Capital Tax Mitigation
Memorandum and Sample Letters

1 Comprehensive family will directed to mitigating future tax liabilities and which includes overriding power of appointment over residue (*see note at the end*)

I   of   in the County of   the husband/wife of   REVOKE any earlier Will or testamentary dispositions of mine AND DECLARE this to be my Will which I make this   day of One thousand nine hundred and ninety-

1. I WISH to be buried where most convenient and my funeral to be conducted in a simple manner [And if a memorial is placed at my grave I DIRECT my Executors to pay the cost from my residuary estate]

or

1. I WISH my body to be cremated my ashes to be scattered and my funeral to be conducted in a simple manner

2. a) I APPOINT my wife/husband and
   of   in the County
   of   and
   of
   in the County of   to be the executors
   and trustees of this Will
   b) THE expression 'my Trustees' when used in this Will means my executors and the trustees or trustee whether original or substituted or added

3. IF a child of mine is under age at the death of the survivor of myself and my wife/husband I APPOINT   and   to be the guardians of that child And I authorise them by deed or the survivor of them by deed or Will to appoint one or two persons to act as guardians in their place after the survivor's death

4. a) I GIVE free of inheritance tax all my chattels to those persons who obtain the first grant of Probate of this Will
   b) I REQUEST them but without imposing any legal obligation
      i) To give effect as soon as possible but not later than two years after my death to any memorandum or notes of wishes of mine about any of my chattels
      ii) Subject to any wishes to make my wife/husband the owner of my chattels (or the balance thereof) if (s)he survives me by three months
      iii) Subject as aforesaid (in particular if my wife/husband does not survive me by three months) to hold my chattels (or the balance thereof) upon the same trusts and with and subject to the same powers and provisions

as apply to and as an addition to the Trust Fund (as defined in Clause 8(c) hereof)

c) IN this Clause 'chattels' has the same meaning as the expression 'personal chattels' in the Administration of Estates Act 1925 (but including any car or other article that I own at the time of my death despite it being regarded for the purposes of taxation or insurance or otherwise as being wholly or partly for business use)

d) ALL expenses for safe custody and insurance of my chattels before giving effect to my wishes and for packing transporting and insuring any chattels for delivery to their recipients shall be paid from my residuary estate

5. I GIVE free of inheritance tax the following cash legacies to the following persons [or charities];

6. a) i) MY Trustees may if they at any time decide pay all or any part of a legacy under Clause 5 to the beneficiary when he or she is under age or to a parent or guardian of the beneficiary And in that event the receipt of the beneficiary or of the parent or guardian shall be a complete discharge to my Trustees

   ii) MY Trustees and the parent or guardian (as the case may be) shall in respect of that legacy have power to use both income and capital (without limitation) for the benefit of the beneficiary and power to invest similar to the one in Clause 13(a) of this Will including power to buy National Savings Certificates

   b) THE receipt of a person who purports to be the treasurer or other officer of a charitable benevolent or philanthropic institution society club or body of persons for a legacy under Clause 5 shall be a complete discharge to my Trustees who shall not thereafter have responsibility for its application

7. a) NOTWITHSTANDING the rest of this Clause:
   i) IF my wife/husband does not survive me the gift under sub-clause (b) shall fail and the terms of the succeeding sub-clauses shall not take effect; and

   ii) IF my wife/husband dies during the period of three months after my death the trusts hereafter declared over the Legacy Fund shall cease and thereupon my Trustees shall stand possessed of the capital and income (including accruing or accrued income not yet received) of the Legacy Fund upon the same trusts and with and subject to the same powers and provisions as apply to and as an addition to the Trust Fund (as defined in Clause 8(c) of this Will)

   b) i) I GIVE to my Trustees a cash sum calculated by paragraph (ii) of this sub-clause to hold upon the trusts and with and subject to the powers and provisions hereafter declared over the Legacy Fund

   ii) THE cash sum in paragraph (i) of this sub-clause is the largest amount that can be given by this Clause without any inheritance tax being payable on the transfer of value of my estate which I am deemed to make immediately before my death

iii) THIS gift shall not carry interest until payment

c) IN this Clause the following expressions have the following meanings:

'The Legacy Fund' means the cash sum given by sub-clause (b) of this Clause and the assets for the time being representing it

'The Trust Period' means the period starting with the date of my death and ending eighty years later (and that period is the perpetuity period applicable hereto)

'The Beneficiaries' means those of the following persons living at my death or born during the Trust Period being my wife/husband and my children and my remoter issue and any person who is or has been a spouse of any child or remoter issue of mine (including of any who have died before me)

d) MY Trustees shall sell or retain any part of the assets of the Legacy Fund that is not money with power to invest any money and to vary investments similar to the one in sub-clause (a) of Clause 13 of this Will

e) MY Trustees shall pay or transfer or otherwise hold (as the case may be) the Legacy Fund and its income to or for the benefit of any one or more of the Beneficiaries at such age or time or respective ages or times in such shares and with and subject to such trusts and dispositive and administrative powers and provisions (including protective and discretionary trusts and powers exercisable at the discretion of my Trustees or any other person or persons) as my Trustees (not being less than two in number) may during the Trust Period by any deed or deeds revocable or irrevocable appoint (regard being had to the law relating to remoteness) PROVIDED:

   i) that no appointment shall invalidate any prior payment or application of any part or parts of the capital or income of the Legacy Fund;

   ii) that no power of revocation reserved to my Trustees in any appointment shall be capable of being exercised after the end of the Trust Period; and

   iii) that my Trustees may during the Trust Period at any time or times by irrevocable deed extinguish or restrict the future exercise of this power of appointment

f) IN default of and until and subject to any appointment by my Trustees under sub-clause (e) of this Clause my Trustees shall hold the Legacy Fund upon the following trusts:

   i) UNTIL the end of the Trust Period UPON TRUST to pay or apply the income of the Legacy Fund with power from time to time to pay or apply the whole or any part or parts of the capital of the Legacy Fund to or for the benefit of any one or more of the Beneficiaries for the time being living PROVIDED THAT my Trustees may (notwithstanding the foregoing discretionary trust in respect of that income) during the period of twenty one years from my death from time to time accumulate the whole or any part of the income of the Legacy Fund at compound interest by investing it and its resulting income in any investments authorised by sub-clause (d) of this Clause and adding the accumulations to the capital of the Legacy Fund

   ii) SUBJECT as aforesaid UPON TRUST for those of my children living at my death if more than one in equal shares

g) MY Trustees shall have a similar power of appropriation over the Legacy Fund (including after any exercise of their power of appointment under sub-clause

(e) of this Clause) to the one in sub-clause (a) of Clause 14 of this Will without needing the consent of anyone

h) ANY of my Trustees may join in exercising any of the trusts and powers under this Clause notwithstanding that he or she is one of the Beneficiaries and will or may benefit as a result

i) I DECLARE but without imposing any binding legal obligation on them that it is my wish first that my Trustees shall regard my wife/husband during her/his lifetime as the primary beneficiary of both the income and capital of the Legacy Fund and secondly that as soon as possible after the death of my wife/husband my Trustees shall exercise their powers over the capital of the Legacy Fund in such manner as will so far as possible correspond with the terms of sub-clause (b) of Clause 10 of this Will

8. a) I GIVE all my property and assets both real and personal movable and immovable whatsoever and wheresoever not otherwise disposed of by this Will or any Codicil to my Trustees UPON TRUST to sell the same or any part thereof which does not consist of money or to retain the same or any part in the condition or state of investment as it is at the time of my death for so long as my Trustees decide without being liable for loss

b) MY Trustees shall from the money from any sale and from my ready money pay my funeral and testamentary expenses and debts and any legacies in this Will or any Codicil

c) MY Trustees shall hold the rest of the said money and the property and investments at any time representing it and any part of my property and assets as remain unsold (hereafter called 'the Trust Fund') upon the trusts and with and subject to the powers and provisions hereafter declared in this Will

9. a) MY Trustees shall pay or transfer or otherwise hold (as the case may be) the Trust Fund and its income to or for the benefit of any one or more of the following persons (including any born after my death) being my wife/husband and my children and my remoter issue and any person who is or has been a spouse of any child or remoter issue of mine (including of any who have died before me) at such age or time or respective ages or times in such shares and with and subject to such trusts and dispositive and administrative powers and provisions (including protective and discretionary trusts and powers exercisable at the discretion of my Trustees or any other person or persons) as my Trustees (not being less than two in number) may by any deed or deeds revocable or irrevocable appoint (regard being had to the law relating to remoteness) PROVIDED:

  i) that no appointment shall invalidate any prior payment or application of any part or parts of the capital or income of the Trust Fund;

  ii) that my Trustees may at any time or times by irrevocable deed extinguish or restrict the future exercise of this power of appointment; and

  iii) that without imposing any binding legal obligation I REQUEST my Trustees in exercising or not exercising or limiting this power of appointment to have regard to the future interests of the Family and for that purpose to discuss their intentions with my wife/husband before acting

b) I DECLARE that my Trustees may exercise their power of appointment under sub-clause (a) notwithstanding

i) that Probate of this Will has not been obtained; or

ii) that the administration of my estate has not been completed and the Trust Fund has not been fully quantified and established; or

iii) that any of them will or may benefit as a result

10. IN default of and until and subject to any appointment by my Trustees under Clause 9 of this Will my Trustees shall hold the Trust Fund and its income upon the following trusts that is to say:

a) i) IF my wife/husband survives me by three months UPON TRUST to pay the income of the Trust Fund to my wife/husband during her/his life

ii) SUBJECT thereto (including when my wife/husband does not so survive me or dies during the following period) UPON TRUST until the end of the period of twenty-three months from my death to pay or apply the income of the Trust Fund to or for the benefit of any one or more of my children and remoter issue for the time being living

b) i) SUBJECT as aforesaid UPON TRUST to pay or transfer or otherwise hold (as the case may be) the capital and income of the Trust Fund to or for my child or children living three months after my death who attain the Vesting Age if more than one in equal shares PROVIDED THAT if any child has died in my lifetime (whether before or after the date of this Will) or within three months after my death or having survived me dies before attaining the Vesting Age and issue of that child are living three months after my death and attain the Vesting Age such issue shall take by substitution if more than one as tenants in common in equal shares the share of the Trust Fund which my deceased child would have taken had he or she been living three months after my death and attained the Vesting Age but so that no issue remoter than a child of my deceased child shall take whose parent is living and so capable of taking

ii) SUBJECT as aforesaid UPON TRUST to pay or transfer or otherwise hold (as the case may be) the capital and income of the Trust Fund to or for the following persons namely

living three months after my death who attain the Vesting Age if more than one in equal shares PROVIDED THAT if any of the said persons has died in my lifetime (whether before or after the date of this Will) or within three months after my death or having survived me dies before attaining the Vesting Age and issue of that person are living three months after my death and attain the Vesting Age such issue shall take by substitution if more than one as tenants in common in equal shares the share of the Trust Fund which such deceased person would have taken had he or she been living three months after my death and attained the Vesting Age but so that no issue remoter than a child of such deceased person shall take whose parent is living and so capable of taking

iii) THE expression 'the Vesting Age' means the age of twenty-five years or if earlier the age of the beneficiary on the day before the twenty-first anniversary of my death and I DECLARE that for the purposes of the Trustee Act 1925 section 31 (or any statutory modification or re-enactment of it) a beneficiary shall be deemed to attain full age on attaining the Vesting Age and references to 'infancy' and 'eighteen years' shall accordingly be varied and the right of my Trustees to pay or apply income to or for a beneficiary who has not attained the Vesting Age shall be exerciseable as my Trustees in their absolute discretion think fit

11. I DECLARE that any adult beneficiary may within two years after my death execute a deed to disclaim all or part (including a fraction or percentage) of his or her entitlements in this Will in which event what is disclaimed shall devolve under this Will as if he or she had died before me

12.a) IN addition to all other powers conferred by law or under this Will my Trustees (not being less than two in number) may at any time or times raise capital out of that part of the Trust Fund of which my wife/husband is then entitled to the income under sub-clause (a) of Clause 10 of this Will for the following purposes:

   i) for paying it to or applying it for the benefit of my wife/husband; or
   ii) for making loans to my wife/husband either with or without security and with or without interest and generally upon such terms and subject to such conditions as my Trustees decide and I DECLARE that my Trustees shall also have freedom to leave them outstanding during her/his life and that my Trustees shall not be liable for any loss to the Trust Fund because of the making of any loans or the failure to recover the amounts thereby owed before or after the death of my wife/husband

   b) I DECLARE that when considering whether or not to exercise the foregoing power for my wife/husband my Trustees shall disregard the interests of any other beneficiaries in the Trust Fund

13. MY Trustees shall have the following powers which they may exercise at any time and from time to time:

   a) POWER to invest trust moneys in both income producing and non-income producing assets of every kind and wherever situated and to vary investments and in those respects to act in the same full and unrestricted manner as if they themselves were absolutely entitled thereto beneficially [And without prejudice to the generality of the foregoing power my Trustees shall not be under any duty to diversify the investments comprised in the Trust Fund whether under Section 6(1) of the Trustee Investments Act 1961 or otherwise]

   b) POWER to retain or purchase as an authorised investment any freehold or leasehold property or any interest or share therein of whatever nature proportion or amount (which shall be held upon trust to retain or sell the same) as a residence for my wife/husband and in the event of any such retention or purchase my Trustees shall have power to apply trust moneys in the erection alteration improvement or repair of any building on such freehold or leasehold property including one where there is any such interest or share And my Trustees shall also have power to decide (according to the circumstances generally) the terms and conditions in every respect upon which my wife/husband may occupy and reside at the property (or have the benefit of the said interest or share therein) PROVIDED ALWAYS and I HEREBY DECLARE that no property or any share or interest in any property retained or purchased pursuant to the terms of the foregoing power is to be sold (or have interests granted thereout) by my Trustees without the consent in writing of my wife/husband during her/his lifetime

c) POWER to borrow money upon such terms and subject to such conditions including in relation to repayment and interest and whether or not upon the security of the Trust Fund or any part thereof and for such purposes in connection with the administration of my estate and the trusts of this Will as my Trustees think fit but no lender shall be concerned about the purpose of any such loan to my Trustees or the circumstances or the propriety thereof

d) POWER to enter into any contract or other dealing or disposition (whether by way of sale purchase exchange mortgage lease loan borrowing or otherwise) with the trustees of any other Will or any settlement or trust or policy (being a contract or other dealing or disposition which apart from this present provision my Trustees could lawfully have entered into if none of them had also been a trustee of such other Will or such settlement or trust or policy) notwithstanding that my Trustees or any one or more of them shall also be trustees or the sole trustee of such other Will or such settlement or trust or policy and in like manner in all respects as though none of my Trustees had been a trustee of such other Will or such settlement or trust or policy

e) POWER to insure under comprehensive or any other cover and against any risks for any amounts (including allowing as they deem appropriate for any possible effects of inflation and increasing building or replacement costs and expenses) any asset which forms part of the Trust Fund irrespective of who may use or enjoy it and the insurance premiums may be discharged by my Trustees either out of income or out of capital (or partly out of one and partly out of the other) as my Trustees in their absolute discretion decide and any moneys received by my Trustees as the result of any insurance insofar as not used in rebuilding reinstating replacing or repairing the asset lost or damaged shall be treated as if they were the proceeds of sale of the asset insured PROVIDED ALWAYS that my Trustees shall not be under any responsibility to insure or be liable for any loss that may result from any failure to do so or for the inadequacy of any policy they effect

14.a) MY Trustees shall have power at any time or times to appropriate any part of my residuary estate or of the Trust Fund (as the case may be) in its then actual condition or state of investment in or towards satisfaction of any legacy or any share in the Trust Fund (whether or not the same is settled including by exercise of their power of appointment in Clause 9) without needing the consent of anyone

b) WHEN placing a value on any of my personal chattels (as defined by the Administration of Estates Act 1925) so appropriated my Trustees may use the same value as has been placed on it by any Valuers they instruct for inheritance tax purposes on the death of myself or of my wife/husband (as the case may be) or such other value as they in their absolute discretion decide is fair

c) AS a supplement to their power in sub-clause (a) of this Clause my Trustees (as the executors of this Will) for the purposes of satisfying in whole or in part the settled legacy in Clause 7 may grant a charge (with or without payment of interest and whether or not repayable on demand) over any part of my residuary estate or of the Trust Fund (as the case may be) to secure the whole or part of that settled legacy And in that event my Trustees (as trustees of the trusts in Clause 7) shall accept the charge for the amount so secured as being in or towards satisfaction of the settled legacy

d) THE powers in this Clause can be exercised by my Trustees notwithstanding that any of them may benefit personally as a result

15. ANY person who does not survive me by three months shall be deemed to have died before me for ascertaining the devolution of my estate and its income

16. IN the administration of my estate and the trusts of this Will:

a) WHERE any payment in the nature of income received after the occurrence of any event (including my own death) would (but for this sub-clause) fall to be treated as accruing partly (or wholly) before that event it shall be treated as accruing wholly after that event

b) INCOME from any investment or other asset which remains unsold shall be treated as if it is income from an investment authorised by Clause 13(a) of this Will

c) NO investment or other asset not producing income shall be treated as if it does

d) MY debts and funeral and testamentary expenses (including inheritance tax payable from my residuary estate) and legacies shall be paid from the capital of my estate without recourse to its income

17. ANY of my executors or trustees being a person engaged in any profession or business shall be entitled (a) to charge and be paid all usual professional or other charges for business transacted time expended and acts done by that person or their firm or company or any partner or employee in connection with the administration of my estate and the trusts of this Will including acts which an executor or trustee not being in any profession or business could or might have done personally and (b) to retain or receive whether or not personally any brokerage or commission of a normal nature for any stockbroking or insurance transaction undertaken by that person or their firm or company

IN WITNESS whereof I have hereunto set my hand the day and year first above written

SIGNED by the above named . . . .
as his/her Will in the presence of us
both present at the same time who
in his/her presence at his/her
request and in the presence of each
other have hereunto subscribed our
names as witnesses:

NOTE

The above will form is comprehensive. Its structure results from the considerations in framing the trusts of the residuary estate in ch 8. It also takes into consideration the other matters dealt with about capital tax mitigation in the memorandum being no 2, p 135 below. In the residuary trusts, under sub-clause (b) of clause 10, both the income and capital interests entitlements of the children or other ultimate beneficiaries are synchronised, on their attaining 'the Vesting Age', probably being twenty-five. The explanation for that is a capital tax one and is contained in the note to form 60, p 201 below.

2 Memorandum directed to capital tax mitigation (*see note at the end*)

This Memorandum discusses, for the purposes of the accompanying draft Will, matters of capital tax and its mitigation. The main tax under consideration is inheritance tax ('IHT') but capital gains tax ('CGT') is also taken into account.

The clauses of the draft Will to which we draw attention are Clauses   and   which we discuss in turn under B, C and D below, after some general observations under A. E contains concluding observations on personal non-taxation aspects of what has been proposed under D.

A *General Observations*

1) An intention behind schemes to mitigate capital taxes liabilities, particularly of IHT, is to increase the amount of assets that are distributed in due time to our children and/or grandchildren or other beneficiaries following the death of the survivor of ourself and our spouse.

   It is simple to treat the ultimate liability for IHT as 40% of the whole which except for the nil% band, index-linked on an annual basis, is the rate of IHT above the nil% band, at present £1 ,000.

   If one imagines a see-saw, there is Mr Lamont or other the Chancellor of the Exchequer for the time being on one end and our, say , children on the other. In those circumstances potentially the most important of our beneficiaries is the Chancellor of the Exchequer to the extent of 40% free of any deductions, with our children each receiving, say,   %, but sharing the expenses of the administration of our estates. Thus, the intention of mitigation is to remove value that would otherwise be received by the Chancellor of the Exchequer from his end of the see-saw and to place it on the end of that of our children.

2) It is possible to do that by making lifetime gifts of substance, in some shape or form, to our children. But that may well be financially difficult having regard to the uncertain needs of ourselves and our spouses in a future of uncertain length. Because of the Finance Act 1989 that has become more difficult, for reasons of CGT, as we will explain.

   By making a potentially exempt transfer ('PET'), which for example can be an absolute gift or a gift under trust with a straight life/income interest, there is no IHT paid on the making of the gift and provided that we survive seven years after making it and provided that there is no reservation of a benefit and no benefit is received back, at *any* time before our death whether direct or indirect, that PET becomes and remains a fully exempt transfer.

   But, as the result of the Finance Act 1989, hold-over relief for CGT purposes is no longer generally available on a gift of assets which is also a PET; business assets and land qualifying for IHT agricultural property relief can in these circumstances continue to attract hold-over relief. And that also is so when there is a lifetime gift which on its making is chargeable to IHT (even though none is payable where it is covered by the nil% band) because, usually, it is a trust gift with discretionary trusts.

It will be appreciated from what is contrasted in the next paragraph that a person would obtain the worst of all worlds if having made a gift which did not enjoy the benefit of hold-over relief for CGT purposes, thus resulting in an immediate CGT liability, he does not survive the seven year period with the further result that that gift which was a PET becomes retroactively a chargeable transfer for IHT purposes, with an IHT liability to be discharged.

3) There is no CGT liability on death. Moreover, beneficiaries receive assets from the executors without a CGT liability being incurred, at the executors' deemed acquisition values, which are the values on death.

4) In relation to IHT, there is the all important exemption for gifts between spouses whether during lifetime or on death. Additionally, provided a person has not made gifts to non-exempt persons within seven years of his death, absorbing his nil% band, there is that band available in all or in part for testamentary gifts to non-exempt persons without incurring a payment of IHT.

5) If at the time of death there are exempt and non-exempt beneficiaries (particularly in the case of the former a surviving spouse) testamentary gifts to non-exempt beneficiaries in excess of the available nil% band will bring forward at once a liability to IHT. That, in our opinion, is not satisfactory and should be avoided. D below discusses what are considered better arrangements.

B   Clause

This 'chattels' clause is not only of practical convenience but is also directed to the terms of the Inheritance Tax Act 1984, section 143, which reads as follows:

> 'Where a testator expresses a wish that property bequeathed by his Will should be transferred by the legatee to other persons, and the legatee transfers any of the property in accordance with that wish within the period of two years after the death of the testator, this Act shall have effect as if the property transferred had been bequeathed by the Will to the transferee.'

This clause can give all one's 'chattels' (that expression means tangible articles of every kind except for any used for business purposes unless there is anything expressed to the contrary) to those persons who are nominated, possibly being the same persons as the executors, except any otherwise given specifically. It envisages that there may be a separate and informal, therefore not strictly legally binding, memorandum or notes of wishes which can subsequently be altered and added to as and when desired, without the need for alterations to the Will itself by Codicil. The decision about the use of such an arrangement is a personal one but, as will be noted from the wording of section 142, the giving of effect to any such expressed wishes, within the two year period, is regarded, for IHT purposes, as if the gifts had been included within the Will and therefore ones direct from the testator to the recipients themselves, without regard to the action in fact taken by the nominal beneficiaries which would otherwise be a transfer or gift onwards by them for IHT purposes.

C Clause

As will be appreciated, if the other spouse survives and becomes entitled to the residuary estate of the testator, or a life interest in it which is regarded as the same for IHT purposes, there is normally no IHT liability because of the exemption for gifts between spouses.

An IHT liability will ultimately become payable on the survivor's death when, put simply, the combined assets will be aggregated and suffer IHT together. Because the spouse exemption applies overall, the first to die will not, on his or her death, have taken advantage of their nil% band for IHT purposes. That band which is index linked each 6 April, for this present tax year runs up to £1 ,000. When applicable on a death that band, to ascertain what part of it is available, needs as has already been referred to, to take into cumulative account the value of gifts made by the testator during the seven years before death. After £1 ,000 the rate of IHT is 40%, irrespective of however large may be the value of the assets.

At the risk of over simplifying matters one can almost say that the proportion of the assets which would have suffered an IHT charge at nil% will be added on to the top of the survivor's assets on their death and charged to IHT at their highest rate. The difference it will be appreciated and therefore the possible saving could be, at present rates, £ , , (40% of £1 ,000).

It would of course be possible to achieve the particular IHT saving by a gift under the particular will of a cash legacy equal to the available amount of the nil% band but allowing for other non-exempt legacies, at the time of death, to the children. But as the primary purpose is to safeguard the survivor financially to the utmost extent that may not be a practical possibility. Accordingly, the object behind the above Clause is to achieve that IHT mitigation by the use of the nil% band but at the same time enabling the survivor to be a beneficiary in respect of the legacy which is constituted on discretionary trusts and yet it will not be treated as assets taxable to IHT on their subsequent death. An explanation of the individual sub-clauses can be given separately.

To achieve the maximum benefit of such arrangements, each spouse requires assets of a value sufficient to cover the nil% band. An examination of the respective assets should be made and, for that purpose, account should be taken only of those assets which are owned by each which may thus include a share being a tenancy-in-common in the matrimonial home but not their ownership if it is a joint tenancy which may therefore need to be changed, very simply, to a tenancy-in-common. Advice may also be required, on the making of the Will, where a spouse has a sufficient value of assets but they are not liquid, in contrast to cash and investments, because they include for example a share in the matrimonial home, as in the case of a tenancy-in-common. In addition, regard should be paid to likely expectations in the future which would thus increase their assets.

D Clause

In A(5) above, mention is made of the unsatisfactory result of bringing forward on to the first death any IHT liability whatsoever.

1) The form of residuary trusts under a Will which takes that matter into account can be structured along the following lines:

   a) The executors and trustees are given a wide 'overriding' power of appointment (thus a right of disposal) to be exercised (if at all) within a stipulated class of beneficiaries which can, for example, include the other spouse, children, remoter issue and possibly the spouses of children or remoter issue. This power can also be released. The variety, manner and occasions for the exercise of this power are wide.

   b) Subject to that power of appointment and subject to any exercise of it and in what manner

      i) If the spouse survives, the 'underlying' trusts confer a life/income interest on that spouse (see (2) below).

      ii) If the other spouse does not survive, there is a discretionary trust over the income for a period of twenty-three months only from the date of the death (see (3) below).

   c) Subject to (a) and (b), the children equally are the beneficiaries, or the issue of any of them who do not survive.

2) We explain the reasons for the combined effect of a) and (b)(i) of (1) above in the following manner:

   a) If the other spouse survives, the spouse exemption for IHT purposes will apply on the death of the testator notwithstanding the presence of the overriding power of appointment.

   b) Should the overriding power of appointment be subsequently exercised by the executors and trustees in favour of others thus extinguishing pro tanto the life interest of the spouse that is regarded as if it was a transfer for IHT purposes and can qualify as PET whose exempt status is confirmed after survival of the spouse by seven years.

   c) Interestingly, the reservation of benefit provisions referred to in A2) above, do not apply because a condition of their application is a gift by the deemed transferor and in the particular circumstances the widow(er) has not made any gift.

   d) If that power is, as is very possible, exercised in favour of the spouse there are no IHT consequences.

   e) The existence of the overriding power of appointment generally creates flexibility and given the wish, including for saving future IHT in respect of the children, would enable them to be by-passed by its exercise in favour of their children whether or not the circumstances require trusts to be constituted of a protective nature.

   f) Although the matter relatively is not a major one it is the case that, in the circumstances of trusts with a straight life interest, they suffer CGT at the sole rate of 25% on disposals when contrasted with a possible rate of 40% for individuals.

3) We explain the reasons for the combined effect of (a) and (b)(ii) of (1) above in the following manner:

a) If the other spouse does not survive, the spouse exemption for IHT purposes cannot of necessity apply.

b) i) Nevertheless, the existence of the overriding power of appointment, as is referred to under (1)(a), generally creates flexibility and given the wish would enable the children to be by-passed by its exercise in favour of their children whether or not the circumstances require trusts to be constituted of a protective nature.

ii) The terms of Clause (a)(ii), with its twenty-three months period, take into account the provisions of the Inheritance Tax Act 1984, section 144. In summary, section 144 provides that so long as assets under a Will are held on trusts without an interest in possession, because they contain like Clause (a)(ii) discretionary trusts, the exercise of the overriding power of appointment, in the desired manner within the period of two years following the death, will not, in itself, result in a charge to IHT which would otherwise be the case.

E Concluding Observations

D above assumes that, for reasons of tax, the surviving spouse will receive a life interest. There is sometimes a tendency to decry the surviving spouse receiving a life interest only as opposed to being entitled to the residuary estate of their deceased spouse absolutely on the grounds that, for IHT purposes, the result is the same. It is nevertheless suggested that, for personal reasons, the possibility of a life interest, with suitable powers for the executors and trustees, including by the presence of an overriding power of appointment, to make over capital, should not be lightly discarded. The decision will be based on personal reasons and not fiscal ones, but a husband might well wish to limit his wife to life interest so that she may have the benefit of considerate executors and trustees of whom she can, if desired, be one. The spouses may also have differing views, even if only of degree, about the eventual destination of their respective assets. Such Wills, in these days of people living longer and widows and widowers marrying again, can thus safeguard the future inheritance of their children, come what may.

Date   199 .

NOTE

The above memorandum, as its title indicates, is directed to capital tax mitigation. That subject is a large and complex one and it has been thought easier to give an explanation by a separate memorandum which can be sent to the client in advance of the draft will or at the same time with it and its covering letter: see the second paragraph within brackets of the sample letter being no 3, p 140 below.

3 Sample letter to accompany draft of will under I (*see note at the end*)

Date

Dear

I enclose a draft of a new Will for your consideration. If there is an opportunity for us to meet to run through the draft together that might be best.

[Having regard to the structure of the draft Will I also enclose a memorandum which is directed to its capital tax mitigation aspect and refers to Clauses 4, 7 and 9.]

I set out below observations intended to be of help in studying draft Will:

Clauses 1, 2, 3, 5, 6, 15 and 17: These Clauses do not need detailed comment. You should consider whether they are as you wish. Clause 17 enables an executor or trustee in a profession or business, such as myself, to employ their firm to undertake the giving of advice and work on behalf of your estate and to make their normal charges. In contrast to, say, a Bank, there is no 'acceptance charge' of any kind because of the appointment.

Clause 4: Personal chattels are what you would expect as including furniture, jewellery and personal items generally. In fact, the expression also includes cars. [B of the accompanying Memorandum gives an explanation.] [This Clause may be useful in enabling you to express informal, though not strictly legally binding, wishes from time to time without the necessity of a formal codicil. The decision about using this formula is one of choice. The reason for mentioning a period of up to two years for giving effect to your wishes is that the legislation provides that, for IHT purposes, the giving of effect to them within that period is treated as if the gifts had been made by you under your Will.] I have available, if you need one, a form to record your wishes which can later be recast when occasion arises.

If you have certain articles of quality which you do not intend to mention in your form of wishes, would you prefer that on your death they should be included within your residuary estate and subject to the trusts of it? In that case please see also my remarks at the end of my observations about Clause 13.

Clause 7: This Clause takes advantage of your nil% band for inheritance tax purposes. C of the enclosed Memorandum gives an explanation. I now deal with the sub-clauses, using their lettering but not in strict sequence:

a) If your wife/husband predeceases you, it follows that the spouse exemption is not available and accordingly Clause 7 will not apply. Equally, if the two of you die in a joint calamity or if she/he also died during say the following three months, the trust is not required and therefore its capital can immediately be distributed to your succeeding beneficiaries.

i) This sub-clause, although expressed as a declaration of wish by you, is all important and would I am sure be treated as sacrosanct by your executors and trustees, all other things being equal. I put matters like that as clearly they must, including in strict law, make their own judgment in accordance with the actual circumstances as exist from time to time, but nevertheless being aware of the wishes you may have expressed.

b) This sub-clause is the way by which this settled legacy is calculated. It is directed to the nil% band at the time of your death.

g) It is Clause 14 which is the power to enable your executors or trustees, in contrast to setting aside cash then to be invested, to satisfy and meet this settled legacy from assets you hold. The power of appropriation under this sub-clause has in contemplation appropriation of assets at the time to meet subsequent distributions from this Legacy Fund.

d) This incorporates investment powers by reference to other provisions in your Will.

c) The definitions are, I think, reasonably clear but you will note that ostensibly, although not overlooking the declaration in (i), the trust can in theory continue for eighty years, the period allowed by the rule against perpetuities. In particular, I would ask you to study and check the persons who are to comprise the class of 'The Beneficiaries'.

f) i) The following is subject, in practice, to the declaration in sub-clause (i). During the time that the trust continues, the trustees are to pay or apply the income for any one or more of the beneficiaries with a like power to use capital for their benefit. Because there may be income surplus to requirements, at any particular time, power has been included for the trustees to accumulate and capitalise any part of the income during a period of twenty-one years from your death, which is the maximum period allowed by law.

f) ii) Finally, this is the trust which deals with the ultimate destination of the trust capital should, inconceivably, the trust run its full period of eighty years or indeed, sadly, come to a premature end because of the deaths of all the beneficiaries. I have provided for the trust capital to go into the estates of your children and thereby be dealt with in accordance with their Wills, failing which the intestacy law provisions that apply to them.

f) i) But, clearly, having regard to the circumstances and the terms of your declaration
& e) in sub-clause (i), there will come a time, most likely following your wife's/ husband's death, when the trust will have served its purpose and should be terminated. There are two ways by which that can be done. First, under the power within sub-clause (f)(i) to which I have previously referred, to make over the capital in appropriate shares to the particular beneficiaries. Secondly, under sub-clause (e), by a deed which can achieve the same result but which nevertheless can, if desired, create suitable trusts where it is thought that the particular beneficiaries should either have limited interests or trusts which provide protective terms.

Clause 8: I have adopted the usual trust for sale formula to enable your executors and trustees to discharge funeral expenses, outstanding debts, inheritance tax (should any be payable), administration expenses and legacies. They would make such sales as they might from time to time consider necessary or advisable: as the wording indicates, the balance of your capital will be retained. In fact Clause 14 provides that in due course assets can be transferred in kind to the ultimate beneficiaries. [I would emphasise that if your wife/husband has predeceased you (or to the extent that any part of her/his life/income interest does not extend to all the capital) and all your children had attained their ages for their entitlements to capital, there need be no continuing trusts. But that is subject to the presence and need to release the overriding power of appointment in Clause 9. Your executors could make over the assets to the children as soon as they had completed their formal duties of administration. There would, in any event, be a temporary continuing trust if any of the children were under the age of capital entitlement or, alternatively, had died leaving young children].

Clause 9: This Clause confers the overriding power of appointment, explained in D of the accompanying Memorandum.

Clauses 10(a)(i) and 16: Your wife/husband is entitled to all income which is received following the moment of your death from (a   part of) your residuary assets, and there is no question, for example, of any part of any dividend, covering a pre-death period, having to be treated as capital. [These circumstances continue until there is any change as the result of the exercise of the overriding power of appointment in Clause 9.]

Clause 10(a)(ii): This trust applies in the event of your wife/husband not being alive. The explanation for it is also contained in D of the accompanying Memorandum.

Clause 10(b)(i) & (iii): Subject to the overriding power of appointment in Clause 9 and its exercise or the release of it and subject to the death of the survivor of the two of you the children are entitled in equal shares, substituting their issue if needs be. The wording prevents their right to income arising before their intended entitlement to capital at twenty-five although that does not prevent the trustees from paying them income before then. Because of a technical capital gains tax matter which I can, if you would like, explain in detail, their entitlements to the receipt of income as of right have, in effect, been delayed until they receive their shares of capital.

Clause 10(b)(ii) & (iii): This envisages circumstances of calamity overtaking all your children including their not attaining their ages of entitlement and dying without issue. In my opinion you should state who are your long-stop beneficiaries.

Clause 11: This Clause confers power on a beneficiary to disclaim within two years after your death all or part of his entitlement. You will note the wording which states what is to happen to what is disclaimed. It might be tax-advantageous for a beneficiary who has prospered to do that.

Clause 12: It is of course the case that under Clause 9 the executors and trustees have their overriding power of appointment which can be exercised to pay capital to your wife/husband. This present power can be considered as more informal and of more immediate use. The trustees have power to use capital, in case of need, for your wife/husband. The wording indicates that for that purpose there would need to be at least two trustees. They will, of course, want to do the best they can for her/him and, as you will observe, I have also included power to make loans. It might be that your wife/husband has assets, but at the particular time she/he is short of liquid finance. Depending on her/his circumstances, and examining this draft Will as a whole, if you felt your wife/husband was being unduly fettered, it would be possible for you to give her/him an absolute cash legacy.

Clause 13: This Clause contains a series of administrative powers for your executors and trustees. I refer briefly to the sub-clauses:-

a) This gives the trustees wide powers of investment which they would, no doubt, exercise with the aid of professional advice. It is generally considered best these days not to fetter the investment powers of trustees.

b) This is, I think, self-explanatory and would give your wife/husband and the trustees ample discretion either in relation to your present house or the acquisition of a future residence for her/his use. Of course, to the extent that capital is locked up in house property your wife's/husband's income under Clause 10(a)(i) will be reduced. (As you and your wife/husband are technically known as tenants in common of the house you will follow that in the event of her/him surviving you she/he will own her/his half-interest absolutely and have a life interest in yours. This arrangement about the ownership of the property may seem unusual but I can assure you that it works in practice and does not give rise to difficulties).

c) Power to borrow which could be of use, possibly temporarily.

d) Power to enter into business arrangements with other family trusts when one or more of your executors and trustees are also trustees of the latter. For example, this could involve a sale of assets to a policy trust which you had effected for the purpose of funding IHT arising on your death or on the death of your wife/husband and which would thus provide your executors and trustees with cash to help meet the IHT liability.

e) Power to insure having regard to conditions prevailing these days.

An additional power can be included about the retention of articles depending on your decision on the matter raised at the end of my observations about Clause 4.

Clause 14: This power enables assets to be transferred in kind to the ultimate beneficiaries. Sub-clause (b) is intended as a convenient method by which a value can be placed on chattels which beneficiaries wish to take. Those who because of their needs take more articles will of course receive less of the other assets. Sub-clause (c) is a means by which the settled legacy in Clause 7 can be satisfied by all or part of your interest in the house. This may not be necessary in your case, but if you are the survivor it may be useful in your wife's/husband's Will if she/he lacks financial liquidity.

I hope that I have made everything reasonably clear but if there are any points which trouble you please do say so. I enclose a stamped addressed envelope for use in case of need for returning the draft Will.

Yours sincerely,

NOTE

The above letter, as its title indicates, is a sample which needs to be adapted not only in relation to the precise terms of the draft will but also according to the circumstances and what is considered suitable for the client in question.

The reference in the second paragraph, within brackets, to an enclosed memorandum directed to capital tax mitigation aspects is to the memorandum being no 2, p 135 above.

4 Will with absolute interests

I   of   in the County of   the husband/
wife of   REVOKE any earlier Will or testamentary dispositions of
mine AND DECLARE this to be my Will which I make this   day
of   One thousand nine hundred and ninety-

1. I APPOINT   of   in the County of
and   of   in the County of   to be
the executors and trustees of this Will

2. I WISH to be cremated/buried

3. IF a child of mine is under age at the death of the survivor of myself and my wife/husband I APPOINT   and   to be the guardians of that child And I authorise them by deed or the survivor of them by deed or Will to appoint one or two persons to act as guardians after the survivor's death

4. a) I GIVE free of inheritance tax all my chattels to   and   jointly
   b) I REQUEST them but without imposing any legal obligation:
      i) To give effect as soon as possible but not later than two years after my death to any memorandum or notes of wishes of mine about any of my chattels
      ii) Subject to any wishes to hold my chattels (or the balance thereof) in accordance with Clause 6 of this Will
   c) IN this Clause 'chattels' has the same meaning as the expression 'personal chattels' in the Administration of Estates Act 1925 (including any car or other article that I own at the time of my death despite it being regarded for the purposes of taxation or insurance or otherwise as being wholly or partly for business use)
   d) ALL expenses for safe custody and insurance of my chattels before giving effect to my wishes and for packing transporting and insuring any chattels for delivery to their recipients shall be paid from my residuary estate

5. I GIVE free of inheritance tax the following cash legacies to the following persons [or charities]:

6. SUBJECT to the payment or discharge of my funeral testamentary and administration expenses and debts and other liabilities (and legacies) I GIVE all my property and assets of every kind and wherever situated as follows:
   a) To my wife/husband absolutely if she/he survives me by three months
   b) If my wife/husband dies before me or survives me by less than three months or if the said gift to her/him fails for any other reason then to my Executors and Trustees:
      i) upon trust either to retain (if they think fit without being liable for loss) all or any part in the same state as it is at the time of my death or to sell whatever and whenever they decide with power when they consider it proper to invest trust moneys and to vary investments in accordance with sub-clause (a) of Clause 8 of this Will
      ii) upon trust to distribute (if and when that is practicable) what is retained or otherwise held and the net proceeds of what is sold together with all income that is received in the manner hereunder
      iii) that is to say to my child or children living three months after my death if more than one in equal shares PROVIDED THAT if any child dies before me or within three months after my death and issue of that child are living three months after my death such issue shall take by substitution if more than one in equal shares per stirpes the share that the deceased child would have taken had he or she been living three months after my death but so that no issue shall take whose parent is then living and so capable of taking

iv) but if no child or remoter issue of mine is living three months after my death then to such of the following persons namely

as are living three months after my death if more than one in equal shares PROVIDED THAT if any of such persons dies before me or within three months after my death and issue of that person are living three months after my death such issue shall take by substitution if more than one in equal shares per stirpes the share that the deceased person would have taken had he or she been living three months after my death but so that no issue shall take whose parent is then living and so capable of taking

7. MY Executors and Trustees in addition to all other powers conferred on them by law or as the result of the terms of this Will shall have the following powers:
   a) For the purposes of any distribution under Clause 6(b) to appropriate all or any part of my said property and assets or the property and assets from time to time held in or towards satisfaction of any share in my residuary estate without needing the consent of anyone
   b) For the purposes of placing a value on any of my personal chattels (as defined by the Administration of Estates Act 1925) so appropriated to use if they so decide such value as may have been placed on the same by any Valuers they instruct for inheritance tax purposes on my death or such other value as they may in their absolute discretion consider fair
   c) To join in exercising any of the foregoing powers notwithstanding that they themselves are Executors and Trustees and may benefit as the result of their exercise
   d) To insure under comprehensive or any other cover against any risks and for any amounts (including allowing as they deem appropriate for any possible future effects of inflation and increasing building or replacement costs and expenses) any asset held at any time by my Executors and Trustees And the premiums in respect of any such insurance may be discharged by my Executors and Trustees either out of income or out of capital (or partly out of one and partly out of the other) as my Executors and Trustees shall in their absolute discretion determine and any moneys received by my Executors and Trustees as the result of any insurance insofar as not used in rebuilding reinstating replacing or repairing the asset lost or damaged shall be treated as if they were the proceeds of sale of the asset insured PROVIDED ALWAYS that my Executors and Trustees shall not be under any responsibility to insure or be liable for any loss that may result from any failure so to do or from the inadequacy of any kind of policy they effect

8. IN the event of a person under the age of majority being entitled to a share of my residuary estate then in addition to all powers conferred by law my Executors and Trustees shall have the following powers which they may exercise from time to time in respect of such share (and the income thereof) until such person attains the age of majority:
   a) Power to invest trust moneys in both income producing and non-income producing assets of every kind and wherever situated and to vary investments and in those respects to act in the same full and unrestricted manner as if they themselves were absolutely entitled thereto beneficially

b) Power to use the income of and to raise capital out of such share and to pay the same to or apply the same for the maintenance education or otherwise howsoever for the benefit of such person and for such purpose payments can be made to such person's parent or guardian Provided that in no circumstances shall the foregoing power or any other power be exercised so as to prevent limit or postpone the entitlement of a beneficiary beyond the attaining of the age of majority

9.   ANY person who does not survive me by three months shall be deemed to have died before me for ascertaining the devolution of my estate and its income

10.   IF at any time an executor or trustee is a professional or business person charges can be made in the ordinary way for all work done by that person or their firm or company or any partner or employee

IN WITNESS whereof I have hereunto set my hand the day and year first above written

SIGNED by the above named   in our
joint presence and then by us in his/her
presence:

NOTE

The precedent under 6, p 148 below, may be more suitable when the surviving spouse is not only to be the sole beneficiary but also the executor.

5 Sample letter to accompany draft of will under 4

Dear

I enclose a draft of a new Will for your consideration. I hope you will find its terms are reasonably straightforward. Nevertheless, if there is an opportunity for us to meet to run through the draft together this might be most convenient. In any event, I am setting out below some observations which I hope will be of help when studying it.

   Turning to the draft Will:

Clauses 1, 2, 3, 5, 9 and 10: These clauses do not need detailed comment. You will be able to check whether they are as you wish. Clause 10 would enable an executor or trustee in a profession or business, such as myself, to employ their firm to undertake the giving of advice and work on behalf of your estate and to make their normal charges. In contrast to, say, a Bank, there is no 'acceptance charge' of any kind because of such appointment.

Clause 4: This clause, with regard to chattels, may not be considered strictly necessary since, under Clause 6, if your wife/husband survives you by the period mentioned in Clause 9 (s)he is to receive all your assets (other than the legacies under Clause 5). It is included because of the words in the clause which may be useful in enabling you to express informal, though not strictly legally binding, wishes from time to time without going to the necessity of making a formal codicil. The decision with regard to using such a formula is one of personal choice. (The reason for mentioning a period of up to two years for giving effect to your wishes is because the legislation provides that for IHT purposes, the giving of effect to them within that period would be treated as if the gifts had been made by you under your Will. I can also let you have in due course a form which will enable you to record any wishes and which can subsequently be added to and altered when occasion arises.)

Clause 6: As I have mentioned your wife/husband is absolutely entitled if (s)he survives you by the period mentioned in Clause 9 and if (s)he does not, then the children are entitled equally, substituting their issue if needs be. If all your children were over eighteen there would be no question of any continuing trusts. Your executors would make over the assets to them as soon as they had completed their formal duties of administration. There would, however, be a temporary continuing trust if any of them was under age or alternatively had died leaving young children. You will need to state who should benefit in the depressing circumstances of calamity affecting you all.

Clause 7: This conveniently follows on from Clause 6 and envisages the possibility of some assets being transferred in kind, and provides a convenient method by which a value can be placed on chattels which beneficiaries wish to take. To the extent that one beneficiary took a greater amount of chattels than the others so (s)he would receive a lesser amount of your other assets. Sub-clause (d) contains a power to insure having regard to conditions prevailing these days.

Clause 8: This clause applies where there is a beneficiary under 18. The trustees are given wide powers of investment which they would, no doubt, exercise with the aid of professional advice. It is generally considered best these days not to fetter the investment powers of trustees. The trustees are also given specific power to use not only income for the benefit of a beneficiary but also, if appropriate, capital, such as for education.

I hope that I have made everything reasonably clear but if there are any points which trouble you please do say so. I enclose a stamped addressed envelope for use in case of need, for returning the draft Will.

Yours sincerely,

NOTE

The foregoing letter, as its title indicates, is a sample which needs to be adapted not only in relation to the precise terms of the draft will but also according to the circumstances and what is considered suitable from the point of view of the testator in question. Testators may range from the very wealthy to those of moderate means, may be young marrieds, or widows and widowers and this letter could also be adapted to accompany draft wills of a childless couple.

6 Will when spouse sole executor and beneficiary with substitutional provisions

I   of   in the County of   the husband/
wife of   REVOKE any earlier Will or testamentary dispositions of
mine AND DECLARE this to be my Will which I make this   day
of   One thousand nine hundred and ninety-

1.   I APPOINT my wife/husband to be the executor of this Will but if my wife/
husband dies before me or renounces probate or dies without having proved my
Will I ALSO APPOINT   of   in the County of
                    and   of   in the County of
            to be the executors and trustees of this Will

2.   I WISH to be cremated/buried

3.   IF a child of mine is under age at the death of the survivor of myself and my
wife/husband I APPOINT   and   to be the guardians
of that child And I authorise them by deed or the survivor of them by deed or
Will to appoint one or two persons to act as guardians after the survivor's death

4. a) I GIVE (free of inheritance tax) all my chattels to my wife/husband if (s)he
        survives me by three months and failing her/him so doing to the (said)
                        and   jointly.
    b) I REQUEST her/him or them but without imposing any legal obligation
        i) TO give effect as soon as possible but not later than two years after my
           death to any memorandum or notes of wishes of mine about any of my
           chattels
        ii) SUBJECT to any wishes to make my wife/husband if (s)he survives me
            by three months the owner of my chattels (or the balance thereof)
        iii) SUBJECT as aforesaid and if my wife/husband does not so survive me to
             hold my chattels (or the balance thereof) in accordance with Clause 8
             of this Will
    c) IN this Clause 'chattels' has the same meaning as the expression 'personal
       chattels' in the Administration of Estates Act 1925 (including any car or other
       article that I own at the time of my death despite it being regarded for the
       purposes of taxation or insurance or otherwise as being wholly or partly for
       business use)
    d) ALL expenses for safe custody and insurance of my chattels before giving effect
       to my wishes and for packing transporting and insuring any chattels for delivery
       to their recipients shall be paid from my residuary estate

5.   SUBJECT to the payment or discharge of my funeral testamentary and
administration expenses and debts and other liabilities I GIVE all my property and
assets of every kind and wherever situated to my wife/husband absolutely if she/
he survives me by three months

6. IF my wife/husband does not so survive me or the said gift to her/him fails for any reason the provisions of Clauses   to   hereof shall take effect

7. I GIVE free of inheritance tax the following cash legacies to the following persons:

8. SUBJECT to the terms of Clause 4 of this Will and to the payment or discharge of my funeral testamentary and administration expenses and debts and other liabilities (and legacies) I GIVE all my property and assets of every kind and wherever situated to my Executors and Trustees:
   a) upon trust either to retain (if they think fit without being liable for loss) all or any part in the same state as it is at the time of my death or to sell whatever and whenever they decide with power when they consider it proper to invest trust moneys and to vary investments in accordance with sub-clause (a) of Clause 10 of this Will
   b) upon trust to distribute (if and when that is practicable) what is retained or otherwise held and the net proceeds of what is sold together with all income that is received in the manner hereunder
   c) that is to say to my child or children living three months after my death if more than one in equal shares PROVIDED THAT if any child dies before me or within three months after my death and issue of that child are living three months after my death such issue shall take by substitution if more than one in equal shares per stirpes the share that the deceased child would have taken had he or she been living three months after my death but so that no issue shall take whose parent is then living and so capable of taking
   d) but if no child or remoter issue of mine is living three months after my death then to such of the following persons namely

   as are living three months after my death if more than one in equal shares PROVIDED THAT if any of such persons dies before me or within three months after my death and issue of that person are living three months after my death such issue shall take by substitution if more than one in equal shares per stirpes the share that the deceased person would have taken had he or she been living three months after my death but so that no issue shall take whose parent is then living and so capable of taking

9. to 12. (Such Clauses are as per Clauses 7 to 10 of the precedent under 4, p 143 above, with a consequential amendment, in a cross reference in Clause 7(a) thereof, resulting in the need to substitute '. . . under Clause 8 . . .' for '. . . under Clause 6(b) . . .')

IN WITNESS whereof I have hereunto set my hand the day and year first above written

SIGNED by the above named   in our
joint presence and then by us in his/her }
presence:

NOTE
As the heading suggests, this precedent is an alternative to the one under 4, p 143 above. It may

be more suitable when the surviving spouse is not only to be the sole beneficiary but also the sole executor.

The sample accompanying letter 5, p 146 above can be readily adapted for explaining this precedent.

Part III. Forms, Clauses and Aids

7 Letter assisting instructions for will

Dear

I shall be very pleased to assist you with the making of a Will. In the first place, it might be helpful if we had a meeting to discuss the matter generally. After the meeting, it would be my intention to submit a draft of a Will which you could consider, and then let me know whether it is in keeping with your wishes.

Having in mind the possibility of our meeting, you might care to think over the answers to the following points:

a) Who are to be your executors? I think you should consider alternative possibilities, to guard against circumstances such as the one referred to under (e) below.

b) Do you want to make known in your Will any wishes with regard to funeral and burial? You should also mention if you wish your eyes and body to be made available for medical purposes.

c) Who are to be the guardian or guardians of your young children, in the event of the deaths of both yourself and your wife?

d) Do you wish to give any small legacies of cash or kind?

e) We can discuss the details when we meet, but I assume that your wife and family are to receive the bulk, if not all, of your assets. I appreciate it is a depressing thought, but you ought to say what is to happen to your assets in the event of a total calamity affecting the family as a whole.

f) I would like a note of the full names of your wife and, also, the full names and ages of your children.

I do not wish to overburden this letter, having regard to the possibility of our meeting. However, the way in which you make your Will could be affected by the implications of inheritance tax (IHT) which subject to the spouse or any other exemptions is the fiscal charge on death. I am, therefore, enclosing:

1. A note, of general comment, in relation to IHT on the making of Wills for spouses.[1]

2. In the light of such note, an Assets Questionnaire in respect of both your wife's assets and your own.[2] I emphasise that the completion of this is not intended to be a time consuming chore. Particularly, as values fluctuate, as do the assets themselves, broad figures and estimates will be sufficient, at any rate in the first instance. Nevertheless, the answers will enable some kind of picture to emerge from which it will be possible to form a view and give appropriate advice.

---

1 Form 8, p 154 below.
2 Form 9, p 156 below.

3. Finally, a note on the IHT exemptions available, should they be of possible interest now or in the future.[3]

I look forward to hearing from you.

Yours sincerely,

NOTE

The foregoing letter, which needs to be adapted to the circumstances and the intellect of the client, assumes that the solicitor has knowledge of his personal background, such as in relation to past marriage, domicile, aliases and personal inclinations, any of which could have a bearing on what he can do and how the will should be drafted. But, whatever the existing knowledge, it may well be considered that a meeting in any event will be required, when opportunity can be taken to raise and discuss any more personal matters.

8 Inheritance tax observations in relation to spouses' wills

It is necessary to be aware of matters relating to inheritance tax (IHT). It is the fiscal charge on death. IHT can also be charged on lifetime gifts. The purpose of this note is to refer to certain features which emerge from the IHT legislation and which affect the making of Wills.

1) As in the case of lifetime gifts, gifts between husbands and wives under their Wills are exempt. Accordingly, to the extent that such gifts are made, there will be freedom from IHT liability.

2) The freedom from IHT, where there are gifts between spouses, applies irrespective of whether the gift is an absolute one or by way of a life/income interest. The result is the same, as in the latter case it is the underlying capital which is regarded as the extent of the gift, for IHT purposes.

3) In due course the then value of whatever may be the combined assets will be taken together for the purpose of assessing the IHT arising on the second death. Almost certainly the combined liability will be greater than if the two sets of assets had been taxed separately. Though this does not affect the widow or widower who will naturally be better off, the result will affect the children or the ultimate inheritors.

4) Inevitably, as a couple grow older the life expectation of the survivor will become shorter and, given estimated figures covering the assets and financial interests of each spouse, it is possible to illustrate such bunching effect of the combined IHT liability as compared with, if one went to the other extreme which is probably not desirable, the IHT on the two sets of assets if taken separately. One usually proceeds on the basis that the prime object of the Wills is to meet the practical circumstances of the survivor, come what may, in these inflationary times when it is impossible to forecast ahead with any degree of confidence.

5) It is worth mentioning two additional matters which we think are of importance:
   a) Leaving aside exempt gifts, in relation to the calculation of IHT, lifetime

gifts made during the preceding seven years are cumulated, each succeeding gift commencing at the point in the IHT table where the last one left off, with the final charge, similarly calculated, on death. Because of the important provisions introduced by the Finance Act 1986 it may in fact be the case that IHT is not paid on the particular lifetime gifts at the times they are made but because the donor dies during the following seven years the IHT liability then arises on the basis they are chargeable and cumulated as from the time they were made. As will be known, each of us has, under the IHT table, a nil% band of between £0 and £

(this figure is index linked each 6 April) and according to the extent that such band has not been absorbed in one's lifetime, it is 'wasteful', for IHT purposes, to give all one's assets to one's spouse because such a gift is exempt in any case and the £   (as adjusted by index linking) nil% band (or what is left of it) is therefore left unused. There is something to be said, when the financial position allows, for giving one's children £   (as so adjusted) or at any rate what may not have already been absorbed of such nil% band in one's lifetime less any other non exempt legacies under one's Will.

b) Even if it is decided not to leave such a legacy to the children there is a very important provision under section 142 of the Inheritance Tax Act 1984. Briefly summarised, and possibly over-simplified, this would enable members of one's family after one's death, given the desire and according to the circumstances, to amend one's Will with the result that for IHT purposes the Will would be treated as if it had been made in its amended form. This could itself introduce a £   (as so adjusted) legacy, or whatever might be an appropriate amount, for the children, or generally adjust the figures in a way more beneficial for IHT purposes.

6) The aim is to make one's Will simple and straightforward. Nevertheless in certain circumstances, with a suitable degree of skilled drafting, it is in fact possible to obtain the best of both worlds. We have in mind that despite the prime object of meeting the practical circumstances of the survivor it may at the same time be possible to take advantage of all or part of the nil% band to the extent not already absorbed by gifts during the preceding seven years. It will be appreciated, from our observations under (5)(a) above, that if one spouse leaves the survivor of them all of his or her assets the nil% band (or what is left of it) will be lost. In our opinion, it is possible, though maybe surprising, to produce, by appropriate drafting, a Will in terms which will enable a slice of assets to take advantage of the nil% band (to the extent not already absorbed) on the first death, without materially affecting the survivor and also in such manner that that slice of assets will not be affected by IHT on the survivor's own death. The aggregate saving in IHT when taking the two deaths together can, for the benefit of the children or ultimate inheritors, be large. We will, on request, be pleased to elaborate on what can be saved by that means in IHT and how that saving can be achieved in the drafting of the Will.

Date:

9 Assets questionnaire and approximate values

	Brief Details	Self	Spouse
		£	£

1. Main freehold or leasehold property.
  a) Is it owned jointly? If so, state whether held in equal (or, if not, what) shares.
  b) Amount of any mortgage now outstanding.
  c) Is it supported by endowment/life policies?			

2. a) i) Agricultural property.
     ii) Is that property subject to any mortgage or charge, including by way of deposit of title deeds with Bank to secure loan or overdraft facilities?
  b) Woodlands not on (a).			

3. Any other property. Is any of it let?			
4. Is there any property (or other assets) in sole name but with someone else (including spouse) having a beneficial interest in it?			
5. The car(s). (Any HP?)			
6. a) Articles including jewellery, silver, antiques, furniture, carpets, paintings. (Are there any articles likely to be of sufficient quality to be of national, scientific, historic or artistic interest?) b) Collections not covered under (a) such as stamps and coins.			
7. Stocks and Shares of Public Companies quoted on Stock Exchange including Unit Trusts.			
8. Interests in family and other unquoted Companies. (Recent Accounts and a copy of any Memorandum and Articles of Association would assist).			
9. a) Interests in Partnership(s)			

	Brief Details	Self	Spouse
		£	£

including business ventures with members of one's family. (A copy of any documents and recent Accounts would assist).

b) Are you a member of Lloyd's?

10. Cash including that on current and deposit accounts. (Are any such accounts joint? If so who feeds them?)

11. Building Society Deposits.

12. Life and endowment policies effected for the benefit of oneself. If so, we would like to see them.

13. Any such policies, and any accident policy, effected for the benefit of others. If so, we would like to see them.

14. Assets abroad whether house property or any other kind.

15. The capital value of trusts, whether or not created under Wills (including any abroad), in which one has a life/income or other definite interest. (Are there any other trusts?) (A copy of the documents would assist).

16. Money lent whether on loan or mortgage. Do you intend such loans to continue or be released?

17. Any other assets (such as Post Office Savings, Bank Accounts, Premium Bonds and National Savings Certificates).

18. a) Pension arrangements whether Company and/or Self Employed (a copy of any Superannuation Scheme or other documentation would assist and also details of any nomination or requests to any of their trustees).

b) Accident policy effected by employer.

19. Family Income Protection Policies.

20. Gifts made during the last seven

	Brief Details	Self	Spouse
		£	£

years including any involving releases of beneficial interests under trusts. [If so, for the purposes of tax calculations we need details of gifts made during the seven years prior to each.]

21. Are any future lifetime gifts of a substantial nature in contemplation by (either of) you?

22. a) Liabilities including mortgages other than that covered under 1 above.
 b) Unusual and contingent liabilities such as guarantees.

23. Possible expectations from others, including those under existing trusts whether or not created under the Will of a deceased person.

24. Are there any persons not members of your immediate family whom you are maintaining?

25. If you have been on active military service, did you suffer any wound or contract any disease which in any way affects your health?

NOTE

As this information may be useful to us when giving advice please let us know your respective dates of birth—

Self . . . .

Spouse . . . .

and also details of your children—

Full names   Dates of birth

Date

NOTE

Questions 1 and 4 Whether the house property is in a sole name or in joint names the beneficial interests need to be ascertained. The decided cases under the Married Women's Property Act 1882, s 17, show that the fact that a property is in the sole name of one spouse raises no presumption that it is the sole property of that spouse; see letter of Senior Registrar, Principal Registry, Family

Division in *Law Society's Gazette* 9 December 1981, p 1404. The interest of the other spouse can, for example, arise from contribution to the purchase price, the making of mortgage payments and the financial and physical making of improvements. There is a helpful article by P A Kay in *Law Society's Gazette* 20 February 1980, p 175. Where there is a beneficial joint tenancy there may be a case for severing it, thereby converting it into a tenancy in common; see chapter 7, at p 84 above and precedents 115 and 116, pp 256 and 258 below.

Question 2 Inheritance Tax Act 1984, s 162(4) covers liabilities which are incumbrances. They reduce the value of the encumbered property. Accordingly if there is a charge to IHT on agricultural property the value of it for the purposes of agricultural property relief will be reduced. An owner should consider, instead, charging other property, if necessary in priority to any charge over his agricultural property.

Questions 5 and 6 Butterworths *Wills, Probate & Administration Service*, at A(736) contains a comprehensive explanation about chattels subject to credit sale, hire purchase, conditional sale or leasing agreements and the testamentary factors to be taken into consideration. The usual description of 'personal chattels' by reference to the definition in Administration of Estates Act 1925, s 55(1)(x), excludes, in the absence of words to the contrary, articles, including cars, used for business purposes.

Questions 8 and 9 Whether the business is incorporated or not thought will be required about continuity in the event of the death of the testator and what appropriate clauses can helpfully be included in his will. In the case of a deceased partner the partnership agreement will be a factor when valuing his share for IHT purposes.

Question 9 Apart from the normal kind of business, often these days husbands and wives run joint business ventures, and as no doubt they are run 'with a view to profit' this would result in there being a partnership (Partnership Act 1890, s 1). When this is so, subject to any agreement to the contrary, a death will dissolve the partnership (Partnership Act 1890, s 33) in which event the partnership should be wound up and the amount due to the deceased partner paid to his or her personal representatives and be received by them as capital. The testator will no doubt wish to consider whether or not the foregoing is what he would wish.

Question 10 Joint bank accounts need clarification in relation to the intentions of the person(s) who feed them. Possibly a person intends the balance to accrue to the survivor on his death, possibly this is not so and the name of the other joint holder has only been added as a signatory.

Question 14 If there are assets abroad, particularly foreign land, a will to be made in the country concerned is advisable.

Question 16 Executors as a matter of principle must require repayment of debts. Hence it is necessary to know the intentions of the testator. See also Form 47 p 190 below.

Question 18 In the case of an employee, his company's pension scheme(s) may provide for a capital sum in the event of his death in service before pension age, of typically four times current salary. In some cases the scheme will provide a pension for the widow of an employee should he predecease her in retirement and, sometimes, a widow's pension from the date of the employee's death if this occurs before retirement. Usually, the death in service benefits are payable to the dependants of the employee in such manner and shares as the trustees of the scheme decide, including to his personal representatives. In such cases it is normal procedure for an employee to be able to complete a form addressed to the trustees indicating how he hopes they will exercise their discretion should the particular circumstances arise. (See O of chapter 3, p 27 above and J of chapter 6, p 80 above).

An employee might also be protected under a Group Permanent Disablement Insurance Scheme which could provide a continuing income, of up to two-thirds of current earnings, to his normal age of retirement. In the case of the self-employed person his pension arrangements will be individual and personal in the sense that they can arise under his partnership arrangements and/or be effected by way of Retirement Annuity Contracts under the provisions of the Income and Corporation Taxes Act 1988, ss 618 et seq.

Question 20 It will be necessary to know to what extent the client has absorbed his IHT nil% band and at what point on the cumulative scale his next set of gifts, including on death, might start. It is to be recognised that in the event of a deceased having made a potentially exempt transfer (PET) within the seven years before his death it will thereby become a chargeable transfer not only giving rise to a charge to IHT for which the beneficiary is primarily liable but also affecting the IHT liability on subsequent gifts and the assets generally on his death.

Apart from considerations of IHT, where beneficiaries will have received gifts during his life, the testator will need to decide whether or not those gifts are to be taken into account on the division of his assets under his will: see Form 75, p 213 below. When there have been payments to a potential testamentary beneficiary it is important also to make certain whether they were gifts or loans and, if the latter, whether they are to be repaid or to be specifically forgiven under the will, hence the concluding words of *question 16.*

Question 24 may be a delicate one. Nevertheless, it is important to know whether there is any person who could qualify as an applicant under the Inheritance (Provision for Family and Dependants) Act 1975, (e) of section 1(1); see p 111 above.

Question 25 has in mind the full exemption from IHT because of 'death on active service, etc'. Where a wound or a disease contributes in any way to premature death, indeed many years afterwards, the exemption is available even though it is not the direct cause of death; see the estate duty case of *Barty-King v Ministry of Defence* [1979] 2 All ER 80, [1979] STC 218.

10 Inheritance tax, exemptions and reliefs and potentially exempt transfers

This Note is not intended to be exhaustive or overdetailed. Part I gives details of the main inheritance tax (IHT) exemptions and reliefs. Additional observations, in respect of some of them, are contained later in this Note with the use of the corresponding numbering. Part II describes and explains potentially exempt transfers.

Part I

1. Transfers during life or on death between husband and wife are generally exempt.
2. a) Transfers during life up to a total value of £3,000 in any one tax year, plus any unused part of the previous year's exemption. If in any one tax year the transferor does not use the whole of this exemption the balance can only be carried forward one year and can only be used after the exemption for that later year has been absorbed.
   b) This exemption also can be set against the value of any underlying trust capital over which the transferor's life/income interest is relinquished.
3. Transfers during life to any one person in each tax year if the total value to that person does not exceed £250. Any number of these small transfers not exceeding a total of £250 per person will be exempt, but this exemption is not available to cover part of a larger gift, and is therefore lost completely if more than £250 is transferred to one person whether by one or more gifts

in the same year. It also cannot be used to augment the £3,000 allowance under 2 above.

4. Transfers made out of the transferor's income which are part of his normal expenditure provided that after allowing for all such transfers the transferor is left with sufficient income to maintain his usual standard of living.

5. a) Transfers in consideration of marriage:
    i) Up to £5,000, if made by a parent of either party to the marriage.
    ii) Up to £2,500, if made by any other ancestor or by a party to the marriage.
    iii) Up to £1,000, if made by any other person.
   b) This exemption, for transfers in consideration of marriage, as in the case of 2(b) above, also can be set against the value of any underlying trust capital over which the transferor's life/income interest is relinquished.

6. Transfers during life if made for the maintenance of a spouse or former spouse or for the maintenance, education or training of a child.

7. Transfers during life if made to a dependent relative of the transferor and are reasonable provision for their care or maintenance.

8. Transfers during life or on death to charities.

9. Transfers during life or on death to recognised political parties, registered housing associations, certain bodies such as National Gallery, British Museum, National Trust and Universities in the United Kingdom and also those for public benefit.

10. There are IHT exemptions and reliefs for works of art etc (heritage property), business property, agricultural property and woodlands.

11. Though not in fact an exemption, the first £ (this figure is index linked each 6 April) worth of transfers, not covered by any of the foregoing exemptions is subject to a nil% rate of IHT. In so far as the £ (as adjusted by index linking) nil% band is not absorbed by lifetime gifts (chargeable when they were made or become chargeable because the transferor does not survive their making by seven years), it is available including on death.

12. A variation by a person, who would otherwise benefit, of all or part of his entitlement as the result of a death, if made within two years after it, does not itself give rise to a charge to IHT and the result of the variation is treated, for IHT purposes, as if made by the deceased. But that is also subject to the appropriate written notice being given to the Revenue within six months after the variation is made.

Additional observations arising out of the foregoing part of this Note.

Each exemption is, with the exception of the £250 annual exemption under No 3 above, independent of the others. Everyone is entitled to all the exemptions. For example, both husband and wife have the annual £3,000 exemption (see No 2). However, the Inheritance Tax Act 1984 does provide that where there are associated operations, two or more transfers may be viewed as one, ie, a later transfer may be deemed to have been made by the original transferor.

The latter provisions under the 1984 Act are widely drawn and must be treated with caution, in particular in their application to husband and wife. No doubt where a wealthy husband gives a sum of money with a direction, or subject to an understanding, that it is to be used in a particular manner, any exemption available to the wife on her later transfer will be disregarded and the payment treated as made by the husband.

Unlike the cases of lifetime transfers under Nos 1, 3, 5, 8 and 9 above, where as under Nos 2 and 4 above a lifetime transfer is made within the £3,000 annual exemption or out of income as part of the transferor's normal expenditure the 'property subject to a reservation' conditions introduced by the Finance Act 1986 must be noted. If such a transfer has been made and, irrespective of the number of years that elapse before the transferor's death, the transferor, prior to the seven-year period before his death, has not relinquished in full possession and enjoyment of the gifted property to the beneficiary or has during that period derived, directly or indirectly, any benefit however small, it will be treated as if he was beneficially entitled to it on his death and accordingly then charged to IHT along with everything else.

1. The exception to this exemption is where the recipient spouse is not domiciled in the United Kingdom. Here, the exemption is limited to £55,000.

2. a) The 'carry forward' of any balance remaining of the £3,000 exemption for the year ending on the previous 5 April extends only to the following tax year and is lost if not used then. For example, if £2,000 has been given and set against the exemption in the year ending 5 April 1990 and £2,000 in the year ending 5 April 1991, the amount available in the year ending 5 April 1992 is £4,000 (not £5,000).

   b) The transferor must give notice to the particular trustees in the form prescribed by the Inland Revenue, within six months of the date of the relinquishment, of the amount of the trust capital available for exemption.

4. The capital element of an annuity cannot be treated as income for the purpose of this calculation. 'Normal' means habitual. The exemption applies to the extent that any part of a transfer can come within the provision. It is not a case of all or nothing.

5. a) It is important to note that the gift must be made in consideration of marriage, not merely on the occasion of marriage.

   b) The transferor must give notice to the particular trustees in the form prescribed by the Inland Revenue, within six months of the date of the relinquishment, of the amount of the trust capital available for exemption.

7. 'Dependent relative' is defined in the same way as for income tax purposes but includes a relative of the transferor's spouse.

Part II

Although a particular lifetime transfer is not exempt it can qualify as a potentially exempt transfer (PET). The concept of a PET was introduced into the inheritance tax legislation by the Finance Act 1986. The matter is important because the potential exemption is in no way limited by the size of the gift.

In essence, a PET is a lifetime gift or release of trust income made by an individual which is treated as if exempt when it is made with no liability for IHT. If the individual survives his gift or release by a period of seven years its exemption from IHT is confirmed. If he dies during that period it is thereby regarded as becoming and having been, when made, a chargeable transfer and is subject to IHT as the result of the individual's death.

If the latter happens IHT will be charged on the value of the gift when it was made. The liability for IHT falls on the beneficiary or recipient(s). Nevertheless, there is what is known as taper relief where the donor survives his gift by three years and which is graduated according to whether he survives his gift by three, four, five or six years.

To qualify as a PET the gift or release must be made for another individual or into a trust which confers a normal straight income interest or into what is known as an accumulation or maintenance trust or into a disabled trust.

A gift will therefore not be a PET and will on its making be a chargeable transfer (assuming of course it is not within the exemptions referred to in Part I above) and thereby give rise to an immediate liability to IHT in the event of it being made into a discretionary trust or, for example, being made to a company or club.

In Part I there is a reference to the 'property subject to a reservation' conditions also introduced into the inheritance tax legislation by the Finance Act 1986. It is to be emphasised that those conditions apply equally to a PET. Thus, if such a transfer or gift, including a PET, has been made and, irrespective of the number of years that elapse before the transferor's death, the transferor, prior to the seven-year period before his death, has not relinquished in full possession and enjoyment of the gifted property to the beneficiary or has, during that period, derived directly or indirectly a benefit however small the gifted property will be treated as if he was beneficially entitled to it on his death and accordingly then charged to IHT along with everything else.

Date

11 Declaration concerning mutual wills

We are making in duplicate this Memorandum, a copy of which will be put with each of our Wills, to place on record that the Wills, which we have just signed or are about to sign, are not intended to be mutual in the legal sense. Accordingly, each of us and the survivor has absolute freedom at any time to alter his or her Will in such manner as he or she shall, alone, decide

DATED this   day of   19

NOTE

Wills can always be revoked. However mutual wills in the technical legal sense are ones which, because a contract or trust is deemed to have been created, should not be revoked by one testator without the consent of the other. Following the death of the first testator, if the surviving testator revokes his mutual will the rights of the former 'beneficiaries' may be enforceable in equity. Though two wills may appear to be mutual in the lay sense there needs to be an inference to make them so in the legal sense, but clearly the matter is one that should be borne in mind. While a man and his wife may work out a pattern for the distribution of their conjoint assets, depending on which of them dies first, it could well more often be the case that they would not wish their wills to be mutual in the legal sense. If the draftsman, in the particular circumstances, feels that there is any risk of this he should take instructions, and this form can be adopted or adapted according to what decision is reached.

Re Cleaver, Cleaver v Insley [1981] 2 All ER 1018, [1981] 1 WLR 939 is a case which illustrates the existence of mutual wills.

12 Commencement of will and alternative for will in expectation of marriage

I   of   in the County of

the husband/wife of

REVOKE any earlier Wills or testamentary dispositions of mine AND DECLARE this to be my Will which I make this   day of   199

I   of   in the County of

REVOKE any earlier Wills or testamentary dispositions of mine AND DECLARE this to be my Will which I make this   day of   199   in expectation of my marriage to
(hereinafter called 'my wife/husband') and which Will shall not be revoked by my marriage to her/him

NOTE

With regard to the second of these forms, by the Wills Act 1837, s 18, a will is revoked by subsequent marriage. Nevertheless, by s 18(3) where it appears from a will that at the time it was made the testator was expecting to be married to a particular person and that he intended that his will should not be revoked by the marriage, it is not revoked by his marriage to that person.

It is the case that such a will would take effect if the testator were to die before the marriage took place, unless it were made conditional upon the marriage in fact taking place. If the latter is desired the words 'Provided that unless and until my said marriage shall have been solemnised this my Will shall in every respect be of no force or effect' should be added.

13 Commencement of English will when there is an overseas will

I   of   in the County of

the husband/wife of

REVOKE any earlier Will or testamentary dispositions of mine (except my Ruritanian Will to which I will refer) AND DECLARE this to be my Will which I make this   day of   199
  1. I STATE as follows:
    a) that I am domiciled in England;
    b) that this Will and the rights of the beneficiaries shall be governed by the law of England; and
    c) that this Will shall not revoke or vary the terms of the Will dated the   day of   199   I made in Ruritania which is limited to the disposal of immovable (and movable) property and assets that I own in Ruritania at my death

NOTE
References should be made to the comments on p 9 above. In the case of this form it is assumed that the testator is domiciled in England.

A testator in considering his testamentary wishes needs to have regard to the laws of the countries where his assets, particularly immovable property, are situated and to the possibility of making separate wills respectively.

Where there are separate wills limited to particular assets it is important that he should have one leading will to dispose of his worldwide assets not otherwise dealt with under separate will. Such leading will can best conform with the law of his current domicile. Care must of course be taken that, in making any new will, general words are not used which unintentionally revoke an earlier overseas will.

14 Commencement of English will of a person domiciled abroad

I   of   Ruritania the wife/husband of

REVOKE any earlier Will or testamentary dispositions of mine (except my Ruritanian Will to which I refer) AND DECLARE this to be my English Will which I make this   day   199
   1. I STATE as follows:
      a) that I am domiciled in Ruritania where I have lived since my marriage to my husband/wife on the   day of
         19   ;
      b) that this Will is limited to the disposal of property and assets whether immovable or movable that I own in England at my death; and
      c) that this Will shall not revoke or vary the terms of any Will or testamentary dispositions that I have made in Ruritania or elsewhere except in so far as any such Will or testamentary dispositions dispose of any property and assets as are referred to in the foregoing declaration under (b) of this Clause

NOTE
Regard should be had to the observations in the note to the preceding form. For the purpose of this form it is convenient to assume the example of an English woman, having assets in England, marrying a foreigner as the result of which she lives abroad and acquires an overseas domicile.

15 Declaration against English domicile by husband

I DECLARE as follows:
   a) that my domicile of origin is in   which was the country/ state of the domicile of my father at the time of my birth:
   b) that I do not regard England as my permanent home as in the event of the death of my wife I intend to leave England: and

c) that notwithstanding the foregoing declarations this Will shall be governed and construed and the rights of all the beneficiaries hereunder shall be regulated according to the law of England

NOTE

A person's domicile is of crucial importance in relation to whether or not a transfer of value, during lifetime or on death, is subject to IHT: see B of ch 9 above. While a declaration cannot override evidence which points to, say, a domicile in England it can be of assistance in covering circumstances such as those in *IRC v Bullock*: see p 106 above.

In contrast, in relation to a woman married before the Domicile and Matrimonial Proceedings Act 1973 note *IRC v Duchess of Portland*: see p 105 above.

16 Funeral wishes etc (specimen clauses)

I WISH to be buried where most convenient and my funeral to be conducted in a simple manner (And if a memorial is placed at my grave I DIRECT my Executors to pay the cost from my residuary estate)

I WISH my body to be cremated my ashes to be scattered and my funeral conducted in a simple manner

I CONFIRM that I have signed a Request that my kidneys be used after my death for transplantation

AFTER certainty of death has been confirmed by a qualified medical practitioner I HEREBY EXPRESS the wishes following:

IF practicable I GIVE my eyes for the benefit of others by corneal grafting medical research or for such other purpose as my Executors may deem appropriate at the time of my death and subject thereto I DESIRE that my body be cremated and my ashes scattered

I REQUEST that my body shall be offered for medical research anatomical examination transplants or other use of organs or parts to the Department of Human Anatomy   if I die within   miles of   but if I do not do so then either to the said Department or such other Department of Anatomy or Medical School as my Executors shall decide and afterwards my body or what remains of it shall be disposed of by the Medical Authority concerned But if this request in whole or in part is not acceptable for any reason I WISH my body or what remains of it to be cremated and my ashes scattered

I DESIRE that my wife/husband or failing my wife/husband my Executors shall decide according to the circumstances what form the simple Funeral or Memorial Service shall take following my death

NOTE
It has been suggested in some books that it is better to leave wishes in a separate letter addressed to, say, a near relative, as sometimes the will is not opened or located until after the funeral. This perhaps justifies the practice, when funeral wishes are expressed in the will, of providing the testator with a copy to keep with his personal papers.

As to use being made of parts of the body for therapeutic purposes (such as corneal grafting and organ transplantation) the Human Tissue Act 1961 should be consulted and that Act is the authority for the removal of eyes. A removal of eyes needs to be carried out very quickly - within about ten hours. The Anatomy Act 1984 enables a person to express a request in the formal manner provided that his body be used after his death for anatomical examination (which involves teaching and research).

It will be recognised that there is no guarantee that the offer of a body for medical research etc will be accepted. Although the age of the individual is immaterial, there are several conditions which could leave the body unsuitable for anatomical examination, the object of which is the study of the normal structure of the body. These include a history of carcinoma or any malignancy, tuberculosis, amputation of limbs, extensive surgery during lifetime, gross obesity, excessive wastage, gangrene, the necessity to carry out a post-mortem and the removal of kidneys and other major organs, for transplant purposes.

As is well known, the executors and family generally are not legally bound by funeral and burial wishes except that a direction against cremation is effective to prevent it taking place. Also, when a deceased person has made a valid request in accordance with the provisions of the Human Tissue Act 1961, s 1(1) that his body or part thereof be used after his death for therapeutic purposes or for purposes of medical education or research then the person lawfully in possession of the body (in many cases this will be the hospital in which he died) may authorise the removal of the part and its use in accordance with the deceased's request without need for consultation with the executors or with any of the deceased's relatives.

There is a very useful commentary on the use and disposal of the body in *Butterworths Wills, Probate and Administration Service*, A[311]-[326].

17 Appointment of executors and trustees

a) I APPOINT   of   in the County of
              and   of   in the County
of   to be the executors and trustees of this Will [but if
the appointment of either or both of them fails (because of death or inability
or unwillingness to act or for any other reason)] I ALSO APPOINT
of   in the County of

b) The expression 'my Trustees' when used in this Will means my executors
and the trustees or trustee whether original or substituted or added

NOTE
Probate will not be granted to a minor. Nevertheless, an appointment of an executor can be worded to take effect on the happening of an event, including the attainment of full age.

A separate executor or executors may be appointed to act over separate assets. In the case of an author, for example, a literary executor is common.

Any number of individuals or trust corporations may be appointed but probate will not be granted to more than four over any part of the estate; Supreme Court Act 1981, s 114(1).

Unless the circumstances are inopportune, it may well be worthwhile to suggest that, where a solicitor is to be appointed as executor and trustee, he should be the first named. This would mean that routine company notices (which are always sent to the first named executor) and, more important, letters of allotment would come to him in preference to, say, the widow.

If the wife is appointed her full names should be mentioned, if that has not been done at the beginning of the will.

It is possible to differentiate between the offices of executors and trustees and to appoint different persons in the case of each. This is not always appreciated and in certain cases there may be something to be said for appointing the spouse as an executor but not as a trustee. 23 *Encyclopaedia of Forms and Precedents* (4th edn) has a precedent at p 824.

See also next form and Form 97, p 231 below.

By the Companies Act 1985, s 360, a company registered in England is prohibited from entering on its register notice of any trust.

It is usually the case, under Articles of Association, that the vote of the first named executor and trustee on the register of the company counts, see for example Regulation 55 of Table A in the Schedule to the Companies (Tables A–F) Regulations 1985, SI 1985/805. The executor and trustee who has the voting rights should of course exercise those rights in concurrence with the others. It is also usually to the first named executor and trustee that any notice will be given. This is deemed to be sufficient notice to the other executors and trustees (see Regulation 112 of Table A). If the matter is of importance the following wording can be added – 'AND I REQUEST that the name of the said   be placed first on the register of any registered and inscribed stocks and securities which from time to time are included in the Trust Fund as hereinafter defined.'

This comment goes beyond the realms of will drafting, but it is suggested that where a non-family or non-professional person is appointed an executor he should receive a token legacy with wording along the following lines – 'AND I GIVE free of inheritance tax the sum of £   to the said   if (s)he shall prove my will (and accept the trusts hereof)'.

18 Appointment of members of a firm as executors and trustees

a) As executors of this Will I APPOINT the partners at the date of my death in the firm of   of   or the firm which at that date has succeeded to and carries on its practice and I express the wish that two and only two of them shall prove my Will and that if possible one of whom shall be

or—

a) As executors of this my Will I APPOINT my wife/husband and the partners at the date of my death in the firm of   of or the firm which at that date has succeeded to and carries on its practice and depending on whether or not my wife/husband proves my Will I express the wish that one or two only of such partners (being or including if possible   ) shall prove my Will it being my wish that there shall be only two proving executors

b) As trustees of the trusts of this Will I APPOINT the persons who obtain the first grant of probate (not being a grant limited to settled land) of my Will

c) The expression 'my Trustees' when used in this Will means my executors and the trustees or trustee whether original or substituted or added

NOTE

This form flows from the work of Mr R T Oerton, which was complimented by the court in *Re Horgan* [1971] P 50 [1969] 3 All ER 1570. See also Form 97 p 231 below.

19 Appointment of guardians

IF a child of mine is under age at the date of the death of the survivor of myself and my wife/husband I APPOINT   and   to be the guardians of that child [And I authorise them by deed or the survivor of them by deed or Will to appoint one or two persons to act as guardians in their place after the survivor's death]

NOTE

This matter is of course an extremely important one and should never be ignored. Reference should be made to the subject of Guardianship on p 115 above.

Although the words in square brackets are included, the Children Act 1989, s 5(4), gives any guardian the power to appoint another guardian to take his place in the event of his own death.

A testator may wish to ensure that the guardians are not out of pocket as the result of their duties and accordingly to provide specifically for the discharge of expenses they incur.

20 Absolute gift of house

a) I GIVE to   (free of inheritance tax and free of mortgage or charge) my property known as   in the County of   or failing which any other property (belonging to me in fee simple or held by me under a lease for a term of years having at least twenty-one years unexpired at my death) where I live at my death AND I DIRECT that my Trustees shall out of the residue of my estate discharge any mortgage or charge thereon AND I DECLARE that if at the time of my death I have entered into a contract for the sale of all or part of my property or failing which all or any part of any other property without having completed the acquisition of a further property (either in fee simple or for a term of years having at least twenty-one years unexpired at my death) intended to be my residence then in addition to or in place of such gift (as the case may be) the said   shall receive a legacy free of inheritance tax equal to the net proceeds of sale

   b) IF the gift made by the preceding sub-clause shall wholly fail then I GIVE to the said   a(n) (additional) legacy of £   free of inheritance tax

NOTE

It is necessary to make sure that the description of the property is sufficient to cover the whole of the property the testator has in mind as the subject matter of the gift. The title deeds should be examined whenever possible.

In (a), despite the Inheritance Tax Act, s 211, it is considered best, except where the gift is to the spouse, to include the words 'free of inheritance tax', if that is the intention, or, if not, that 'this gift shall bear its own share of any inheritance tax (and all other like taxes and duties) payable on or by reason of my death'; see p 71 above.

Also in (a), the words 'free of mortgage or charge' are important. In the absence of any such words liability for any mortgage or charge would fall on the beneficiary; Administration of Estates Act 1925, s 35.

   See form 27 and the note to it p 175 below where in addition to the mortgage or charge there is a policy charged by way of collateral security.

21 Life interest in house

   a) I GIVE (free of mortgage or charge) my property known as
      in the County of   (hereinafter called 'my property') to my
      Trustees UPON TRUST (subject to the written consent of my wife during her life) to sell it with power to postpone sale for such a period as my Trustees think proper and to invest the net proceeds of sale in or upon any of the investments authorised by Clause   hereof and to pay the income of the investments and also the net rents and profits of my property until sale to my wife during her life PROVIDED NEVERTHELESS that any income received after her death shall be applied as if it had accrued after her death and accordingly no apportionment is to be made

   b) I DIRECT that so long as my property remains unsold and during the lifetime of my wife my Trustees shall allow my wife if she so wishes to live there she paying all outgoings and keeping the buildings adequately insured under comprehensive cover and in reasonable repair decoration and condition AND I DECLARE that my Trustees shall not be responsible during the lifetime of my wife to see to the insurance repair decoration and condition and that my Trustees shall not be liable for any loss or damage that may happen to my property from any cause whatsoever

   c) I ALSO DIRECT that after the death of my wife my property or its proceeds of sale or the investments representing the same shall fall into and form part of my residuary estate and shall be held by my Trustees upon the trusts hereafter declared concerning the same

d) IN ADDITION to the investment powers of my Trustees under Clause

hereof I EMPOWER them to lay out the proceeds of sale of my property or any property substituted under this present power in the purchase of any freehold or leasehold property to be held upon trusts for the benefit of my wife corresponding in all respect with the trusts hereinbefore expressly and by reference declared

e) PROVIDED ALWAYS and I HEREBY DECLARE as follows:

i) If at the time of my death I am no longer the owner of

aforesaid but own another property either freehold or leasehold (such leasehold property having a term of not less than twenty years unexpired at that time) then for the purposes of the foregoing subclauses of this Clause the name of such other property (if more than one such other property then whichever of them my Trustees in their absolute discretion decide) shall fall within the said definition of 'my property'

ii) If at the time of my death I am not the owner of a property falling within the said definition or have entered into a contract to dispose of it then for the purpose of the provisions of this Clause there shall be substituted a settled cash legacy of an amount equal to the gross sale price of my property which legacy shall be held upon trusts for the benefit of my wife corresponding in all respects with the trusts hereinbefore expressly and by reference declared as if it had been the net proceeds arising from the sale by my Trustees of my property

NOTE

Where the person to be entitled to use the house is also to be entitled to the income of the residuary estate it will no doubt be considered easier and better in place of such a clause to cover the position under the trustees' investment powers: see Form 80 p 218 below.

See note to preceding form.

22 Use of house so long as required

I GIVE (free of mortgage or charge) to my Trustees my property known as   in the County of   (hereinafter called 'my property') upon trust to grant to my wife (unless within three months after my death my wife by notice or memorandum in writing to my Trustees informs them that she does not want one) a lease of my property for a term of years (but nevertheless determinable by notice in writing given to or by my wife or her personal representatives should she cease to use my property as her permanent home) at a nominal rent and generally subject to such covenants and upon such conditions as to payment of outgoings and as to insurance repair and decoration and otherwise as my Trustees in their discretion think fit and subject as aforesaid upon trust to convey and transfer my property subject to and with the benefit of any lease to my (son)

or—

I GIVE (free of inheritance tax and free of mortgage or charge) to my (son)
my property known as   in the County of
(hereinafter called 'my property') subject to the condition that
my said (son) shall permit my wife it she so wishes and without payment to use
my property as a personal residence (but not otherwise) during her lifetime subject
to her being responsible for keeping the same properly insured under comprehensive
cover for the payment of outgoings and for maintaining my property in reasonable
repair decoration and condition

or—

I GIVE (free of inheritance tax and free of mortgage or charge) to my Trustees
my property known as   in the County of
(hereinafter called 'my property') UPON TRUST to sell the same with power to postpone
sale for such a period as my Trustees shall think proper and to stand possessed
of the net proceeds of sale and the net rents and profits until sale upon the trusts
hereafter declared concerning the Trust Fund and the income thereof respectively
PROVIDED NEVERTHELESS that during the lifetime of   and until
such time as he shall cease to use and occupy my property personally or to pay
the outgoings or to keep the buildings adequately insured under comprehensive cover
and in reasonable repair decoration and condition my Trustees shall not sell it without
the consent in writing of the said

NOTE
The above forms, which are a matter of choice according to the circumstances, are intended to
cover the situation where the occupier of the house is *not* entitled to the income as a whole of
the residuary estate.

The forms also presuppose that the right of occupation will end upon the house ceasing to be used.

The difficulty in the framing of suitable clauses is because, as a result of a series of interlocking
provisions in the Settled Land Act 1925 a person having a right to occupy may have the powers
of a tenant for life under that Act, and fetters and restrictions on such powers are void.

The forms can, of course, be subject to a series of adaptations.

The term of the lease under the first of these forms will be related to the expectation of life of
the person concerned, but the difficulty about creating leases is that with so many possible changes
in the law one never quite knows what the ultimate effect will be. Reference can conveniently be
made to note 3, p 51 above.

The second of these forms is aimed at creating a licence to occupy outside the Settled Land Act
1925. It presupposes that there is a satisfactory family relationship between mother and son. So
far as the form is intended to circumvent the Act one should not be over-confident: see for example
the somewhat curious Court of Appeal cases of *Bannister* v *Bannister* [1948] 2 All ER 133 and *Binions*
v Evans [1972] Ch 359, [1972] 2 All ER 70.

The third form is drafted with the object of imposing an immediate binding trust for sale, thereby
taking the trusts and right of occupation outside the Settled Land Act 1925.

The Capital Gains Tax Act 1979, s 104 which extends s 101 will enable the capital gains tax exemption
to be obtained if the conditions, including the house being the main residence of the beneficiary,
are satisfied. In the circumstances envisaged the beneficiary's right of occupation will doubtless be
an interest in possession for IHT purposes. In that connection, reference should be made to B of
ch 6, p 70 above.

See Form 21 and the note to it, p 170 above, where in addition to the mortgage or charge there is a policy charged by way of collateral security.

23 Absolute gift of interest in house

I GIVE to my wife/husband my share in the property (and in its future proceeds of sale) known as   in the County of   and in such other freehold or leasehold properties (and in their respective proceeds of sale) where I live at the time of my death

NOTE
It often happens that a testator knows that his house is in the joint names of himself and his wife, but for some reason does not know whether it is held by them as joint tenants or tenants in common. They may have no children and desire that the survivor should become the absolute owner. This is a belt and braces clause to cover the possibility of there being a tenancy in common.

If the house is held under a joint tenancy as opposed to a tenancy in common and though it is desired that the survivor of such persons should become the full owner, it may be considered sensible to sever the joint tenancy and to have a clause on the foregoing lines. If the interest of the deceased then devolves under the will it will be possible to guard against the deaths occurring as the result of the same calamity by the inclusion of a survivorship clause (see Form 94, p 229 below). For a mutual notice to sever a joint tenancy and a deed of severance, see precedents 115 and 116, pp 256 and 258 below.

In the foregoing respects see commentary in ch 7, at p 84 above.

Consideration should be given to the presence of a mortgage or charge secured on the property.

24 Life interest in interest in house

I GIVE my share in the property known as   in the County of   or failing which in any other freehold or leasehold property owned jointly by me and my wife/husband where I live at the time of my death and in the respective proceeds of sale thereof (hereinafter called 'the Property Fund' which expression shall include any property investments and cash from time to time representing the same) to my Trustees upon the following trusts and directions:
a) Upon trust to sell (but subject to the provisions of sub-clause (d) of this Clause) or retain the same or any part thereof for so long as my Trustees shall in their absolute discretion decide without being liable for loss
b) To pay any income from the Property Fund to my wife/husband during her/his lifetime
c) After the death of my wife/husband the Property Fund shall fall into and form part of my residuary estate
d) During the lifetime of my wife/husband no steps shall be taken by my Trustees

to enforce the trust for sale applicable to any such freehold or leasehold property or to realise my share therein or to obtain any rents or profits without the written consent of my wife/husband and that until sale my Trustees shall allow my wife/husband to live there for so long as she/he wishes but upon the terms that she/he shall pay all outgoings payable and keep the property in reasonable repair and condition and adequately insured under comprehensive cover AND I DECLARE that my Trustees shall not be responsible for seeing to such repair and condition or for the effecting and keeping up of such insurance or for the breach of any obligations imposed upon my wife/husband

e) If my wife/husband at any time requests in writing my Trustees to join in selling any such freehold or leasehold property or any other property purchased pursuant to this sub-clause my Trustees shall do so and at any time thereafter at the like request of my wife/husband shall apply all or some part according to the request of my wife/husband of the net proceeds of sale representing my said share in or towards the purchase of another freehold or leasehold property or flat or a share therein selected by her/him for use as her/his residence (including then or thereafter meeting the cost of alterations improvements and repairs to buildings) such acquired asset or share to be held upon trusts for the benefit of my wife/husband corresponding in all respects with the foregoing trusts and directions

f) My Trustees shall also have in relation to the Property Fund the same powers of investment as those contained in Clause   of this Will

NOTE

When the person entitled to enjoy the interest in the house is also entitled to the income of the residuary estate it will no doubt be considered easier and better, in place of such a clause, to cover the position under the trustees' investment powers: see Form 80 p 218 below.

As drafted, it has been assumed that the life tenant is the spouse and therefore, prima facie, there will be freedom from IHT. Consideration will need to be given to any mortgage or charge over the property.

The reference in sub-clause (f), regarding investment powers, is to those in (a) of Form 80 p 218 below.

25 Gift of house to spouse and children in stipulated shares

IF my wife/husband survives me I GIVE free of inheritance tax where applicable and free of mortgage or charge my property known as   in the County of   and any other freehold or leasehold properties where I live at the time of my death to my Trustees UPON TRUST (subject to the written consent of my wife/husband during her/his life) to sell the same with power to postpone any sale for such a period as my Trustees think fit and to hold the net proceeds of sale and the net rents and profits until sale UPON TRUST as to a
share for my wife/husband absolutely and as to the remaining   share for those persons who are beneficiaries under Clause   (b) of this Will upon the same

trusts and in the same manner and shares [without regard to the overriding power of appointment under Clause   and any exercise of it]

NOTE
This form assumes that the testator wishes to adopt the kind of arrangements referred to in ch 7, at p 86, except that the above circumstances assume that the testator is the sole owner of the house.

26 Gift of interest in house to spouse and children in stipulated shares

IF my wife/husband survives me I GIVE free of inheritance tax where applicable my beneficial share in the property known as   in the County of   and in any other freehold or leasehold properties owned jointly by me and my wife/husband where I live at the time of my death and in the future proceeds of sale thereof as to a   share for my wife/husband absolutely and as to the remaining share for those persons who are beneficiaries under Clause   (b) of this Will upon the same trusts and in the same manner and shares [without regard to the overriding power of appointment under Clause   and any exercise of it]

NOTE
As in the case of the preceding form it assumes that the testator wishes to adopt the kind of arrangements referred to in ch 7, at p 86. Consideration should be given to the presence of a mortgage or charge secured on the property.

27 Declaration that mortgage or charge is to be discharged from proceeds of insurance policy

I DECLARE that the amount owing at the time of my death under any mortgage or charge secured on my said property and all interest which may accrue to the time of its discharge and the costs and expenses for its discharge shall be paid to the extent of what is thereby required out of the proceeds of any insurance policy which is charged by way of collateral security or is otherwise connected with the said mortgage or charge or failing any such policy or to the extent that the proceeds of it are not sufficient for that purpose out of my residuary estate AND I ALSO DECLARE that the benefit of the foregoing first declaration shall be free of inheritance tax

NOTE
The above form assumes the possibility that there is an outstanding loan secured by a mortgage or charge with a policy also charged by way of collateral security which policy will mature on the death. No doubt the mortgagee will take repayment of the loan from the policy proceeds. This

form makes it clear that, despite the Administration of Estates Act 1925, s 35, the beneficiary of the property shall to the extent required enjoy the benefit of the policy proceeds.

28 Right to purchase interest in house

a) I DECLARE that (notwithstanding her/his appointment as an executor and trustee of this Will) my wife/husband shall have the option (exercisable not later than two months after the date on which probate with respect to my estate is obtained by notice in writing to my Executors and Trustees) to purchase my share in the property (and its future proceeds of sale thereof) known as   in the County of   and in such other freehold or leasehold properties (and in the proceeds of sale thereof) where I live at the time of my death

b) The purchase price shall be a sum equal to the value at the time of my death of the property (which is the subject of the said notice) in the open market and with vacant possession ('the open market value') provided that where the sale is of a share and not the whole the purchase price shall be a sum equal to that proportion of the open market value which my share bears to the whole

c) Subject to taking into account the provisions of sub-clause (b) of this Clause the purchase price shall be fixed (whether or not under the guidance of professional valuers instructed jointly by both parties) by agreement between them and failing agreement shall be determined by arbitration

d) Completion of the purchase and sale shall take place within six weeks after the time of such agreement or determination

e) If so requested in writing by my wife/husband all expenses shall be paid by my Trustees from my residuary estate in exoneration of any liability on the part of her/him

NOTE

This form envisages that, in the context of their IHT calculations and the pattern of their respective wills, the wealthier of the two spouses is to have the opportunity of buying the interest of the other, following the death, in the matrimonial home. This would, for example, provide the executors and trustees of the deceased with cash with which to meet legacies to beneficiaries, who are non-exempt for IHT purposes, such as their children.

29 Absolute gift of jewellery

I GIVE free of inheritance tax to   all my jewellery and all other articles of a like nature including tiaras rings necklaces earrings brooches pendants bracelets and watches

NOTE

It often happens that a lady wishes to leave her 'jewellery' to, say, her daughter. The above is an attempt to place a comprehensive definition on how far the expression extends.

See also para (b) of and note to next form.

30 Absolute gifts of specific chattels

a) I GIVE free of inheritance tax the following specific legacies:

b) ALL expenses for safe custody and insurance before giving effect to these gifts and for packing transporting and insuring for delivery to those persons their articles shall be paid from my residuary estate

NOTE
The reason for the inclusion of this form is the declaration under (b). It is not always appreciated that in the normal course of events it is for a beneficiary to make his own arrangements for the collecting of his gift and this in practice can sometimes spoil its effect: see *Re Fitzpatrick, Bennett v Bennett* [1952] Ch 86, [1951] 2 All ER 949 and *Williams, Mortimer and Sunnucks* (16th edn) pp 927-928.

31 Gifts of chattels, specific and general, including where there is a memorandum of wishes

a) I GIVE free of inheritance tax the following specific legacies to the following persons:

b) I GIVE free of inheritance tax all my chattels (but subject to the gifts under sub-clause (a) of this Clause in so far as they take effect) to those persons who obtain the first grant of Probate of this Will

c) I REQUEST them but without imposing any legal obligation
   i) TO give effect as soon as possible but not later than two years after my death to any memorandum or notes of wishes of mine about any of my chattels
   ii) SUBJECT to any wishes to make my wife/husband the owner of my chattels (or the balance thereof) if she/he survives me by three months

or

   ii) SUBJECT to any wishes to make my wife/husband the owner of those chattels which they in their absolute discretion regard as being unsuitable to be treated as subject to the provisions of paragraph (iii) of this sub-clause on account of their particular nature or lack of durability or small value or for any other reason if she/he survives me by three months
   [iii) SUBJECT as aforesaid (in particular if my wife/husband does not survive me by three months) to hold my chattels (or the balance thereof) upon the same trusts and with and subject to the same powers and provisions

(including the power under Clause ( ) hereof) as apply to and as an addition to the Trust Fund (as defined in Clause ( ) of this Will)]

d) IN this Clause 'chattels' has the same meaning as the expression 'personal chattels' in the Administration of Estates Act 1925 (but including any car or other article that I own at the time of my death despite it being regarded for the purposes of taxation or insurance or otherwise as being wholly or partly for business use)

e) ALL expenses for safe custody and insurance of my chattels before giving effect to my wishes and for packing transporting and insuring any chattels for delivery to their recipients shall be paid from my residuary estate

NOTE

'Personal chattels' as defined by the Administration of Estates Act 1925, s 55(1)(x) means carriages, horses, stable furniture and effects (not used for business purposes), motor cars and accessories (not used for business purposes), garden effects, domestic animals, plate, plated articles, linen, china, glass, books, pictures, prints, furniture, jewellery, articles of household or personal use or ornament, musical and scientific instruments and apparatus, wines, liquors and consumable stores, but does not include any chattels used at . . . death . . . for business purposes nor money or securities for money.

Updated wording, in keeping with modern circumstances (television sets etc), can be found in 23 *Encyclopaedia of Forms and Precedents* (4th edn) 838.

It is suggested, in the definition, under (d) above, that the car should be dealt with specifically. On the one hand, it may be 'used for business purposes', and therefore not, in fact, covered by the definition in s 55(1)(x) and on the other, probably being a major chattel when compared in value with his run-of-the-mill articles, the testator may wish that it should form part of his residuary estate.

Apart from the matter of the car, it is important, depending on the terms of the will as a whole, that the testator should give thought to his individual kinds of chattels including his business articles, such as his typewriter and office equipment and also articles he may have bought principally for investment purposes such as gold, silver, pictures and antiques.

Thought will need to be given about who should be the beneficiaries under (b) to give effect to any expressed wishes made in accordance with (c). As illustrated, they could be those persons who prove the will. Equally they could be nominated members of the family or the survivors of them.

For the IHT effects, in respect of the use of (b) and (c) of this form, see s 143 and p 79 above. The next form, being a memorandum of wishes over chattels, can be used, as and when desired, by the testator.

32 Memorandum of wishes over chattels

TO

In Clause   of my Will dated   199   I have given you all my chattels of every description

Nevertheless I have requested you but without imposing any legal obligation to give effect as soon as possible but not later than two years following my death to any memorandum or notes of wishes of mine with regard to any of my chattels

Accordingly I am making this Memorandum to record whom I wish to receive the articles specifically mentioned or otherwise described below

Articles   *Recipients*

Dated this   day of   199

NOTE
This form links up with the previous form and can be used by a testator, as and when desired.

33 Life interest in selected chattels

a) I GIVE to my Trustees my selected articles (as defined in sub-clause (d) hereof) to hold upon the following trusts and with and subject to the following powers and provisions:
   i) UPON TRUST to allow my wife/husband to have the use and enjoyment of my selected articles during her/his life she/he at her/his own cost keeping them insured in the names of my Trustees for their full value for insurance purposes against loss or damage by fire and theft with insurers decided by my Trustees and in good repair and preservation reasonable wear and tear excepted
   ii) SUBJECT to the foregoing interest of my wife/husband UPON TRUST to hold my selected articles upon the same trusts and with and subject to the same powers and provisions as apply to and as an addition to the Trust Fund (as defined in Clause   (c) of this Will)
b) I DECLARE that it shall not be obligatory on my Trustees to require any inventory thereof to be made and that my Trustees shall not be concerned during the lifetime of my wife/husband to see to the insurance thereof or be liable for any loss or damage that may happen thereto from any cause whatsoever
c) I ALSO DECLARE that my Trustees may at any time during the life of my wife/husband (subject to her/his written consent) sell my selected articles or any of them and that my Trustees shall have power (if so requested by my wife/husband) to apply the net proceeds of any such sale and any insurance moneys not required for repair in the purchase of other articles of a similar kind to be held upon the trusts declared under sub-clause (a)(i) hereof but subject thereto the said proceeds or moneys shall be held upon the trusts declared under sub-clause (a)(ii) hereof otherwise to take effect following the death of my wife/husband
d) For the purposes of this Clause 'my selected articles' means . . .

NOTE

This form may be desired in the case of valuable personal chattels, in which event it can be adapted to deal solely with such chattels of value. Invariably the settling of chattels en bloc gives rise to practical difficulties and should be discouraged.

34 Fiduciary power over chattels available for distribution by executors and trustees

a) I GIVE free of inheritance tax all my chattels to my Trustees to hold with and upon the powers trusts and provisions in this Clause

b) MY Trustees shall have power during the period of two years after my death to distribute any or all of my chattels to any person or persons as they in their discretion choose

c) ALL income received by my Trustees as the result of their holding any of my chattels before the particular exercise of their power in sub-clause (b) shall be regarded as belonging to it

d) I DECLARE but without imposing any legal obligation that when exercising their power under sub-clause (b) my Trustees shall have regard to any memorandum or notes of wishes of mine

e) SUBJECT to the power in sub-clause (b) and its exercise my Trustees shall distribute my chattels (or the balance thereof) to my wife/husband if s/he survives me failing which my Trustees shall hold them upon the same trusts and with and subject to the same powers and provisions as apply to and as an addition to the Trust Fund (as defined in Clause   hereof)

f) IN this Clause 'chattels' has the same meaning as the expression 'personal chattels' in the Administration of Estates Act 1925 (but including any car or other article that I own at the time of my death despite it being regarded for the purposes of taxation or insurance or otherwise as being wholly or partly for business use)

g) ALL expenses for safe custody and insurance of my chattels while held by my Trustees and for packing transporting and insuring any chattels for delivery to their recipients shall be paid from my residuary estate

NOTE

This form is based on *Re Beatty's Will Trusts* [1990] 3 All ER 844, where a testatrix had by her will given personal chattels and cash to her trustees with a power to allocate, divide or make over any part of them within two years of her death among any person or persons at their discretion. Anything not so distributed was to become part of her residuary estate. After the death of the testatrix, the trustees made distributions but later the residuary beneficiaries questioned the validity of their power to do so.

Hoffman J said the relevant clauses in the will were not effective to impose any trust to distribute the chattels or money over which they operated but conferred 'in lieu thereof' a fiduciary power. So the trustees were under a duty to consider whether the power should be exercised and to act in accordance with what they believed was the purpose which would cause the testatrix to create the powers.

The powers were fiduciary. They were not general or special powers but were what is known as trust powers of the kind dealt with in depth in *Re Park, Public Trustee v Armstrong* [1932] 1 Ch 580.

The argument on behalf of the residuary beneficiaries was that, even if the powers would have been valid as part of a settlement, they were invalidated by the rule that a testator could not delegate the making of his will.

In the opinion of Hoffman J, in *Chichester Diocesan Fund and Board of Finance (Incorporated) v Simpson* [1944] AC 341, [1944] 2 All ER 60, their Lordships would have been fully aware that for centuries testators had been in the habit of creating general and special powers of appointment and the validity of a power to appoint to anyone other than the donee had almost certainly been upheld in *Re Park*.

The judge therefore held that the powers were valid and that there was no rule of law to invalidate them merely because they happened to be part of a will.

Sub-clause (c) has been included to delay the surviving spouse having an interest in possession in the chattels during the time they are held by the executors and trustees. Thus advantage can be taken of s 144 (see p 91 above) and the retrospective benefit of the surviving spouse exemption, under s 18, in the case of those chattels received by the surviving spouse either as the result of the exercise by the executors and trustees of their power in sub-clause (b) or the default provisions in sub-clause (e).

35 Gift of chattels to more than one person with provision for settling dispute about division

I GIVE free of inheritance tax to such of them   and
                     as survive me all my personal chattels as defined by Section 55(1)(x) of the Administration of Estates Act 1925 if both of them so as to be divided equally between them in such manner as they shall jointly agree PROVIDED THAT if there shall be any difference about the manner of that division of my personal chattels such difference shall be settled by my Trustees in such manner as my Trustees shall think proper and the decision of my Trustees shall be final and binding And I empower my Trustees if they consider it appropriate to sell any of my personal chattels and to divide the net proceeds of sale equally between the said
                     and

36 Powers in relation to gifts to persons under age

a) My Trustees may if they at any time decide pay transfer or deliver all or any part of a legacy under Clauses   and   to the beneficiary when he or she is under age or to a parent or guardian of the beneficiary and in that event the receipt of the beneficiary or of the parent or guardian shall be a complete discharge to my Trustees

b) My Trustees and the parent or guardian (as the case may be) shall in respect of that legacy have power to use both income and capital (without limitation) for the benefit of the beneficiary and power to invest similar to the one in Clause   ( ) of this Will including power to purchase National Savings Certificates

NOTE

The form is included in order to meet the case of small legacies to, say, godchildren. The receipt of a person under age is a good discharge to the trustees if there is suitable provision for it in the will: *Re Somech, Westminster Bank Ltd v Phillips* [1957] Ch 165 at 167 and 168. The Family Law Reform Act 1969 reduced the age of majority from 21 to 18.

The reference in (b) regarding investment could be to the kind in (a) of Form 80, p 218 below.

37 Gift of shareholding etc

a) I GIVE to   (free of inheritance tax and free of charge) all my shares (including debentures if any) and loan accounts in
   and the benefit of any other loans which remain owing to me at my death by the company together with any undrawn remuneration and fees and all dividends and interest already accrued due or accruing at my death but then unpaid

b) I DECLARE that if any shares which would have been comprised in this gift (whether or not acquired after the date hereof) have prior to my death been acquired by another company in consideration whether in whole or in part of shares of that other company this gift shall (additionally) take effect as if the name of that other company had been included in sub-clause (a) hereof in addition to the name of

NOTE

The wording of any gift, in accordance with this form, needs to be tailor-made to meet the circumstances. An examination of a recent set of accounts of the company would assist. Likewise, considerations should be given to whether or not the gift will or will not bear its own share of the IHT liability. For IHT purposes, the shares may have the benefit of relief for business property, see p 35 above, and the right to pay the liability by instalments, see p 25 above.

38 Gift of interest in business

I GIVE to my wife/husband my share and interest in the stock equipment and other assets including book debts goodwill and bank balances in the business of

which we carry on in partnership under the name of
but this gift is subject to my share and interest in the liabilities
of the business

NOTE

Reference is to be made to comments referable to Question 9, p 159 above. The assumption is that
the husband and wife, whether or not they recognise the fact, are running a joint business venture
such as dealers in antiques. It is suggested that any such clause can best be drafted with a copy
of the latest accounts in mind since this will disclose the nature of the assets. The clause can be
elaborated by reference to 'all the machinery plant stock-in-trade vehicles and all effects of every
kind'. It is assumed, although that may not be the case, that the business has a separate bank account.
In any event the practicalities will need to be considered and whether along with such gift there
should also be a cash legacy to help support the running of the business. Consideration must be
given to the ownership and title of the business premises. At its simplest, this can state that 'the
foregoing gift shall (not) include any interest in the premises upon which the business is conducted
at the date of my death'.

Care should be taken to check whether the beneficial interests in the premises are held as joint
tenants or as tenants in common since the jus accrescendi will apply to the former and take effect
irrespective of any survivorship period mentioned in the will.

A wide range of forms is included in 23 *Encyclopaedia of Forms and Precedents* (4th edn) 965ff.

Though reference can be made to Form 79, p 216 below and the note to it, it is suggested that
as in this form where the circumstances make that possible it is better to give a specific legacy
of a business interest than to allow it to become part of the residuary estate and subject to continuing
trusts.

It is inadvisable for executors and trustees to carry on a testator's business, without specific authority,
because they should only do so pending winding it up.

39 Gift of interests in Lloyd's

a) I GIVE to   my Lloyd's assets (as defined in sub-clause (b) [and
   sub-clause (c)] hereof) and all income and gains in respect thereof received
   after my death and all profits of my underwriting accounts open at the time
   of my death irrespective of the periods the said income and gains and accounts
   cover But this gift is subject to inheritance tax and like liabilities as mentioned
   in sub-clause   ( ) hereof

b) My Lloyd's assets for the purposes of the foregoing gift shall comprise the
   following:
   i) any assets of mine used in or held in reserve for my business as an
      underwriting member of Lloyd's and the syndicates in which I participate
      including investments and cash deposited with the Corporation of Lloyd's
      and any held in the special reserve fund and in the premiums reserve
      fund and in the personal reserve fund and any other funds and accounts
      connected with my said business; and
   ii) any benefits arising from any stop loss or indemnity arrangements and

any estate protection plan to facilitate the winding up of my Lloyd's business respectively in force on my behalf at the time of my death

[c] i) My Lloyd's assets for the purposes of the foregoing gift shall also where applicable include the Relevant Part of my Charged Assets

ii) My Charged Assets are any assets of mine which are charged at my death as security to my bank or any other company or persons for the giving or granting of any bank or other guarantee or letter of credit or the like to the Corporation of Lloyd's for the purposes of my Lloyd's deposit And the Relevant Part thereof is that part which is of a value at my death equal to the then aggregate of the maximum amount or amounts payable under any such bank or other guarantee or letter of credit or the like

iii) For the purposes of the foregoing paragraph (ii) my Trustees shall as soon as possible after my death select at their absolute discretion from my Charged Assets those of them which are to comprise the Relevant Part for which purpose my Trustees shall so far as is possible place on them such values as apply for inheritance tax purposes on my death but without regard for business property relief]

The amount of the income and gains and profits referred to under sub-clause (a) shall be arrived at after allowing for all liabilities and expenses in connection with my said business and after taking into account any losses which may have arisen during the relevant periods

The foregoing gift of the said income and gains and profits shall be subject to all liabilities for tax including basic and higher rate tax and capital gains tax and any other tax attributable thereto respectively irrespective of whoever is accountable therefore and in exoneration of my residuary estate but shall carry with it the benefit of all tax repayments attributable to the same received after my death

Provided always that this gift shall bear its own share of any inheritance tax (and all other like taxes and duties) payable on or by reason of my death

NOTE

A large part of insurance business in the United Kingdom is carried on by members of Lloyd's. The number of members is about 26,500. Although members join together to conduct their business through syndicates, all of them are individually and personally liable on the policies to which their names are attached. Each member is thus in business and trades as an individual on his own account with unlimited liability.

A gift of Lloyd's assets cannot give the beneficiary the right to carry on a deceased's business at Lloyd's.

Underwriting interests qualify, on the death of a member, for the 50% of business relief under s 103 et seq of the Inheritance Tax Act 1984 and for payment of IHT by interest-free instalments. These are very material factors for a member of Lloyd's to consider when making his will. Should the member, whether specifically or as part of his residuary estate, give his Lloyd's interests to his surviving spouse, because the spouse exemption for IHT purposes will apply, no advantage will therefore be derived from the 50% business relief. When the financial circumstances allow, there is a strong case for a member giving his Lloyd's interests under his will to other members of his family. This will not result in themselves becoming members of Lloyd's. They will receive whatever assets are due on the winding up of the deceased member's business interests in Lloyd's.

An explanation about Lloyd's assets is in *Butterworths Wills, Probate and Administration Service*, A [757]-[760] which should be consulted.

40 Designation by farmer under a tenancy created before 12 July 1984 of successor under the Agricultural Holdings Act 1986 and gift of farming assets

a) I HEREBY DESIGNATE for the purposes of the Agricultural Holdings Act 1986 my wife/son/daughter   as the person whom I wish to succeed me as tenant of   Farm of which I am the tenant farmer

b) SUBJECT to my wife/my said son/my said daughter succeeding me as tenant I GIVE to her/him my business and assets of a farmer including live and dead stock and agricultural vehicles machinery equipment and effects of every description and bank balances but such gifts shall be subject to all debts and liabilities of my business at my death

c) PROVIDED ALWAYS that the gift under sub-clause (b) of this Clause shall bear its own share of any inheritance tax (and all other like taxes and duties) payable on or by reason of my death

NOTE

This form will need to be adjusted according to the practical circumstances and the wishes of the testator.

It will be appreciated that the farming interests of the testator will qualify for the 50% business relief under s 103 et seq and for payment of IHT by interest-free instalments. Should the gift be made to the surviving spouse, because the spouse exemption for IHT purposes will apply, no advantage will therefore be derived from the 50% business relief.

41 Legacy free of or subject to IHT

I GIVE free of inheritance tax to   (*amount of cash or description of asset*)

or—

I GIVE to   (*amount of cash or description of asset*) PROVIDED ALWAYS that this gift shall bear its own share of any inheritance tax (and all other like taxes and duties) payable on or by reason of my death

NOTE

Reference should be made to sub-chapter C p 71 above. When it is desired to have an overriding provision to make all legacies in the will free of IHT, rather than to use those words in reference to each legacy, see Form 95, p 230 below.

42 Cash legacy equal to IHT nil% band

a) IF my wife/husband survives me I GIVE to   a legacy of
cash being the largest amount that I can give by this Clause without any
inheritance tax being payable on the transfer of value of my estate which
I am deemed to make immediately before my death
b) THIS gift shall not carry interest until payment

NOTE
The legacy under this form is gauged by the extent of the IHT nil% band at the time of the testator's
death. The assumption by the conditional words at the beginning is that the legacy will not be
required in the event of the spouse *not* surviving and accordingly the estate of the testator being
non-exempt as a whole for IHT purposes. Reference to the use of the IHT nil% band should be
made to sub-chapter H, p 77 above.

43 Cash legacy equal to IHT nil% band upon discretionary trusts under which spouse is a beneficiary

a) NOTWITHSTANDING the rest of this Clause:
  i) IF my wife/husband does not survive me the gift under sub-clause (b)
  shall fail and the terms of the succeeding sub-clauses shall not take effect;
  and
  ii) IF my wife/husband dies during the period of three months after my death
  the trusts hereafter declared over the Legacy Fund shall cease and thereupon
  my Trustees shall stand possessed of the capital and income (including
  accruing or accrued income not yet received) of the Legacy Fund upon
  the same trusts and with and subject to the same powers and provisions
  as apply to and as an addition to the Trust Fund (as defined in Clause   (c)
  of this Will)
b) i) I GIVE to my Trustees a cash sum calculated by paragraph (ii) of this
  sub-clause to hold upon the trusts and with and subject to the powers
  and provisions hereafter declared over the Legacy Fund
  ii) THE cash sum in paragraph (i) of this sub-clause is the largest amount
  that can be given by this Clause without any inheritance tax being payable
  on the transfer of value of my estate which I am deemed to make immediately
  before my death
  iii) THIS gift shall not carry interest until payment
c) IN this Clause the following expressions have the following meanings:
  'The Legacy Fund' means the cash sum given by sub-clause (b) of this Clause
  and the assets for the time being representing it
  'The Trust Period' means the period starting with the date of my death and
  ending eighty years later (and that period is the perpetuity period applicable
  hereto)
  'The Beneficiaries' means those of the following persons living at my death

or born during the Trust Period being my wife/husband and my children and my remoter issue and any person who is or has been a spouse of any child or remoter issue of mine (including of any who have died before me)

d) MY Trustees shall sell or retain any part of the assets of the Legacy Fund that is not money with power to invest any money and to vary investments similar to the one in sub-clause (a) of Clause   of this Will

e) MY Trustees shall pay or transfer or otherwise hold (as the case may be) the Legacy Fund and its income to or for the benefit of any one or more of the Beneficiaries at such age or time or respective ages or times in such shares and with and subject to such trusts and dispositive and administrative powers and provisions (including protective and discretionary trusts and powers exercisable at the discretion of my Trustees or any other person or persons) as my Trustees (not being less than two in number) may during the Trust Period by any deed or deeds revocable or irrevocable appoint (regard being had to the law relating to remoteness)

PROVIDED:

i) that no appointment shall invalidate any prior payment or application of any part or parts of the capital or income of the Legacy Fund

ii) that no power of revocation reserved to my Trustees in any appointment shall be capable of being exercised after the end of the Trust Period; and

iii) that my Trustees may during the Trust Period at any time or times by irrevocable deed extinguish or restrict the future exercise of this power of appointment

f) IN default of and until and subject to any appointment by my Trustees under sub-clause (e) of this Clause my Trustees shall hold the Legacy Fund upon the following trusts:

i) UNTIL the end of the Trust Period UPON TRUST to pay or apply the income of the Legacy Fund with power from time to time to pay or apply the whole or any part or parts of the capital of the Legacy Fund to or for the benefit of any one or more of the Beneficiaries for the time being living PROVIDED THAT my Trustees may (notwithstanding the foregoing discretionary trust in respect of that income) during the period of twenty one years from my death from time to time accumulate the whole or any part of the income of the Legacy Fund at compound interest by investing it and its resulting income in any investments authorised by sub-clause (d) of this Clause and adding the accumulations to the capital of the Legacy Fund

ii) SUBJECT as aforesaid UPON TRUST for those of my children living at my death if more than one in equal shares

g) MY Trustees shall have a similar power of appropriation over the Legacy Fund (including after any exercise of their power of appointment under sub-clause (e) of this Clause) to the one in sub-clause (a) of Clause   of this Will without needing the consent of anyone

h) ANY of my Trustees may join in exercising any of the trusts and powers under this Clause notwithstanding that he or she is one of the Beneficiaries and will or may benefit as a result

i) I DECLARE but without imposing any binding legal obligation on them that it is my wish first that my Trustees shall regard my wife/husband during her/his lifetime as the primary beneficiary of both the income and capital of the Legacy Fund and secondly that as soon as possible after the death of my wife/husband my Trustees shall exercise their powers over the capital of the Legacy Fund in such manner as will so far as possible correspond with the terms of sub-clause (b) of Clause   of this Will

NOTE

The reasons for using this form are explained in H of ch 6, p 77 above. It is included, as clause 7, in the precedent no 1, p 127 above. There is explanation of it for client purposes in the sample letter, being no 3, p 140 above.

44 Cash legacies to take effect only on the death of the survivor of spouses

I GIVE free of inheritance tax to the following persons the following cash legacies:

To   the sum of
               THOUSAND POUNDS ($£$)
To   the sum of
               THOUSAND POUNDS ($£$)

PROVIDED ALWAYS that each of the said legacies shall not take effect in the event of my predeceasing my wife/husband and for the purpose of this proviso should I and my wife/husband die in circumstances rendering it uncertain which of us survived the other I shall be deemed to have died after/before him/her

NOTE

This form meets the circumstances where a husband and wife wish each beneficiary to receive a legacy under one or other, but not both, of their wills.

45 Settled legacy for the life of the beneficiary

a) I GIVE free of inheritance tax to my Trustees the sum of
POUNDS ($£$) to hold upon the trusts and with and subject to the powers and provisions declared in this clause

b) MY Trustees shall invest such sum and for such purposes and generally shall have a similar power to the power to invest and to vary investments as is contained in Clause   of this Will

c) MY Trustees shall have the power under Clause   of this Will to appropriate any part of my residuary property and assets in or towards satisfaction of the said cash legacy

d) THE said cash sum and the property and assets for the time being representing

the same are hereinafter in this clause called '   's settled
legacy'

e) MY Trustees shall stand possessed of   's settled legacy UPON
TRUST to pay the income thereof to   during her/his life

f) SUBJECT as aforesaid my Trustees shall stand possessed of   's
settled legacy upon similar trusts to those contained in sub-clauses (b) and
(c) of Clause   of this Will as if those trusts were herein repeated

g) FOR the purpose of avoiding doubt I DECLARE that in relation to
                    's settled legacy subject to such modifications of wording
as may be necessary similar powers and provisions to those contained in Clauses
        and   of this Will are to apply

46 Cash legacy which is index-linked

I GIVE free of inheritance tax to   the sum of
PROVIDED NEVERTHELESS that:

a) For the said amount of   there shall be substituted an amount
arrived at by increasing the said amount by the same percentage as the percentage
increase in the Retail Prices Index as hereinafter defined as the result of
comparing the month of my death with the month during which this Will
is made and if the result is not a multiple of £1,000 rounding it up to the
nearest amount which is such a multiple

b) i) For the purposes hereof the Retail Prices Index shall mean the Index of
Retail Prices published by the Department of Employment or any official
publication substituted therefor and in the event of any change after the
date hereof in the reference base used to compile the said Index the figure
taken to be that at which the said Index stands after such change shall
be the figure at which the said Index would have stood if the reference
base current at the date hereof had been retained

ii) If at the time of my death the said Retail Prices Index has been abolished
or adjusted or in any way changed in any manner which would frustrate
my intentions to increase this legacy then my Trustees may use such other
yardsticks or their own judgment to arrive at such increase as may be
appropriate for the purposes of arriving at the amount of the legacy

NOTE
There will be cases where a testator wishes to give a cash legacy of substance to, say, an employee
who has rendered continuing services and does not want that person to suffer as the result of the
fall in the purchasing power of the £. It is assumed, with justification, that it is unlikely that in
current conditions the £ will increase its purchasing power.

From the beginning of 1987 the Department of Employment set a new base for the Retail Prices
Index (RPI) whereby January 1987 = £100. At that time 'the old base' which was set at 100 in
January 1974 stood at 394.5.

The RPI figure for each month is published by the Department of Emplo
or third Friday of the following month. Details are published in *The Times* and sc

To compare the current RPI (new base) with a past RPI (old base), it will be
the current RPI to the old base. In that event, the following calculation should

$$\frac{\text{Current RPI (new base)}}{100} \times 394.5 = \text{Current RPI (old base}$$

eg for March 1991: $\frac{131.4}{100} \times 394.5 = 518.37$

In *Whillans's Tax Tables*, published each year by Butterworths, there is a ret
with January 1987 at 100 and on a monthly basis moving back (to June 1947,
on that figure.

47 Release of money owing

I RELEASE (free of inheritance tax)   from the liability to repay
£   or such of that amount as is owed by him to me at my death
including interest thereon

NOTE
A release of debt is equivalent to a cash legacy of its amount. Not infrequently a testator will have
made loans, whether on a permanent or temporary basis, to members of his family. It is important
to discover from him his intentions about the future of any debt in the event of his death to avoid
misunderstanding and possible distress.

48 Gift(s) to employee(s)

I GIVE free of inheritance tax to   and   the sum
of £   (each) provided that (in each case) (s)he shall be in my
employment at the time of my death and not be under notice to leave whether
given or received AND I DIRECT that:
   a) Such gift(s) shall be in addition to such moneys as may be due for salary
      and wages at my death: and
   b) My Trustees shall have power in their absolute discretion to reduce any such
      legacy by an amount equal to all or part (as my Trustees shall decide) of
      the net amount of any redundancy payment for which my estate may be liable
      under the Employment Protection (Consolidation) Act 1978 (or any statutory
      modification or re-enactment thereof)

NOTE
It is of course possible to make gifts to employees generally in which event it will be necessary
to consider the following matters:

a) Whether there should be a sliding scale according to length of service and the relative amounts of wages or salaries.
b) Whether there should be a minimum qualifying period of service at time of death.
c) Whether the gifts should apply to both full-time and part-time employees.
d) Whether they should apply to both indoor and outdoor employees.
e) What the position should be in the case of employees who retire after the date of the will but before the death.

The 1978 Act, s 93(1)(b) proceeds on the assumption that the death of an employer is an event which terminates the contract of employment. However, under Schedule 12, para 14, the employee is not entitled to a redundancy payment if he has unreasonably refused a personal representative's written offer to renew or re-engage where this would take effect within eight weeks of the death and either the provisions of the contract would be the same or the offer constitutes an offer of suitable employment. In the case of domestic staff in a private household such offer may be made by the person to whom the management of the household has passed (except in the case of a sale or other disposition for valuable consideration): see Schedule 12, para 21.

As the result of Schedule 12, para 6, where a personal representative is liable for a redundancy payment and the liability had not accrued before the death it is treated as a liability of the deceased employer which had accrued immediately before the death.

There is a Redundancy Fund to which every person liable to make an employer's National Insurance contribution in respect of any person over eighteen must also make a Redundancy Fund contribution, and an employer who has paid a redundancy payment is entitled to a rebate from the Redundancy Fund.

It seems, therefore, that any redundancy payment made by the personal representatives is a proper debt at the date of death which can be included in the Inland Revenue Account as a deduction. On the other hand, any rebate obtained from the Secretary of State (who controls the Redundancy Fund) would be an asset of the estate and would have to be shown in the Account.

49 Gifts to charities, societies and clubs

I GIVE to the (charity and its address) the sum of
£ for its general purposes
I GIVE free of inheritance tax to the (society/club and address) the sum of £
with freedom to spend such capital sum
The receipt of a person who purports to be the treasurer or other officer of a charitable benevolent or philanthropic institution society club or body of persons for a legacy given by this Will or any codicil hereto shall be a complete discharge to my Trustees who shall not thereafter have responsibility for its application

NOTE
A gift to charity, as opposed to one for non-charitable purposes, is not subject to the rule against perpetuities. When there is a gift to a non-charitable association there will be no question of perpetuity if there is freedom to spend the capital of the legacy: for example *Re Lipinski's Will Trusts* [1976] Ch 235, [1977] 1 All ER 33.

Care should always be taken to ensure that any such beneficiary is accurately described. In *Re Recher's Will Trusts, National Westminster Bank Ltd v National Anti-Vivisection Society Ltd* [1972] Ch 526, [1971] 3 All ER 401 Brightman J indicated that it was a professional adviser's most elementary duty not only to get the name right but to ensure that the particular association was still in existence and not to rely on possibly inaccurate information supplied by the client. It may therefore be considered good practice, as a general rule, to exchange letters with the association concerned without disclosing the name of one's client. A letter on the following lines could meet the case:

'Dear Sir/Madam,

We act on behalf of a person who is making a Will and under it (in certain circumstances) there is intended to be a (small) legacy of cash for the benefit of your charity/society/club.

We shall be obliged if you will let us have a note of the wording that is considered appropriate in the case of gifts to your charity/society/club.

We shall also be obliged if you will confirm whether or not it is recognised, by the authorities, in law as a charity.

When you reply please quote our above mentioned reference.

Yours faithfully,

The Secretary,

. . . .

. . . .

An annual list of charities known as the Charities Digest is published by the Family Welfare Association, 501-505 Kingsland Rd, Dalston, London E8 4AU.

Charities Aid Foundation, 48 Pembury Road, Tonbridge, Kent TN9 2BR gives guidance about charities.

50 Cash legacy for charities chosen by the executors and trustees

a) I GIVE to my Trustees the sum of   THOUSAND POUNDS (£   ) to be paid to or for such charity or charities or other charitable object or objects in England and Wales as my Trustees may in their absolute discretion select and to be paid to or for such charities or charitable objects if more than one in such proportions or amounts as my Trustees decide

b) I DESIRE but without imposing any legal obligation that my Trustees shall have regard to any expressions of wishes of mine of which they shall be aware particularly contained in any memorandum or notes

c) THE receipt of a person who purports to be the treasurer or other officer of a charity or object in whose favour they exercise their said discretion shall be a complete discharge to my Trustees who shall not thereafter have responsibility for the application of their payments

51 Gift aid legacy for charity

a) I GIVE free of inheritance tax (if applicable) to my wife/husband/[a named person] if she/he survives me by three months and failing her/him doing so to those persons being my executors who obtain the first grant of Probate of my Will the sum of   POUNDS (£   )

b) IN the case of my wife/husband/[a named person] I REQUEST her/him but without imposing any legal obligation to pay the sum to such charity or charities or for such other charitable purposes in England and Wales as she/he selects and if more than one in such amounts as she/he decides but I WISH her/him to give effect as soon as possible but not later than two years after my death to any memorandum or notes of wishes of mine

c) IN the case of my executors I DECLARE that:
   i) the sum shall be held upon trust to pay to such charity or charities or for such other charitable purposes in England and Wales as they select and if more than one in such amounts as they decide; and
   ii) the receipt of a person who purports to be the treasurer or other officer of a charity or object in whose favour they exercise their discretion shall be a complete discharge to them and they shall not thereafter be concerned about the application of their payment

NOTE

Until the Finance Act 1990, s 25, income tax relief for gifts to charity was only available for gifts under covenant for a period capable of lasting more than three years: ICTA 1988, s 660. By s 25 an *individual* is entitled to claim income tax relief for single charitable gifts of cash of at least £600. The scheme for allowing tax relief is to regard each gift as made after deduction of basic rate income tax and to treat the grossed up amount of the gift as if it is a covenanted payment to charity by the individual. Thus, for example, if a higher rate taxpayer gives £600 that payment is regarded as paid net of tax and therefore £800 gross. To enable the charity to reclaim the tax of £200 the payment should be accompanied by Form R190 (SD). The taxpayer can obtain higher rate relief on his gross gift.

Gift Aid does not by implication apply to gifts by will. Nevertheless by the testator making the legacy to an individual such as the spouse enables the latter to qualify for the foregoing tax relief. If, instead of the surviving spouse, the recipient beneficiary is a non-exempt beneficiary for IHT purposes, being a named person who is an alternative contemplated in (a) and (b) of the above form, Gift Aid will likewise be available and the gift onwards can, for IHT purposes, take advantage of s 143 provided that the testator has expressed his wishes; see p 79 above. The gift should be stated as being 'free of inheritance tax'. If the legacy is to the executors although Gift Aid is not available it can best be made under a trust, as contemplated in (c) of the above form, to take advantage of the IHT exemption under s 23 (gifts to charities).

52 Legacy and arrangements for dogs after the death

a) I WISH   to make proper arrangements for my dogs and bitches ('my dogs') so that they will be saved from cruelty

b) I GIVE free of inheritance tax any dogs I own at the time of my death to
upon trust that within a period of six months following
my death s/he will find good homes for all or any of them (including having
the right to keep any for her/himself) or to put all or any of them down

c) I DECLARE that within that period of six months my Trustees shall have power
from time to time to raise capital out of my estate not exceeding in the aggregate
the sum of £   and to pay the amounts to the said
so that during that period she can use the money to house
(including in their present or other kennels) feed and generally to care for
my dogs and discharge any cost whatsoever in relation to their disposal in
whatever manner may ultimately be decided by her/him

d) THE said   shall be entitled to be reimbursed out of my estate
all her out of pocket expenses in every respect in connection with the foregoing
duties and I DECLARE that in the event of him/her accepting the foregoing
duties in relation to my dogs s/he shall be paid free of inheritance tax a personal
legacy of £

e) PROVIDED ALWAYS and I DECLARE that following any payments to the said
my Trustees shall not thereafter be concerned about their
application

NOTE

This form assumes that the testator has a number of dogs. It can be adapted where there is a
single dog or a cat or other animals to be taken care of after the death.

53 Provisions for annuity

a) I GIVE free of inheritance tax to   a legacy of £

b) I GIVE free of inheritance tax to (the said)   an annuity of
£   during his/her life AND I DIRECT that the annuity shall commence
from that date not exceeding six months after my death as my Trustees decide
and the annuity shall accrue from day to day and shall be paid by equal quarterly
or half-yearly payments as my Trustees also decide

c) MY TRUSTEES shall have power to provide for the payment of the annuity
or discharge their obligation in respect of it by any one or more of the following
methods that is to say:

i) By setting apart as an Annuity Fund out of my residuary estate investments
the income of which shall in the opinion of my Trustees be sufficient
at the time of setting apart to pay the annuity and the likely expenses
of so doing (in which event the investment powers referred to in Clause
of this Will shall apply to the Annuity Fund) and any annuity so provided
for shall cease to be a charge upon my residuary estate and become charged
solely on the income and capital of the investments so purchased or set
apart and accordingly the balance of my residuary estate may be distributed
discharged from the annuity and upon the cesser of the annuity the Annuity

Fund shall fall into and form part of my residuary estate and any surplus income of the Annuity Fund after payment of the said annuity shall be applied in the same manner as the income of my residuary estate but nevertheless with power for my Trustees during the twenty-one years following my death to retain temporarily or accumulate (by investing and adding to the capital of the Annuity Fund) the whole or any part of the surplus income although all or part of it can in any future year be treated by my Trustees as income of the Annuity Fund arising in that year PROVIDED ALWAYS that if my Trustees set aside an Annuity Fund they shall have power then or thereafter to take out of my residuary estate if not previously distributed additional cash capital of such amount as having regard to all the circumstances they deem appropriate for the purpose of providing a cash float to enable them so to arrange matters that the said   can not only receive the annuity payments less tax at the basic rate from time to time in force but also sums equal to the estimated amounts of any income tax repayments subsequently obtainable by him/her in respect thereof which sums shall when the repayments are obtained be reimbursed to my Trustees to be replaced in and form part of the said cash float AND I DECLARE that upon the cesser of the annuity (or earlier if my Trustees decide that it is no longer required) any cash float shall fall into and form part of my residuary estate and that in no circumstances shall my Trustees be liable in any manner in relation to the provision of the cash float and the failure for any reason to recover any moneys due from the said   or his/her personal representatives either before or after his/her death

ii) By buying in their names an annuity from any life office or public company in the name of the said   to satisfy the annuity

iii) By commuting the annuity with the consent in writing of the said   and paying to him/her such capital sum out of my residuary estate as they may in their absolute discretion decide having regard to the circumstances

NOTE

The precedents often provide that an annuity is to commence, say, three months from the date of death and be paid quarterly. It is suggested that the executors and trustees should have some scope for adjusting the date of the payments and the period they cover, if stock exchange investment(s) are to be set aside as an annuity fund under (c)(i) above. The testator, because of the inevitable delay in the receipt by the annuitant of the first payment, may think it proper to give a small legacy to cover the intervening period following his death.

In the above form there has been omitted under (c)(i) a very common direction to resort to the capital of the annuity fund if there is a deficit in the amount of the income to meet the annuity. This can of course be included but it is important to recognise that the annuitant would be assessed to income tax on the capital so used because in his hands it would be income and not capital.

It sometimes causes surprise and indeed resentment when the annuitant finds that the payments he receives are to be made net and not gross. To overcome any temporary financial hardship the proviso under (c)(i) above may be found useful.

If a will provides for an annuity, (b) under Forms 56 and 57, p 198 and p 199 below, should be altered to read '. . . pay or provide for my funeral and testamentary expenses and debts and any legacies and annuities given by this Will. . .'

An annuity charged on the capital of an estate will not only delay final completion of the administration of the estate as the fund to support it will be retained until the death of the annuitant but the fund itself will also suffer IHT on the death of the annuitant, who will have had an interest in possession, with the need for aggregation with the annuitant's own free assets: see s 49(1) and also s 50(2)–(4). Accordingly, consideration should be given to the use of methods (ii) or (iii). If the trustees decide to use method (ii) the annuitant would have the right to demand the capital sum itself. It is also the case that where trustees buy the annuity, the tax advantages, in relation to its 'capital element', under ICTA 1988, s 656, are not available; see s 657(2)(c).

54 Receipt and disposal of lump sum death in service benefit under approved pension scheme with discretionary trusts if wife survives

IF my Trustees receive any money as the result of my being at my death a member of the   Staff Pension and Life Assurance Scheme I DECLARE that that money shall be treated as capital money to be held by my Trustees if my wife is alive when the money is received upon the trusts and with and subject to the powers and provisions as are declared in the next clause of this Will and if my wife is not then alive upon the same trusts and with and subject to the same powers and provisions as apply to and as an addition to the Trust Fund (as defined in Clause   (c) of this Will)

[*Succeeding clause*]

THE trusts powers and provisions referred to in the preceding clause of this Will that are to apply if my wife is alive to any money received by my Trustees from the   Staff Pension and Life Assurance Scheme are as follows:

a) IN this Clause the following expressions have the following meanings:

'The Pension Fund' means the said money and the assets for the time being representing it
'The Trust Period' means the period starting with the date of my death and ending eighty years later And that period is the perpetuity period applicable to the trusts under this Clause
'The Beneficiaries' means those of the following persons living at my death or born during the Trust Period being my wife and my children and my remoter issue and any person who is or has been a spouse of any child or remoter issue of mine (including of any who have died before me)

b) MY Trustees shall sell or retain any part of the assets of the Pension Fund that is for the time being not money with power to invest any money and to vary investments similar to the one in sub-clause (a) of Clause   of this Will

c) MY Trustees shall pay or transfer or otherwise hold (as the case may be) the Pension Fund and its income to or for the benefit of any one or more of the Beneficiaries at such age or time or respective ages or times in such shares and with and subject to such trusts and dispositive and administrative powers and provisions (including protective and discretionary trusts and powers exercisable at the discretion of my Trustees or any other person or persons) as my Trustees may during the Trust Period by any deed or deeds revocable or irrevocable appoint (regard being had to the law relating to remoteness) PROVIDED:

  i) that no appointment shall invalidate any prior payment or application of any part or parts of the capital or income of the Pension Fund;
  ii) that no power of revocation reserved to my Trustees in any appointment shall be capable of being exercised after the end of the Trust Period; and
  iii) that my Trustees may during the Trust Period at any time or times by irrevocable deed extinguish or restrict the future exercise of this power of appointment

d) IN default of and until and subject to any appointment by my Trustees under sub-clause (c) of this Clause my Trustees shall hold the Pension Fund upon the following trusts:

  i) UNTIL the end of the Trust Period UPON TRUST to pay or apply the income of the Pension Fund with power from time to time to pay or apply the whole or any part or parts of the capital of the Pension Fund to or for the benefit of any one or more of the Beneficiaries for the time being living PROVIDED THAT my Trustees may (notwithstanding the foregoing discretionary trust in respect of that income) during the period of twenty-one years from my death from time to time accumulate the whole or any part of the income of the Pension Fund at compound interest by investing it and its resulting income in any investments authorised by sub-clause (b) of this Clause and adding the accumulations to the capital of the Pension Fund
  ii) SUBJECT as aforesaid UPON TRUST for those of my children living at my death if more than one in equal shares

e) MY TRUSTEES shall have a similar power of appropriation over the Pension Fund (including after any exercise of their power of appointment under sub-clause (c) of this Clause) to the one in sub-clause (a) of Clause   of this Will without needing the consent of anyone

f) ANY of my Trustees may join in exercising any of the trusts and powers under this Clause notwithstanding that he or she is one of the Beneficiaries and will or may benefit as a result

g) I DECLARE but without imposing any binding legal obligation on them that it is my wish first that my Trustees shall regard my wife during her lifetime as the primary beneficiary in relation to (both) the income (and capital) of the Pension Fund and secondly that as soon as possible after the death of my wife my Trustees shall exercise their powers over the capital of the Pension

Fund in such manner as will so far as possible correspond with the trusts of sub-clause   ( ) of Clause   of this Will

NOTE
Reference should be made to sub-chapter J of ch 6, p 80 above.

55 Request to trustees of a pension scheme about disposal of death in service benefit

(Name) Staff Pension and Life Assurance Scheme
To the Trustees of the above Scheme.

It is my wish that in relation to any lump sum (or other) benefits which become payable in the event of my death under the discretionary trust provisions of the above Scheme you should [pay the same to   /have regard to the terms of my Will and the beneficiaries under it as at the time of my death]. I hereby revoke any previous request by me in this respect. Nevertheless I accept that the decisions to be made are your responsibility. I have lodged my Will with Messrs   of   . They will be able, should the circumstances arise, to supply you with such relevant information as you may request.

Dated this   day of   199

(Signature of Member)

NOTE
This form is intended as an aide memoire and may help to emphasise the additional need to examine a testator's pension arrangements, including what happens if he dies in service, at the time he is making his will.

Reference should be made, as in the case of the preceding form, to sub-chapter J of ch 6, p 80 above. The preceding form assumes that the particular request will be for payment to be made to the personal representatives of the deceased member. The Rules of the Scheme need however to be examined to make sure that the pension trustees have power to do so.

56 Gift of residue upon trust to sell or retain

a) I GIVE all my property and assets both real and personal movable and immovable whatsoever and wheresoever not otherwise disposed of by this Will or any Codicil to my Trustees UPON TRUST to sell the same or any part thereof which does not consist of money or to retain the same or any part in the condition or state of investment as it is at the time of my death for so long as my Trustees decide without being liable for loss

b) MY TRUSTEES shall from the money from any sale and from my ready money pay my funeral and testamentary expenses and debts and any legacies in this Will or any Codicil

c) MY TRUSTEES shall hold the rest of the said money and the property and investments at any time representing it and any part of my property and assets as remain unsold (hereafter called 'the Trust Fund') upon the trusts and with and subject to the powers and provisions hereafter declared in this Will

NOTE

The Law of Property Act 1925, s 25(4), provides that a trust either to retain or sell land shall be construed as a trust to sell the land with power to postpone. The implied power of postponement extends only to land so that express provision needs to be included to protect the trustees in respect of personalty (see s 25(1)).

Where part of the residuary estate is given to the spouse or an exempt body such as a charity, IHT on the chargeable part must be borne by such chargeable part irrespective of the provisions of the will (see Inheritance Tax Act 1984, s 41).

57 Gift of residue upon trust for sale

a) I GIVE all my property and assets both real and personal movable and immovable whatsoever and wheresoever not otherwise disposed of by this Will or any Codicil to my Trustees UPON TRUST to sell call in and convert into money such parts as are not already money at such time or times and in such manner as they shall think fit with power to postpone the sale calling in and conversion of the whole or any part thereof for so long as my Trustees decide without being liable for loss

b) MY TRUSTEES shall from the money from any sale calling in and conversion and from my ready money pay my funeral and testamentary expenses and debts and any legacies in this Will or any Codicil

c) MY TRUSTEES shall hold the rest of the said money and the property and investments at any time representing it and any such part of my property and assets as remain unsold and unconverted (hereafter called 'the Trust Fund') upon the trusts and with and subject to the powers and provisions hereafter declared in this Will

NOTE

See comments in note to preceding form.

58   Gift of residue upon administration trusts

a) I GIVE all my property and assets both real and personal movable and immovable whatsoever and wheresoever not otherwise disposed of by this Will or any Codicil to my Trustees to hold upon the administration trusts contained in Form 8 Part II of the Statutory Will Forms 1925 which form is herein incorporated

b) My TRUSTEES shall hold my property and assets and the money property and assets at any time representing it (hereafter called 'the Trust Fund') upon the trusts and with and subject to the powers and provisions hereafter declared in this Will

NOTE

The administration trusts can be included in order to cut down the length of a will. They give the trustees power to discharge funeral expenses, outstanding debts, administration expenses, inheritance tax (the reference to duties being changed by Schedule 6, para 1 and Finance Act 1986, s 100(1)) and legacies. They include the usual power of sale should the trustees consider sales necessary or advisable, and powers of management and investment in accordance with the investment clause in the will.

It should be observed that where in the next succeeding clause the person or persons to benefit are to take the assets absolutely, no trust is in fact created (unless of a temporary nature where for example one or more of the persons have not attained vested interests) and the assets can be transferred to the beneficiaries as soon as the executors have completed their formal duties of administration.

59   Life interest to spouse and capital to children and/or issue

MY Trustees shall hold the Trust Fund upon the following trusts that is to say:

a) UPON TRUST to pay the income of (a   share of) the Trust Fund to my wife/husband during her/his life

b) SUBJECT as aforesaid UPON TRUST to pay or transfer or otherwise hold (as the case may be) the capital and income of the Trust Fund to or for my child or children living three months after my death (who attain the age of   years) if more than one in equal shares PROVIDED THAT if any child has died in my lifetime (whether before or after the date of this Will) or within three months after my death or having survived me dies before attaining the age of   years and issue of that child are living three months after my death (and attain the age of twenty years) such issue shall take by substitution if more than one as tenants in common in equal shares the share of the Trust Fund which my deceased child would have taken had he or she been living three months after my death (and attained the age

of   years) but so that no issue remoter than a child of my
deceased child shall take whose parent is living and so capable of taking

NOTE

The above is the conventional form where the spouse's interest is limited to a life interest.

For the considerations in framing the trusts of the residuary estate, reference should be made generally
to ch 8, p 88 above, to form 1 being a comprehensive will form, p 127 above, and the next form
in relation to the contingent age for capital and income entitlement.

For IHT purposes, the giving of a life interest or an absolute one to a surviving spouse has the
same exempt effect: see s 49(1) and s 18(1). There may be personal considerations and circumstances
which encourage the giving of a life interest: see p 88 above.

By s 1(3) and Schedule 1, Family Law Reform Act 1969, the Trustee Act 1925, s 31, was amended
with the result that subject to and after the cesser of the prior life interest a child would be entitled
to receive income as of right on attaining 18, instead of 21 as previously. If the testator prefers
a later age then reference should be made to the next form.

60 Declaration synchronising the capital and income entitlements of children for the purposes of Capital Gains Tax Act 1979, section 147A(2)(d)

THE expression 'the Vesting Age' means the age of twenty-five years or if earlier
the age of the beneficiary on the day before the twenty-first anniversary of my death
and I DECLARE that for the purposes of the Trustee Act 1925 section 31 (or any
statutory modification or re-enactment of it) a beneficiary shall be deemed to attain
full age on attaining the Vesting Age and references to 'infancy' and 'eighteen years'
shall accordingly be varied and the right of my Trustees to pay or apply income
to or for a beneficiary who has not attained the Vesting Age shall be exercisable
as my Trustees in their absolute discretion think fit

NOTE

Depending on the individual ages of the children at the particular death the above form assumes
that there may be some whose trusts comply with the conditions of s 71 for an accumulation and
maintenance trust see p 91 above. Where the trusts are in accordance with the Trustee Act 1925,
s 31, a child attains an interest in possession and therefore his entitlement to income at eighteen
as the result of which the conditions of s 71 for an accumulation and maintenance trust thereafter
cease to apply. It follows, for capital gains tax purposes, that on his subsequently becoming absolutely
entitled to his share of capital at a later age the trustees and himself will not be able to claim hold-
over relief for capital gains tax purposes at that time except in limited circumstances, see CGTA
1979, s 147A in particular sub-s 2(d). Hence this form by varying the terms of s 31 enables the
conditions of s 71 to apply until the capital entitlement age, not exceeding twenty-five being attained,
so making hold-over relief available; see s 71(4)(a).

This form is included as para (iii) at the end of clause 10(b) of the comprehensive family will,
being form 1, at p 131 above. Accordingly, for its context and use, reference should be made to
that form and that clause.

61 Declaration resulting in income of the contingent share of a beneficiary who is under age being his for income tax purposes

The Trustee Act 1925 section 31 (or any statutory modification or re-enactment of it) shall not apply to the foregoing trusts and accordingly the income of the contingent share of the Trust Fund of each beneficiary as it arises shall belong to the beneficiary absolutely And thereafter during any period when the beneficiary is under the age of eighteen years my Trustees may pay or apply the whole or any part or parts of that income (whether or not it has been invested in accordance with their power under Clause   of this Will) to or for the benefit of the beneficiary in such manner as my Trustees shall think fit.

NOTE

The Court of Appeal decision of *Re Delamere's Settlement Trusts, Kenny v Cunningham-Reid* [1984] 1 All ER 584, [1984] 1 WLR 813, supports the conclusion that where any accumulated and capitalised income is the absolute and indefeasible property of a beneficiary who is under age that applies also for income tax purposes. Reference should be made to the comment on p 94 above.

The wording of this form is directed to avoiding the liability to additional rate tax under ICTA 1988, s 686, by making it clear that the income as it arises is the income of the beneficiary, before being distributed, for the purposes of s 686(2)(b).

62 Life interest to spouse and capital to children with declaration limiting their interests to protected ones

MY Trustees shall hold the Trust Fund upon the following trusts that is to say:

a) UPON TRUST to pay the income of the Trust Fund to my wife/husband during her/his life

b) SUBJECT as aforesaid UPON TRUST to hold the Trust Fund and its income for such of them my children namely

living three months after my death if more than one in equal shares with the qualification in the case of each of them that if he or she is then living the declaration and trusts comprised in the next clause of this Will shall apply PROVIDED THAT if any child has died in my lifetime or within three months after my death and issue of that child are living three months after my death and attain the age of twenty years such issue shall take by substitution if more than one as tenants in common in equal shares the share of the Trust

Fund which my deceased child would have taken (for which purposes the said qualification in the case of my children shall be ignored) had he or she been living three months after my death but so that no issue remoter than a child of my deceased child shall take whose parent is living and so capable of taking

[*Succeeding clause*]

a) IN connection with the qualification referred to in Clause   (b) of this Will I MAKE the declaration in sub-clause (b) about the share of the Trust Fund of each of my children

b) I HEREBY DECLARE that if my child survives me by three months his or her share shall be held upon the following trusts and with and subject to the following powers and provisions:
   i) UPON TRUST to hold the income thereof on protective trusts for the benefit of my child during his or her life
   ii) SUBJECT as aforesaid UPON TRUST to hold the capital and income thereof on those trusts that would have applied under Clause   (b) of this Will to the share of the Trust Fund of my child had he or she not been living three months after my death
   iii) IN addition to all other powers my Trustees shall have power (with the consent in writing of my wife/husband during her/his life in so far as the exercise of the power may affect her/his life interest under Clause   (a) hereof) at any time or times to raise capital out of my child's share of the Trust Fund for the purpose of paying or applying it to or for the benefit of him or her and I ALSO DECLARE that when considering whether or not to exercise this power my Trustees shall disregard the interests of any other beneficiaries in respect of his or her share and I FURTHER DECLARE that in particular my Trustees may exercise the foregoing power for the benefit of my child should he or she so request in connection with any appropriation of any of my personal chattels under the terms of Clause   of this Will which may accordingly be made in his or her favour free of any trust notwithstanding the trusts of this Clause

NOTE
It is possible that the children in question although adults, following the deaths of their parents, may become entitled to substantial assets at a time when they are financially inexperienced. The purpose of the above forms is to enable their shares of capital to remain under the control of the trustees who will then be enabled to educate the children in investment and financial matters, no doubt with the aid of investment advisers. When the time is considered ripe capital in the form of investments can be made over to a child absolutely. It is thought that the foregoing practical considerations will override the fact that, as the law stands at present, there would be a charge to capital gains tax, under CGTA 1979 s 54(1), without the likelihood of hold-over relief because of s 147A(2)(a); there being then no charge to IHT, see IHTA 1984, ss 49(1) and 88(2)(b).

63 Division of residue between spouse and children and/or issue on attaining 21 or marriage

MY TRUSTEES shall hold the Trust Fund upon the following trusts that is to say:

a) UPON TRUST to pay or transfer a   share of the capital of the Trust Fund to my wife/husband And my Trustees (unless my wife/husband otherwise requests in writing) shall appropriate my interest or share of whatever proportion nature or amount in (and in the future proceeds of sale thereof) any freehold or leasehold property at which I reside at the time of my death in (if the value thereof is at least equal to my wife's said share) or towards satisfaction of the same

b) SUBJECT as aforesaid UPON TRUST to pay or transfer or otherwise hold (as the case may be) the capital and income of the Trust Fund to or for my child or children etc etc (eg as per (b) of Form 59 above)

NOTE

The assumption behind this form is that the testator has decided to give some share of his assets to his children on his death. It must be emphasised that, even when an equal division between the spouse and children is directed, the children will in fact receive less, because s 41 states that notwithstanding the terms of any dispositions none of the IHT attributable to the value of property comprised in residue shall fall on any gift of a share of residue if or to the extent that the transfer is exempt with respect to the gift. If closer equality of distribution is required, it will thus be necessary to adjust and increase the fraction to which the children are to be entitled which would thereby of course also increase the IHT liability on the death.

64 Life interest to spouse and capital to children on surviving the spouse and attaining a specified age substituting if necessary their issue who attain 21 or a higher specified age or marry

MY TRUSTEES shall hold the Trust Fund upon the following trusts that is to say:

a) UPON TRUST to pay the income of (a   share of) the Trust Fund to my wife/husband during her/his life

b) SUBJECT as aforesaid UPON TRUST to pay or transfer or otherwise hold (as the case may be) the capital and income of the Trust Fund to or for my child or children living three months after the death of the survivor of myself and my wife/husband and attain the age of   years if more than one in equal shares PROVIDED THAT if any child has died in my lifetime (whether before or after the date of this Will) or in the lifetime of my wife/husband or having survived me and my wife/husband shall not be living three months after the death of the survivor of us or shall fail to attain the age of   years leaving issue living three months after the death of the survivor of myself my wife/husband and himself or herself who attain the age of   years (or marry under that age) or shall be living on the Perpetuity Day (as hereafter defined) such issue shall take by substitution if more than one as tenants in common in equal shares the share of the Trust Fund which such deceased child would have taken had he or she survived both me and my wife/husband and attained the age of   years but so that no issue remoter than a child of such deceased child shall take whose parent is living and so capable of taking And for the foregoing purpose the Perpetuity Day shall mean the day on which shall expire the period of eighty years from my death

NOTE

The capital interests of the beneficiaries, under (b) of this form, are expressed to be contingent on their being alive at the death of the surviving spouse. If the spouse is, under (a), to receive less than the whole income, while the trustees can exercise any available powers of appropriation, such as under (a) of Form 92, p 227 below, to set aside separate funds, this will not, in itself, accelerate the rights of the ultimate beneficiaries to receive capital. If that is in fact desired, wording along the lines of (b) of Form 59, p 200 above will be necessary, at any rate in relation to that part of the capital not supporting the current income interest of the surviving spouse.

65 Life interest to spouse and capital to children or remoter issue per stirpes and including provision for spouse of deceased child

MY TRUSTEES shall hold the Trust Fund upon and subject to the following trusts and powers that is to say:

a) UPON TRUST to pay the income of the Trust Fund to my wife/husband during her/his life

b) SUBJECT as aforesaid UPON TRUST to pay or transfer or otherwise hold (as the case may be) the capital and income of the Trust Fund to or for my child or children living three months after my death and attaining the age of   years if more than one in equal shares PROVIDED THAT if any child has died in my lifetime (whether before or after the date of this Will) or within three months after my death or having survived me shall die before attaining the age of   years and issue of that child are living three months after my death (and attain the age of twenty years) such issue shall take by substitution if more than one as tenants in common in equal shares the share of the Trust Fund which such deceased child would have taken had he or she been living three months after my death and attained the age of   years but so that no issue remoter than a child of such deceased child shall take whose parent is living and so capable of taking AND PROVIDED THAT in priority to the substitutional trusts by this sub-clause declared my Trustees may when any child of mine shall die before me or within three months after my death leaving a widow or widower him or her surviving pay to such widow or widower during her or his life the whole or such part as they may from time to time think fit of the income of the share of the Trust Fund which such deceased child would have taken had he or she been living three months after my death and attained the age of   years But so that my Trustees may at any time or times by deed or deeds wholly or partially release the power by this proviso conferred upon them

NOTE

The reason for this form is that from one's personal observations it is invariably the case that in the event of the death of a child, the child's own children are to be entitled to his share with no benefit going to the child's widow. Thus, any possibility of her benefiting depends on whether her husband happens or does not happen to survive his parent(s). The proviso under (b) is an attempt to suggest a method whereby the daughter-in-law, or son-in-law for that matter, can derive some limited benefit.

Because of the possible income rights of a child's widow(er) the share in which the widow(er) has a discretionary interest in income will be subject to the IHT regime in respect of settlements without an interest in possession: Inheritance Tax Act 1984, Part III, Ch III.

66 Life interest upon protective trusts

MY TRUSTEES shall hold the Trust Fund upon and with the following trusts and power that is to say:

a) UPON TRUST to hold the income of the Trust Fund upon protective trusts for the benefit of   for the period of his life

b) SUBJECT as aforesaid UPON TRUST to pay or transfer or otherwise hold (as the case may be) the capital and income of the Trust Fund to or for

c) IN addition to all other powers conferred by law or under this Will my Trustees (not being less than two in number) may at any time or times raise capital out of the Trust Fund for the purpose of paying it to or applying it for the benefit of the said   AND I DECLARE that when considering whether or not to exercise this power my Trustees shall disregard the interests of any other beneficiaries in the Trust Fund

NOTE

The Trustee Act 1925, s 33(1), provides that where income is held on protective trusts for 'the principal beneficiary' he is to receive it until such time as he, in summary, attempts to alienate his future right to it. In that event, during the rest of his former period of entitlement, a discretionary trust over the income comes into being in respect of which the principal beneficiary is included within the class of beneficiaries.

Thus, protective trusts, where appropriate, secure the income position of the beneficiary.

S 88 of the 1984 Act eliminates the IHT charge that would otherwise arise under s 52(1) on the forfeiture and termination of the principal beneficiary's interest in possession and provides that any such termination shall be disregarded. It also follows that a payment or application of capital, under the power contained in (c) of this form, will not give rise to an IHT charge. S 88 applies to settled property 'which is held on trusts to the like effect as those specified in section 33(1) of the Trustee Act 1925'. Because of the words 'to the like effect' it is considered best when drafting the wording not to depart from the trusts of s 33(1) unless, for any strong reason, it is necessary to do so.

67 Interests during life of a disabled beneficiary

MY TRUSTEES shall hold the Trust Fund upon and with the following trusts and powers that is to say:

a) DURING the lifetime of my son   UPON TRUST to pay or apply the whole or any part of the income of the Trust Fund to him or for his benefit or to or for the benefit of my other children and remoter issue from time to time living in such respective shares and in such respective manner as my Trustees shall from time to time in their absolute discretion think fit PROVIDED THAT my Trustees shall have power (notwithstanding the foregoing discretionary trust in respect of such income) during so much of the period of twenty-one years from my death as my said son is living to accumulate that part of the said income of the Trust Fund which has not been so paid or applied and adding it to the capital thereof

b) SUBJECT as aforesaid UPON TRUST to pay or transfer or otherwise hold (as the case may be) the capital and income of the Trust Fund to or for

c) IN ADDITION to all other powers conferred by law or under this Will my Trustees may during the lifetime of my said son at any time or times raise capital out of the Trust Fund for the purpose of paying it to or applying it for the benefit of my said son and my other children and remoter issue from time to time living in such shares and in such manner as my Trustees shall from time to time in their absolute discretion think fit

d) NOTWITHSTANDING anything that hereinbefore appears I DECLARE as follows:
   i) that my Trustees in considering and exercising their powers under sub-clauses (a) and (c) of this Clause for the benefit of my said son may disregard the interests of any other beneficiaries in the Trust Fund and its income
   ii) that on no account shall the power over capital under sub-clause (c) of this Clause be exercised so as to allow the total amount or value of the capital of the Trust Fund paid to or applied for the benefit of persons other than my said son to exceed the total amount or value of such capital paid to or applied for the benefit of my said son

NOTE
S 89 of the 1984 Act applies in the case of settled property where there is, in this case at the time of death, a person—
   a) incapable, by reason of mental disorder within the meaning of the Mental Health Act 1983, of administering his property or managing his affairs, or
   b) in receipt of an attendance allowance under s 35 of the Social Security Act 1975 or the Social Security (Northern Ireland) Act 1975.
S 89(1) and (2) provides that such a disabled person is to be treated for IHT purposes as having an interest in possession in trust capital despite there being in fact no interest in possession provided that the trusts secure that not less than half of the settled property which is applied during his life is applied for his benefit. It is thought that the reference to settled property is to its capital only - thus, the purpose of declaration (ii) in (d) of the above form.

The Capital Gains Tax Act 1979, Sch 1, para 5, provides that where settled property is held on trusts for a mentally disabled person the trustees may obtain the same annual exemption for capital gains tax purposes (£5,500 during 1991/92) as applies to individuals. The conditions are similar to but not the same as the IHT conditions. Under para 5(1) the trusts must secure that, during the lifetime of the mentally disabled person, not less than half of the property which is applied is applied for his benefit, *and* he is entitled to not less than half of the income arising from the property, or no such income may be applied for the benefit of any other person.

68 Division of residue between branches of family

MY TRUSTEES shall hold the Trust Fund UPON TRUST to divide the same into two equal moieties and to hold such moieties upon the following trusts that is to say:

a) As to one such equal moiety for the children of my son
namely   and   living at my death who attain the age of twenty-five years if more than one in equal shares absolutely but also as provided in sub-clause (c) of this Clause And subject as aforesaid (in the event of the foregoing trusts failing or determining) such moiety shall be paid or transferred to my said son absolutely

b) As to the other such equal moiety as to one-half thereof for my daughter
                            absolutely And subject as aforesaid (as to the whole but only in so far as the gift for my said daughter shall not take effect) for the children of my said daughter namely   and
living at my death who attain the age of twenty-five years if more than one in equal shares absolutely but also as provided in sub-clause (c) of this Clause And subject as aforesaid (as to the whole) such moiety shall be paid or transferred to my said daughter absolutely

c) Provided that if any grandchild has died in my lifetime or having survived me fails to attain the age of twenty-five years leaving issue living at the death of the survivor of myself and himself or herself who attain the age of twenty-one years or marry under that age such issue shall take by substitution if more than one as tenants in common in equal shares the share of the Trust Fund which the deceased grandchild would have taken had he or she survived me and attained the age of twenty-five years but so that no issue remoter than a child of the deceased grandchild shall take whose parent is living and so capable of taking

d) Provided also that if the foregoing trusts affecting either moiety under sub-clauses (a) and (b) of this Clause after taking into account the provisions of sub-clause (c) shall completely fail or determine such failed or determined moiety shall be added to the other moiety which has not so failed or determined and be held and disposed of accordingly

e) Each of them my said children and grandchildren for the purposes of this Clause shall be deemed to attain full age on attaining the age of twenty-one years and references to 'infancy' in the Trustee Act 1925 section 31 and any statute re-enacting or replacing the same shall be construed accordingly and references to 'twenty-one years' in the said section 31 (as originally enacted) shall be read as such

NOTE

This is sample wording available for adoption and adaptation according to what may be desired.

69 Eighty-year overriding power of appointment over residue having regard to section 144

a) MY Trustees shall pay or transfer or otherwise hold (as the case may be) the Trust Fund and its income to or for the benefit of any one or more of the following persons (including any born after my death) being my wife/husband and my children and my remoter issue and any person who is or has been a spouse of any child or remoter issue of mine (including of any who have died before me) at such age or time or respective ages or times in such shares and with and subject to such trusts and dispositive and administrative powers and provisions (including protective and discretionary trusts and powers exercisable at the discretion of my Trustees or any other person or persons) as my Trustees (not being less than two in number) may by any deed or deeds revocable or irrevocable appoint (regard being had to the law relating to remoteness) PROVIDED:
   i) that no appointment shall invalidate any prior payment or application of any part or parts of the capital or income of the Trust Fund;
   ii) that my Trustees may at any time or times by irrevocable deed extinguish or restrict the future exercise of this power of appointment; and
   iii) that without imposing any binding legal obligation I REQUEST my Trustees in exercising or not exercising or limiting this power of appointment to have regard to the future interests of the Family and for that purpose to discuss their intentions with my wife/husband before acting

b) I DECLARE that my Trustees may exercise their power of appointment under sub-clause (a) notwithstanding
   i) that Probate of this Will has not been obtained; or
   ii) that the administration of my estate has not been completed and the Trust Fund has not been fully quantified and established; or
   iii) that any of them will or may benefit as a result

NOTE

This form is drafted having regard to the provisions of s 144, p 91 above.

Reference should be made to C of ch 8, p 89 above. The trusts over residue for the spouse and children in default of and subject to any appointment by the trustees are contained in the next form. The two forms are the main part of the pattern of arrangements contemplated by forms 1, 2 and 3, pp 127 to 143 above, comprising a comprehensive family will, a memorandum directed to capital tax mitigation and a letter to accompany draft will.

Great care will be needed since a precondition of the use of s 144 is that not only must the property be settled by the will but there must *not* have been any interest in possession. The presence of the power of appointment will *not* itself preclude an interest in possession subsisting in the trusts in default of appointment.

The existence of the power of appointment also confers flexibility so that the trustees can make the best possible division, both from the points of view of personal and fiscal considerations including taking into account any intervening changes which could not have been foreseen. Accepting the decision of a testator to use such form, it would be convenient and helpful if he at the same time as making his will, made an informal but non-binding memorandum of wishes, to be up-dated by him as and when he desires, expressing his personal views on how the trustees should exercise their power of appointment, everything being equal.

70 Trusts over residue for spouse and children in default of and subject to any appointment by the executors and trustees

IN default of and until and subject to any appointment by my Trustees under Clause of this Will my Trustees shall hold the Trust Fund and its income upon the following trusts that is to say:

a) i) IF my wife/husband survives me by three months UPON TRUST to pay the income of the Trust Fund to my wife/husband during her/his life

ii) SUBJECT thereto (including when my wife/husband does not so survive me or dies during the following period) UPON TRUST until the end of the period of twenty-three months from my death to pay or apply the income of the Trust Fund to or for the benefit of any one or more of my children and remoter issue for the time being living

b) i) SUBJECT as aforesaid UPON TRUST to pay or transfer or otherwise hold (as the case may be) the capital and income of the Trust Fund to or for my child or children living three months after my death who attain the Vesting Age if more than one in equal shares PROVIDED THAT if any child has died in my lifetime (whether before or after the date of this Will) or within three months after my death or having survived me dies before attaining the Vesting Age and issue of that child are living three months after my death and attain the Vesting Age such issue shall take by substitution if more than one as tenants in common in equal shares the share of the Trust Fund which my deceased child would have taken had he or she been living three months after my death and attained the Vesting Age but so that no issue remoter than a child of my deceased child shall take whose parent is living and so capable of taking

ii) SUBJECT as aforesaid UPON TRUST to pay or transfer or otherwise hold (as the case may be) the capital and income of the Trust Fund to or for the following persons namely

living three months after my death who attain the Vesting Age if more than one in equal shares PROVIDED THAT if any of the said persons has died in my lifetime (whether before or after the date of this Will) or within three months after my death or having survived me dies before attaining the Vesting Age and issue of that person are living three months after my death and attain the Vesting Age such issue shall take by substitution if more than one as tenants in common in equal shares the share of the Trust Fund which such deceased person would have taken had he or she been living three months after my death and attained the Vesting Age but so that no issue remoter than a child of such deceased person shall take whose parent is living and so capable of taking

iii) THE expression 'the Vesting Age' means the age of twenty-five years or if earlier the age of the beneficiary on the day before the twenty-first anniversary of my death and I DECLARE that for the purposes of the Trustee Act 1925 section 31 (or any statutory modification or re-enactment of it) a beneficiary shall be deemed to attain full age on attaining the Vesting Age and references to 'infancy' and 'eighteen years' shall accordingly be varied and the right of my Trustees to pay or apply income to or for a beneficiary who has not attained the Vesting Age shall be exercisable as my Trustees in their absolute discretion think fit

NOTE
The above form contains the trusts which are to apply in default of and subject to any appointment by the trustees under the power of appointment contained in the preceding form. Likewise reference should be made to C of ch 8, p 89 above. It is part of the pattern of arrangements contemplated by forms 1, 2 and 3, pp 127 to 143, comprising a comprehensive family will, a memorandum directed to capital tax mitigation and a letter to accompany draft will.

71 Direction against lapse when child dies before testator

SUBJECT as aforesaid UPON TRUST to hold the capital and income of the Trust Fund for my children namely   and   in equal shares PROVIDED that if any of them dies before me I DIRECT that the gift of his or her share of the capital and income of the Trust Fund shall not lapse but shall go and devolve in the same way as if he or she had survived me and died immediately after my death PROVIDED that this direction shall take effect by way of direct gift to the persons or person beneficially interested under the Will or on the intestacy of my deceased child (as the case may be) and in the same manner thereunder but shall not make the foregoing gift part of his or her estate so as to be liable for his or her debts or to inheritance tax payable on his or her death

NOTE
It is surprising that a direction in the foregoing form is not used more frequently. If a child survives the testator, and in such manner to comply with any survivorship clause in the testator's will, he will have complete freedom of testamentary disposition over his inheritance, including for the benefit of his own spouse even if he himself dies shortly afterwards. Yet, if he predeceases the testator then, by the chance of timing, the child's family, in particular his widow, may also suffer the loss of his potential inheritance. So far as the testator is concerned, having survived his child he will be able, if necessary, to review the terms of his own will should he not like the effect for example of his deceased child's will. The actual circumstances will need to be considered. If desired the operative effect of the direction can be made conditional on the spouse or children of the deceased child being alive at the testator's death although of course by that means alone it will not necessarily follow that they will thereby be the substitute beneficiaries since that would depend on the terms of any will of the deceased child. If this direction is used there will need to be an addition to the wording of the survivorship clause in the testator's will, p 229 below, such as 'PROVIDED ALWAYS that this Clause shall not apply to the gift and trusts under sub-clause ( ) of Clause   of this Will'.

The use of this form will not have any IHT effect in relation to the estate of the deceased child.

72 Accruer clause

IF the trusts hereinbefore declared over any share of the Trust Fund shall fail or determine then from the date of the failure or determination that share (and any share or part of a share which may accrue thereto by virtue of this provision) shall accrue and be added to the other share or shares of the Trust Fund (and equally if more than one) the trusts of which shall not at that date have failed or determined and be held upon the like trusts and subject to the like powers and provisions as those affecting such other share or shares

NOTE
The assumption from the above wording is that all the shares of the trust fund are equal. If they are not the words in the second set of brackets can be altered to read: '(and if more than one in the proportion in which those shares then bear to each other)'.

73 Trusts when similar to previously expressed trusts

MY TRUSTEES shall hold the other moiety of the Trust Fund and the income thereof upon like trusts and subject to like powers and provisions in favour of   and his children and remoter issue and otherwise as are hereinbefore declared concerning the first moiety and its income as if the same trusts powers and provisions were herein repeated with the substitution of the name of the said   for that of the said

74 Exclusion of sections 1 and 19 of the Family Law Reform Act 1987

I DECLARE that the provisions of this Will shall be construed as though sections 1 and 19 of the Family Law Reform Act 1987 had not been enacted

NOTE

This form is a means by which illegitimate children and illegitimate remoter issue can be excluded from being beneficiaries. It will be appreciated that the exclusion of an illegitimate child could give rise to an application under the Inheritance (Provision for Family and Dependants) Act 1975.

Possibly wording on the following lines might be considered more satisfactory: '. . . for our children Matthew Mark Luke and John and such other child and children of my wife and myself born after the date hereof . . .'. On the assumption that the four Apostles are their joint children, the 'such' would seem to make it clear that any future children must likewise be joint offspring.

75 Declarations against or for ademption of testamentary gifts by lifetime gifts

I DECLARE that any lifetime gift made by me whether before or after the date of this Will to any of my children or any other beneficiary hereunder shall not be brought into account by him or her (or by any other person) against any testamentary gifts and benefits under this Will or any Codicil
or—
NOTWITHSTANDING the provisions for equality under Clause   (b) of this Will I DECLARE that if at any time any lifetime gift of any kind of a value at the time of the gift in excess of   HUNDRED POUNDS (£   ) has been or is made by me or my wife/husband since the   day of   One thousand nine hundred and ninety-   to any of my children or any other beneficiary a sum equal to the value of the gift at the time it is made (or the aggregate value of any such gifts if more than one) shall be brought into account by that child or other beneficiary (or by any other person or persons who shall take by substitution his or her share) as part of that child's or other beneficiary's share of the capital of the Trust Fund And for the purposes of this Clause as a whole when any gift is not one of cash my Trustees shall decide in such manner as they may in their absolute discretion consider fair whether its value exceeded the said sum of £   and if so what sum is to be brought into account

NOTE

Gifts made before the date of a will are not, in the absence of intention to the contrary, required to be brought into account under the doctrine against double portions. What specific provision will be required by a testator will depend on his wishes and the circumstances. The above forms enable a choice to be made. The second form can be adapted and completed, according to what may be desired and is intended to produce a working arrangement whereby, for example, run-of-the-mill presents are not to be brought into account and how values are to be arrived at when any gift is not one of cash.

76 Power for beneficiary to disclaim all or part of his entitlements

I DECLARE that any adult beneficiary may within two years after my death execute a deed to disclaim all or part (including a fraction or percentage) of his or her entitlements in this Will in which event what is disclaimed shall devolve under this Will as if he or she had died before me

NOTE
For the use of this form reference should be made to D of ch 9, p 101.

77 Power to transfer capital or make loans to spouse

a) IN addition to all other powers conferred by law or under this Will my Trustees (not being less than two in number) may at any time or times raise capital out of that part of the Trust Fund of which my wife/husband is then entitled to the income under sub-clause (a) of Clause   of this Will for the following purposes:
  i) for paying it to or applying it for the benefit of my wife/husband; or
  ii) for making loans to my wife/husband either with or without security and with or without interest and generally upon such terms and subject to such conditions as my Trustees decide and I DECLARE that my Trustees shall also have freedom to leave them outstanding during her/his life and that my Trustees shall not be liable for any loss to the Trust Fund because of the making of any loans or the failure to recover the amounts thereby owed before or after the death of my wife/husband
b) I DECLARE that when considering whether or not to exercise the foregoing power for my wife/husband my Trustees shall disregard the interests of any other beneficiaries in the Trust Fund

NOTE
The exercise of this power will not give rise to a charge to IHT; ss 49(1) and 53(2). The exercise may well give rise to a charge to CGT; see S of ch 5, p 65 above.

78 Power to apply income and capital for the benefit of capital beneficiaries

MY TRUSTEES shall have the following powers in addition to all other powers over any share of the Trust Fund:

a) SUBJECT always to the prior interest of my wife/husband under Clause ( ) of this Will the statutory power under the Trustee Act 1925 section 31 but with the right to pay or apply income for a beneficiary who is under age being exerciseable in every respect as my Trustees think fit and free from any necessity to restrict the amount of income to be paid or applied when other income is also available

b) POWER (with the consent in writing of my wife/husband during her/his lifetime insofar as the exercise of the power may affect her/his life interest under Clause ( ) of this Will) at any time or times to raise capital from the actual or potential share of the Trust Fund of any beneficiary and pay it to or apply it for the maintenance education or otherwise for the benefit of the beneficiary PROVIDED ALWAYS that the amount so paid or applied shall in due time be brought into account by the beneficiary or by any other person or persons who take by substitution the share of the beneficiary And PROVIDED FURTHER and notwithstanding anything that hereinbefore appears that my Trustees shall in no circumstances exercise this power or any other power other than for the personal benefit of the beneficiary to be benefitted nor in particular in such manner as to prevent limit or postpone the entitlement of that beneficiary to the presumptive interest in possession in his or her share of the capital of the Trust Fund

or—

a) POWER under the Trustee Act 1925 section 31 to apply income for maintenance and to accumulate surplus income during a minority but as if the words 'my Trustees think fit' were substituted in sub-section (1)(i) thereof for the words 'may in all the circumstances be reasonable' and as if the proviso at the end of sub-section (1) thereof was omitted

b) POWER under the Trustee Act 1925 section 32 to pay or apply capital for advancement or benefit but as if proviso (a) to sub-section (1) thereof stated that 'no payment or application shall be made to or for any person which exceeds altogether in amount the whole of the presumptive or vested share or interest of that person in the trust property or other than for the personal benefit of that person or in such manner as to prevent limit or postpone his or her interest in possession in that share or interest'

and—

c) POWER to exercise any of the foregoing powers notwithstanding that any of my Trustees may benefit personally as a result

NOTE
The above form gives alternative choices in relation to both (a) and (b). It has been assumed that if the surviving spouse is living (s)he has a life/income interest in the Trust Fund and therefore any exercise of the power under (a) will take effect following the termination of that interest, and that the power under (b) will require from the spouse, written consent for its exercise.

If the power under (b) is exercised, the transfer which would otherwise give rise to a charge to IHT under s 52(1) can qualify as a PET under s 3A because of s 3A(7): see p 46 above. It is also the case that under s 57 the transferor's exemptions under s 19 (£3,000 annual exemption) and under s 22 (gifts in consideration of marriage) can be set against the value of the underlying trust capital over which the transferor's life/income interest is relinquished; see s 57(3)–(5) for the terms and conditions applicable. It has been assumed that the main trusts of the will are in a form as comply with the conditions of s71. As the result of the principles which emerge from *Pilkington v IRC* [1964] AC 612, [1962] 3 All ER 622, HL, trustees may exercise their statutory power of advancement under the Trustee Act 1925, s 32 or any like power to create a sub-settlement for the benefit of a beneficiary. Though such other settlement may be for the overall benefit of the beneficiary, it need not necessarily provide that the beneficiary has an interest in possession not later than age 25. Accordingly, the question arises whether the existence, in itself, of the power of advancement will breach the conditions of s 71.

Although the second proviso in the alternative form (b) above is intended to protect the position, *Lord Inglewood v IRC* [1983] STC 133, CA, makes it clear that the existence of the statutory power of advancement or a similar power to like effect does not thereby create a breach of the conditions of s 71.

At one time the Inland Revenue were of the opinion that where a payment out of capital is made for the benefit of a beneficiary (other than for one whose interest is indefeasibly vested) of a type or for a use which constitutes recurring expense (eg school fees, including their commutation for a number of years, holidays and leisure expenses) in contrast to being for the acquisition of capital assets (eg house purchase, setting up in business and possibly car purchase), such a payment constituted income in the hands of the beneficiary and accordingly was chargeable to income tax. The Inland Revenue supported their opinion by reference to such cases as *Brodie's Will Trustees v IRC* (1933) 17 TC 432; *Lindus and Hortin v IRC* (1933) 17 TC 442; *Cunard's Trustees v IRC* [1946] 1 All ER 159, (1946) 27 TC 122, CA, and, *Jackson's Trustees v IRC* (1942) 25 TC 13. The unfortunate result would be, on the basis of that opinion, that the trustees need to deduct tax at basic rate (Income and Corporation Taxes Act 1988, ss 348 and 349) and, therefore, being paid out of capital, the tax on the grossed-up amount received by the beneficiary should be paid to the Inland Revenue; as a corollary the gross payment would be included within the beneficiary's income for tax purposes.

There has been the helpful and instructive decision of the Court of Appeal in *Stevenson v Wishart* [1987] 2 All ER 428, [1987] STC 266 which held that if trustees, in exercise of their power over capital, chose to make regular payments out of capital rather than release a single sum of a large amount that did not create an income interest for income tax purposes. Fox LJ, in the course of his judgment, gives three working examples which can be helpfully studied. One example was where property is held upon trust for a beneficiary absolutely upon attaining the age of 30. If the trustees, in exercise of their section 32 power, instead of making a single advance of a substantial amount make regular payments of capital to the beneficiary because they do not want him to have too much capital too quickly, the payments are capital payments and not income for income tax purposes.

79 Powers in relation to a business including farming

NOTWITHSTANDING the foregoing trusts my Trustees may in their absolute discretion whether or not in their own names or in the name of a company including one incorporated by them for that purpose carry on any trade or business including the business of farming which is carried on by me either alone or in partnership at the time of my death with any partner or partners whom I may have therein at my death or who may be admitted as hereafter provided AND I DECLARE that in carrying on any such trade or business my Trustees shall have the following powers viz:

a) To retain and employ in the trade or business or withdraw therefrom the whole or any part of my capital employed therein at my death and to use for the purposes of the trade or business any further part of the capital of the Trust Fund which they may think expedient

b) To charge or concur in charging the assets of the trade or business with the payment of any debts incurred in carrying on the same including moneys borrowed from a bank for the purpose of the trade or business together with any liability for interest thereon

c) Notwithstanding the trust contained in sub-clause ( ) of Clause   to set aside from time to time as a reserve fund for reserves replacements maintenance improvements and contingencies such part of the profits (whether earned before my death or to be earned thereafter) of the trade or business as my Trustees think fit and to retain and utilise the same in such manner as my Trustees think proper PROVIDED THAT if at any time my Trustees determine that the reserve fund or any part of it is no longer required and distribute it the amount distributed shall be treated as either income or capital of the Trust Fund or as partly one and partly the other as my Trustees decide. But no part of the profits earned more than twenty-one years after my death shall be treated as capital

d) To enter into any agreement or arrangement with any partner or partners in the trade or business for the extension renewal or curtailment of the partnership or alteration in the terms thereof and to admit or concur in admitting into partnership my wife my son (if he is not already a partner) or any person or persons whom my Trustees regard as being suitable on such terms as they decide

e) To employ in the trade or business such assistants whether qualified or not and others (including my wife/husband) during such period at such remuneration (whether or not wholly or to any extent dependent upon profits) and upon such terms and conditions in all respects as they decide

f) To leave the management of the trade or business to any partner or partners and accordingly to be free from any obligation of attending to the day-to-day management and otherwise beyond requiring an accounting and meeting at least once in every accounting year

g) To leave the management of the trade or business to any manager or managers whom my Trustees may appoint for that purpose at such remuneration (whether or not wholly or to any extent dependent upon profits) and upon such terms and conditions and with such powers authorities and discretion as my Trustees may delegate or otherwise agree

h) At any time to discontinue the trade or business and to wind up its affairs

i) To sell the trade or business upon such terms generally as they shall decide

PROVIDED ALWAYS AND I DECLARE that my Trustees shall not be liable to my estate or any person interested therein for any loss that may be incurred in carrying on the trade or business and that my Trustees and each of them shall be fully indemnified out of my estate against all liability which they may incur in connection therewith

NOTE
Trustees should be given proper specific power to undertake the running of a business, as their normal investment powers would not be sufficient for such purposes.

The reference in sub-clause (c) is to the sub-clause and clause in the will that provide for the income/ life interest in the residuary estate. That sub-clause could also have a cross-reference to sub-clause (c).

It is to be noted that if the power under (c) over income in fact amounts to a dispositive power, in contrast to an administrative power, as discussed in *Pearson v IRC* [1981] AC 753, [1980] 2 All ER 479, HL then that could preclude the person who would otherwise enjoy the life/income interest, as of right, in the residuary estate having an interest in possession for IHT purposes.

The wording to be used in the case of any particular business will need to be tailor-made in relation to the particular circumstances. Reference can conveniently be made to Form 38, p 182 above and the note to it. Clearly if the testator is a partner of a business, partnership arrangements and what happens in the event of his death should be taken into account. If the business is one where, from the professional point of view, there is no objection to it being conducted through a company, trustees may well wish for their own protection to be able to form one for that purpose. The opening words of the foregoing form allow for this.

80 Investment powers including power to retain or purchase a residence

MY Trustees shall have the following powers which they may exercise at any time and from time to time:
   a) POWER to invest trust moneys in both income-producing and non-income-producing assets of every kind and wherever situated and to vary investments and in those respects to act in the same full and unrestricted manner as if they themselves were absolutely entitled thereto beneficially [And without prejudice to the generality of the foregoing power my Trustees shall not be under any duty to diversify the investments comprised in the Trust Fund whether under section 6(1) of the Trustee Investments Act 1961 or otherwise]
   b) POWER to retain or purchase as an authorised investment any freehold or leasehold property or any interest or share therein of whatever nature proportion or amount (which shall be held upon trust to retain or sell the same) as a residence for my wife/husband and in the event of any such retention or purchase my Trustees shall have power to apply trust moneys in the erection alteration improvement or repair of any building on such freehold or leasehold property including one where there is any such interest or share And my Trustees shall also have power to decide (according to the circumstances generally) the terms and conditions in every respect upon which my wife/ husband may occupy and reside at the property (or have the benefit of the said interest or share therein) PROVIDED ALWAYS and I HEREBY DECLARE that no property or any share or interest in any property retained or purchased pursuant to the terms of the foregoing power is to be sold (or have interests granted thereout) by my Trustees without the consent in writing of my wife/ husband during her/his lifetime

NOTE

Trustees are required to invest their trust funds. An investment, in trust law, requires the provision of income for those entitled to it and therefore does not include the purchase of assets not producing income; *Re Wragg* [1919] 2 Ch 58 at 64, 65. Accordingly, sub-clause (a) gives the trustees wider powers with which to exercise their judgement, subject to the necessity for professional advice, see the Trustee Investments Act 1961, s 6 in particular sub-s (2). Any kind of investment can be authorised specifically; *Re Harari's Settlement Trusts* [1949] 1 All ER 430.

Apart from spelling out fully the particular powers of the trustees, sub-clause (b) in its terms overcomes the possibility that while wide investment powers authorise the purchase of land as an investment they do not in themselves authorise the purchase of a house for the purpose of providing a home for a beneficiary: see *Re Power's Will Trusts, Public Trustee v Hastings* [1947] Ch 572, [1947] 2 All ER 282.

It might be considered that the fairly smooth wording of sub-clause (b) is jarred by the insertion of wording specifically providing for the trust to retain or sell. It is felt best to include such wording as it is thought that in its absence (on the authority of *Re Hanson, Hanson v Eastwood* [1928] Ch 96) the property would become subject to the Settled Land Act 1925. S 25(4), Law of Property Act 1925, provides that a trust either to retain or sell land shall be construed as a trust to sell the land with power to postpone the sale.

Hallett *Conveyancing Precedents*, at 1029 and 1030, sets out a sombre warning that trustees for sale may be placed in serious difficulty in failing to sell an asset if they receive an offer in excess of its value. Accordingly, if it is felt that in any case this should be guarded against, it may be convenient if the consent in writing of a named person, such as the surviving spouse, is required for any sale, hence the proviso at the end of (b).

Sansom v Peay [1976] 3 All ER 375 [1976] STC 494 is authority for the capital gains tax exemption under the Capital Gains Tax Act 1979, s 104 applying in such circumstances. It is not necessary that the beneficiary should have a specific right of occupation. It is sufficient that the trustees pursuant to their rights in fact allow him to do so.

81 Power to invest in nominated company

I DECLARE:
   a) that for the purposes of their investment powers under Clause   my Trustees shall have power to retain and hold shares stock and debentures in   and may make loans to that company with or without interest and with or without security and upon such terms generally as my Trustees in their absolute discretion agree
   b) that if at or following my death whether by reason of amalgamation reconstruction takeover or otherwise the majority of the ordinary shares or stock of that company is held by another company the powers under sub-clause (a) shall also apply to that other company
   c) that in the event of their exercising the foregoing powers my Trustees shall not be liable to my estate or any person interested therein for any loss of any kind that may result and
   d) that without prejudice to any protection or indemnity otherwise available my Trustees shall not be liable for any loss sustained by investing or retaining an investment in any company and its shares producing no income or little

income whether or not that investment forms the whole or a major part of the Trust Fund

NOTE
Any investment can be authorised expressly by the will; *Re Harari's Settlement Trusts* [1949] 1 All ER 430.

S 6(1) of the Trustee Investments Act 1961 requires trustees in general in choosing investments to have regard to the need for diversification of investments of the trust, in so far as is appropriate to the circumstances of the particular trust and to the suitability to the trust of investments of the description proposed and of the investment proposed as an investment of that description. Nevertheless, there will be cases where it is desirable that a large investment in a single company, such as a family one, should be retained in the interests of the beneficiaries as a whole.

82 Power to place investments or other assets in name of nominee

a) MY TRUSTEES shall have power to place or purchase any investment or other asset in the names or name of any persons or person or company (whether or not resident in the United Kingdom) as nominees or nominee of them my Trustees and to remunerate such nominees or nominee

b) MY TRUSTEES shall not in any circumstances be liable for allowing any investment or other asset to remain for any period however long in the name of a nominee and for any loss which may arise by reason of their doing so

NOTE
The general rule is that trust property must be under the sole control and in the names of the trustees. While any decisions are for the trustees alone, it could well facilitate matters in the case of a large trust for the investments to be in the name of a nominee.

This power could also be useful where there is land abroad or shares in overseas companies which, as the result of local law, cannot be placed into the names of the English executors.

83 Power to delegate investment management and power to place investments in name of nominee

a) MY Trustees shall also have the following powers which they may exercise at any time and from time to time in relation to all or any part of the Trust Fund:
   i) POWER to employ the services of an Authorised Manager;
   ii) POWER to delegate the exercise of their power to invest trust moneys (including for the purpose of holding or placing them on deposit pending investment) and to vary investments to an Authorised Manager; and

    iii) POWER to allow any investment or other asset to be held in the names or name of an Authorised Manager as nominees or nominee of my Trustees

b) IN relation to the exercise of each of the foregoing powers:

    i) The expression 'Authorised Manager' means any company or any persons or person (whether or not being or including one or more of my Trustees) that my Trustees in their absolute discretion consider suitable for the purposes of the exercise of their respective powers and for obtaining investment advice

    ii) My Trustees shall decide the terms and conditions in every respect including the period thereof and the commission fees or other remuneration payable therefor which commission fees or other remuneration shall be paid out of the capital and income of that part of the Trust Fund in respect of which they are incurred or of any property held on the same trusts

c) PROVIDED ALWAYS AND I DECLARE that my Trustees shall not be liable for any loss arising from any act or omission by an Authorised Manager in whose favour they shall have exercised their powers under this Clause

NOTE

As a matter of law and practice trustees in exercise of their powers of investment should obtain proper professional advice after which they themselves make their investment decisions. At the same time the general rule is that trust property including investments should be under the sole control and in the names of the trustees.

As a matter of business, having regard to current conditions in the City of London, the view may well be taken that any set of trustees having chosen carefully their stockbrokers or other professional investment advisers can derive better investment advantage by delegating to them their power to make and implement investment decisions. Also, by placing the investments into the name of the nominee company of the investment managers concerned, the paperwork including the need for the circulation of and signing by the trustees of sale transfers and dividend mandates will be reduced.

84 Provisions applicable to trustees where there is a substantial company holding

MY Trustees may with a view to qualifying one or more of them to act as a director or directors of any company of which any shares or stock form part of the Trust Fund transfer to any one or more of my Trustees such a number of shares in such company as may be necessary to qualify that trustee to act as a director of such company and any shares so transferred shall be held by that trustee upon the trusts hereof and on that trustee ceasing to act as a director of such company the shares so transferred to him shall forthwith be re-transferred to my Trustees

ANY of my Trustees who shall be or become a director or the holder of any other office or employment in any company any of whose shares shall form part of the Trust Fund or which is controlled by another company any of whose shares form part of the Trust Fund shall be entitled to retain for his own use and benefit any fees or remuneration received by him in connection with such office or employment notwithstanding that his appointment to or retention of such office or employment may be directly or indirectly due to the exercise or non-exercise of any votes in respect of shares forming part of the Trust Fund

NOTWITHSTANDING anything hereinbefore contained I DECLARE that my Trustees although they may do so shall not be bound or required to interfere in the management or conduct of the business of any company of which any shares or stock form part of the Trust Fund

NOTE

The assumption is that the testator is a major shareholder, and possibly a working director, in a particular company and that he wishes his executors and trustees to perpetuate the family involvement in it despite his death.

Consideration should be given to the exclusion of the need for diversification powers required by the Trustee Investments Act 1961, s 6(1); see the words in square brackets at the end of (a) of Form 80, p 218 above – and the specific power to hold an investment in a nominated company – see Form 81, p 219 above.

With regard to the concluding declaration see *Re Lucking's Will Trusts, Renwick v Lucking* [1967] 3 All ER 726, [1968] 1 WLR 866.

85 Power (simple) to retain or purchase chattels

MY TRUSTEES shall have power to retain or purchase as authorised investments any personal chattels (as defined by the Administration of Estates Act 1925) for use enjoyment or possession by my wife/husband and in the event of any such retention or purchase my Trustees shall have power to obtain valuations and cause inventories to be made and to repair improve and alter the form or fashion of any of them and to meet any costs and expenses in the exercise of their powers out of the capital and income of the Trust Fund in such manner as they shall in their absolute discretion determine And my Trustees shall also have power to decide (according to the circumstances generally) the terms and conditions in every respect including in relation to insurance upon which my wife/husband may use enjoy or possess any such personal chattels PROVIDED ALWAYS and I HEREBY DECLARE as follows:

- i) None of such personal chattels retained or purchased pursuant to the terms of the foregoing power which is used enjoyed or possessed by my wife/husband shall be sold by my Trustees without her/his consent in writing during her/his lifetime
- ii) Notwithstanding anything contained in this clause my Trustees shall not be obliged to make or cause to be made any valuations or any inventory of any such personal chattels and shall not be liable for any loss injury or damage that may happen to them from any cause whatsoever and any failure on the part of anyone to effect or maintain any insurance

NOTE

The above form contains a run-of-the-mill power over chattels to be added to the usual investment powers contained in a will. This is in contrast to the next form.

86 Power (elaborate) to retain or purchase chattels

a) I DECLARE that without prejudice to the generality of their investment powers under Clause   ( ) my Trustees may retain and purchase chattels of every description And in respect thereof they shall have the following powers:
   i) Power to retain the chattels in question under their joint control and custody or the control and custody of any of them or to store the same (whether in a depository or warehouse or elsewhere);
   ii) Power to lend all or any of the chattels to any person or persons or body or bodies (including a museum or gallery) upon such terms and conditions as my Trustees decide;
   iii) Power to cause inventories to be made;
   iv) Power to insure against loss or damage by fire burglary and theft and such other risks and for such amounts as my Trustees may from time to time decide;
   v) Power generally to make such arrangements for their safe custody repair insurance and use as having regard to the circumstances my Trustees may from time to time think expedient;
   vi) Power to exchange such chattels or any of them or alter the form or fashion thereof or substitute other chattels for the same or any of them or let the same or any of them for a period (not exceeding seven years) to a person who covenants with my Trustees to keep the same in repair and insured and not (without the consent of my Trustees) to assign or part with the possession thereof;
   vii) Power to sell the chattels or any of them; and
   viii) Power to treat any money received as the result of any insurance insofar as not used in reinstating replacing or repairing any chattel lost or damaged as if it was the proceeds of sale of the chattel insured
b) In the case of any of the chattels of which a person of full age and capacity is entitled to the use but when such person's interest is less than an absolute one my Trustees shall also have the following powers:
   i) Power to cause an inventory of such chattels to be made in duplicate with a view to one part being signed by the beneficiary for retention by my Trustees and the other part to be kept by the beneficiary and to cause any such inventory to be revised as occasion shall require and the parts thereof altered accordingly;
   ii) Power to require the beneficiary to arrange at his or her expense for the safe custody repair and insurance of such chattels in such manner as my Trustees think expedient; and
   iii) Power (where it is not practicable so to require the beneficiary) to make such arrangements as are referred to under paragraph (v) of sub-clause (a) of this Clause
c) My Trustees shall also have power to meet any expenses which they may incur in the exercise of any of the powers referred to in this Clause out of the Trust Fund and its income or such one or more of any different parts of the Trust Fund and the income thereof as they shall decide
d) Notwithstanding anything contained in this Clause my Trustees shall not be

obliged to make or cause to be made any inventories of any such chattels that may be held and shall not be liable for any loss injury or damage that may happen to any such chattels from any cause whatsoever and any failure on the part of anyone to effect or maintain any insurance

NOTE
The powers contained in this form are more elaborate than the powers under the previous form which can be included as additions to the usual investment powers contained in a will. The above form can be used where there are articles of artistic or historic importance and adjusted to meet the particular circumstances.

87 Power to borrow

MY TRUSTEES shall have power to borrow money upon such terms and subject to such conditions including in relation to repayment and interest and whether or not upon the security of the Trust Fund or any part thereof and for such purposes in connection with the administration of my estate and the trusts of this Will as my Trustees think fit but no lender shall be concerned about the purpose of any such loan to my Trustees or the circumstances or the propriety thereof

NOTE
The power for trustees to borrow under the Trustee Act 1925, s 16, is a restricted one. The above power could be useful in modern conditions.

88 Power to enter into transactions with other trusts having common trustees

MY TRUSTEES shall have power to enter into any contract or other dealing or disposition (whether by way of sale purchase exchange mortgage lease loan borrowing or otherwise) with the trustees of any other Will or any settlement or trust or policy (being a contract or other dealing or disposition which apart from this present provision my Trustees could lawfully have entered into if none of them had also been a trustee of such other Will or such settlement or trust or policy) notwithstanding that my Trustees or any one or more of them shall also be trustees or the sole trustee of such other Will or such settlement or trust or policy and in like manner in all respects as though none of my Trustees had been a trustee of such other Will or such settlement or trust or policy

NOTE
In view of the need for avoiding any conflict of duty, as a general rule trustees should not enter into business relationships with other trustees where there are persons who are common trustees of both sets of trusts. This could cause inconvenience: see the observations on p 62 above.

89 Power to insure

MY TRUSTEES shall have power to insure under comprehensive or any other cover and against any risks and for any amounts (including allowing as they deem appropriate for any possible effects of inflation and increasing building or replacement costs and expenses) any asset which forms part of the Trust Fund irrespective of who may use or enjoy it And the insurance premiums may be discharged by my Trustees either out of income or out of capital (or partly out of one and partly out of the other) as my Trustees in their absolute discretion decide and any moneys received by my Trustees as the result of any insurance insofar as not used in rebuilding reinstating replacing or repairing the asset lost or damaged shall be treated as if they were the proceeds of sale of the asset insured PROVIDED ALWAYS that my Trustees shall not be under any responsibility to insure or be liable for any loss that may result from any failure to do so or for the inadequacy of any policy they effect

NOTE
The above form extends very materially the power to insure under the Trustee Act 1925, s 19, and may be more in keeping with modern conditions.

90 Powers of management over landed property

IN ADDITION to their powers under Clause   of this Will and in addition to any powers of management conferred by law my Trustees shall have the following powers:
  a) Power to sell exchange convey lease mortgage charge agree to let license and otherwise conduct the management of any landed property which is part of the Trust Fund and generally have all the rights and powers in respect thereof as if they my Trustees were absolutely entitled thereto beneficially and may in that behalf make any outlay out of income or capital (or partly out of one and partly out of the other) as they shall decide
  b) Power in relation to any freehold or leasehold property which (or its future proceeds of sale) is part of the Trust Fund to apply capital or income (or partly one and partly the other) for the purposes of the erection improvement or repair of any building on any such property as they decide
  c) Power to cultivate improve and manage any freehold or leasehold farm or any subject to a tenancy held by me at the time of my death either alone or in partnership
  d) Power to sell the live and dead stock on any such farm and the crops raised on the same and any other produce
  e) Power to buy live and dead stock seeds and manures
  f) Power to buy and sell machinery implements vehicles motor cars and equipment

of every kind for use whether wholly or partly or for ancillary purposes in any way connected with any such farm

g) Power to erect add to convert rebuild reconstruct and demolish buildings of any kind

h) Power generally to manage any such farm as my Trustees may from time to time and in such manner decide

NOTE

The Law of Property Act 1925, s 28(1), confers upon trustees for sale the same powers of management of a tenant for life under the Settled Land Act 1925. Such powers are limited, as for example those of leasing under s 41 of the latter Act. Accordingly, the powers in the above form could be important if landed property of any kind, including commercial property, is likely to be held.

91 Powers personal to the trustees

NOTWITHSTANDING any general rules of law to the contrary my Trustees and each of them shall have the following powers which may be exercised at any time and from time to time:

a) Power for any of my Trustees to purchase from my Trustees (not being less than two in number) any asset comprised in the Trust Fund provided that:

   i) in the case of investments quoted on any Stock Exchange in the United Kingdom the purchase price is not less than the middle market price thereof at the time of the execution of the transfer;

   ii) in the case of investments not so quoted the purchase price is not less than their open market value as certified by the auditors of the company or by some properly qualified person whom my Trustees shall appoint for such purpose; and

   iii) in the case of any other asset the purchase price is not less than the open market value as certified by a properly qualified valuer whom my Trustees shall appoint for such purpose

And provided also that in cases within (ii) and (iii) any such auditors properly qualified person or valuer in their or his report for such purpose have not advised against the sale by my Trustees for any reason whatsoever

b) Power to be employed and remunerated as a director or other officer or employee or as agent or adviser of any company or other corporation or undertaking or firm whatsoever at any time with any connection with assets comprised in the Trust Fund

c) Power to retain as remuneration fees or profits received by him or her in any such capacity as is mentioned under sub-clause (b) of this Clause notwithstanding that his or her situation or office as such director officer employee agent or adviser may have been obtained or may be held or retained in right or by means or by reason of his or her position as one of my Trustees or any shares stock property rights or powers comprised in or connected with the Trust Fund

AND I DECLARE that my Trustees although they may do so shall not be bound or required to interfere in the management or conduct of the business of any company of which any shares or stock form part of the Trust Fund

NOTE

This form is intended to overcome a number of legal difficulties with which a trustee may, personally, otherwise be faced.

1. The basic rule is that a trustee must not make a profit from his position as trustee; see for example the statement of the rule by Russell J in *Williams v Barton* [1927] 2 Ch 9.
2. A further consequence of that rule is that a trustee cannot have any dealings with the trust property except in his capacity as a trustee; see *Keech v Sandford* [1726] Sel Cas Ch 61.
3. Likewise, a trustee is accountable for any profit or other advantage he obtains from his fiduciary position; see *Phipps v Boardman* [1967] 2 AC 46, [1966] 3 All ER 721, HL.
4. With regard to the concluding declaration see *Re Lucking's Will Trusts, Renwick v Lucking* [1967] 3 All ER 726, [1968] 1 WLR 866.

92 Power of appropriation

a) MY Trustees shall have power at any time or times to appropriate any part of my residuary estate or of the Trust Fund (as the case may be) in its then actual condition or state of investment in or towards satisfaction of any legacy or any share in the Trust Fund (whether or not the same is settled including by exercise of their power of appointment in Clause   ) without needing the consent of anyone

b) WHEN placing a value on any of my personal chattels (as defined by the Administration of Estates Act 1925) so appropriated my Trustees may use the same value as has been placed on it by any Valuers they instruct for inheritance tax purposes on the death of myself or of my wife/husband (as the case may be) or such other value as they in their absolute discretion decide is fair

c) AS a supplement to their power in sub-clause (a) of this Clause my Trustees (as the executors of this Will) for the purposes of satisfying in whole or in part the settled legacy in Clause   may grant a charge (with or without payment of interest and whether or not repayable on demand) over any part of my residuary estate or of the Trust Fund (as the case may be) to secure the whole or part of that settled legacy And in that event my Trustees (as trustees of the trusts in Clause   ) shall accept the charge for the amount so secured as being in or towards satisfaction of the settled legacy

[d) NOTWITHSTANDING the provisions of sub-clause (b) of this Clause my Trustees in respect of any of my personal chattels which being articles of national scientific historic or artistic interest are treated on the particular death as a conditionally exempt transfer for the purposes of the Inheritance Tax Act 1984 section 30 (or any statutory modification or re-enactment thereof) shall in respect of any appropriation place such lesser value as they in their absolute discretion consider fair after taking into account all facts and surrounding circumstances as they consider relevant including the fact that inheritance tax for which conditional exemption was obtained will be payable by the beneficiary on there being a subsequent chargeable event]

THE powers in this Clause can be exercised by my Trustees notwithstanding that any of them may benefit personally as a result

NOTE
Where there is a large cash legacy it is often decided, in order to help save the legatee the trouble of investing his money, to hand over securities in all or part satisfaction of it. Without this clause his formal consent to such an arrangement will be required. By the Stamp Duty (Exempt Instruments) Regulations 1987, SI 1987/516, subject to a written certificate in the manner prescribed, the appropriation of property within the terms of the Finance Act 1985, s 84(4) (death: appropriation in satisfaction of a general legacy of money) is exempt from stamp duty.

This form may also be helpful in the case of appropriations generally. (b) [and (d)] are intended to provide a working formula when chattels are taken as part of a beneficiary's entitlement. As a general rule, apart from the need to be fair between the beneficiaries as a whole, any appropriation should be based on valuations as at the date of the appropriation. In the case of quoted stocks and shares there is no difficulty about valuation. In the case of chattels which have already been valued for IHT purposes, it is considered that, on a rough and ready basis, the same valuation should also be used for any appropriation of chattels made during the course of an administration [It is considered that it would not be fair that a beneficiary should take a conditionally exempt article at 100% of its value when in his hands it will be subject to a charge to IHT should he ever sell it or otherwise breach the conditions for exemption.]

c) is included as Clause 14(c) of form no 1, p 127 above, being the comprehensive family will. It assumes the possibility that the testator cannot take advantage of his nil% band for IHT purposes for satisfying the discretionary trust legacy, under its Clause 7, without recourse to his interest in the family home. (c) is intended as a means of overcoming that difficulty.

93 Exclusion of apportionment rules

IN connection with the administration of my estate and the trusts of this Will:
   a) Where any payment in the nature of income received after the occurrence of any event (including my own death) would (but for this sub-clause) fall to be treated as accruing partly (or wholly) before that event it shall be treated as accruing wholly after that event [Provided that:
      i) This sub-clause shall not apply to any payment in the nature of income received after my death as a result of my having been an Underwriting Member of Lloyd's
      (AND/OR)
      ii) My Trustees shall have power (to be exercised in writing) at any time or times within [one year] from any such event to declare this sub-clause to be inapplicable either generally or in regard to particular payments]
   b) Income from any investment or other asset which remains unsold shall be treated as if it is income from an investment authorised by Clause   of this Will
   c) No investment or other asset not producing income shall be treated as if it does
   d) My debts and funeral and testamentary expenses (including inheritance tax payable from my residuary estate) and legacies shall be paid from the capital of my estate without recourse to its income

NOTE

Without this clause, dividends etc received after the date of death need to be apportioned as between capital and income, the income often going to the surviving spouse. Inevitably during the early months immediately following the death, the dividends etc received cover, in whole or in part, a period prior to the date of death, and so the surviving spouse would receive little or no income. This clause might be considered fair, and it will help generally in simplifying the accountancy side of the administration.

For tax purposes, when a dividend is received after death, no apportionment is made. No part of the payment should be included in the Tax Return of the deceased's income to the date of death (*IRC v Henderson's Executors* (1931) 16 TC 282). There is however an exception where a particular company has declared a dividend before the death with payment not postponed to a post-death date, so that it in fact belonged to the deceased before his death. Dividends received post-death will therefore generally be included in the Tax Return made by the personal representatives. Where there is a non-apportionment clause, the effect will be that dividends received after death will belong to the life tenant and be grossed up and treated as his or her total income for the particular tax year, for higher rate tax purposes. Where the income is likely to be large it may be advisable not to exclude the effect of the Apportionment Act 1870, if necessary compensating the life tenant with a cash legacy. This could be the case where the testator is an underwriting member of Lloyd's or in a business where he receives delayed remuneration, such as commission and bonuses. Either or both of the two provisos to (a) of this form can be included, when appropriate.

This clause, apart from excluding the operation of the Apportionment Act 1870, is intended to exclude the operation of the equitable rules emanating from *Howe v Earl of Dartmouth* (1802) 7 Ves 137, *Re Earl of Chesterfield's Trusts* (1883) 24 Ch D 643 and *Allhusen v Whittell* (1867) LR 4 Eq 295. Briefly, the first can attribute a lesser income than that received from a wasting or unauthorised asset, the second is a corollary of the first and can cause income to be due to the life tenant from capital which does not, in fact, produce income, such as a reversionary interest, and the third can deny to the life tenant the benefit of income from capital that is realised to meet capital taxes, debts and legacies.

Where the rules of equitable apportionment, not having been excluded, require apportionments to be made the resulting sums are capital. Accordingly, for example, any sum attributed to the life tenant should not be included in his Tax Return.

This clause is also intended to exclude an effect of *Re Joel's Will Trusts, Rogerson v Brudenell-Bruce* [1967] Ch 14, [1966] 2 All ER 482, which held that where a class of persons was entitled to a fund on attaining a specific age the death or birth of a member of such class gave rise to an apportionment, so that each member enjoyed only that portion of the income attributable to the time when he was alive.

94 Survivorship clause

ANY person who does not survive me by (   ) month(s) shall be deemed to have died before me for ascertaining the devolution of my estate and its income

NOTE

This form is worded having in mind s 92(1). It provides in effect that where a will lays down a condition of survival of a period of not more than six months, for IHT purposes, whether the primary beneficiary so survives or not the resultant gift is to be treated as taking effect from the time of death.

Other statutory provisions that should be noted are:

a) The Law of Property Act 1925, s 184, provides, with regard to the devolution of property, that where two or more persons have died in circumstances rendering it uncertain which of them survived the other(s), the younger shall be deemed to have survived the elder.

b) Ss 4(2) and 54(4) state, for the purposes of IHT on death, that where it cannot be known which of two or more persons who have died survived the other or others they shall be assumed to have died at the same instant.

It will probably be the case that the inclusion of a survivorship clause meets the wishes of the testator who should consider and state the destination of any particular testamentary gift in the event of the death of the primary beneficiary. As the result of the Wills Act 1837, s 33, had he, for example, made a gift of a piece of jewellery to a child, which was not made conditional on survivorship, and that child predeceased him leaving issue living at the testator's death, the gift would not lapse but fall into the child's estate as if the child had in fact survived the testator. Although s 33 was amended by the Administration of Justice Act 1982, to produce what may well be a fairer result so far as concerns the issue of the deceased child, the foregoing observations remain valid.

There can be circumstances where the presence of a period for survival can increase the aggregate IHT liability. That is when the less wealthy has not sufficient assets to take full advantage of the nil% band.

c) S 18(3) allows the spouse exemption to apply if the period for survival does not exceed twelve months.

d) S 141 provides quick succession relief against IHT for the free estate of a deceased and settled property in which he had an interest in possession, see p 22 above.

95 Payment and incidence of IHT on legacies and lifetime chargeable transfers previously PETs

I DIRECT that the gifts made by Clauses   and   of this Will and any Codicil shall be free of inheritance tax [and all other taxes and duties (if any) payable on or by reason of my death (including any payable outside the United Kingdom)]

I ALSO DIRECT that any inheritance tax or additional inheritance tax payable as the result of a gift or settlement which I have made from assets that belonged to me absolutely shall be borne by my residuary estate in exoneration of the beneficiary or beneficiaries thereof and that the resultant gift because of this direction shall also have the benefit of the first direction under this Clause

PROVIDED ALWAYS and I HEREBY EXPRESSLY DECLARE that the prior provisions of this Clause shall not apply to any of my assets (whether or not specifically given under this Will or any Codicil) in respect of which my Trustees (who shall have an absolute discretion whether or not to do so) claim exemption from inheritance tax on my death under Chapter II of Part II of the Inheritance Tax Act 1984 (or any statutory modification or re-enactment thereof) which provides for conditional relief for articles of national scientific historic or artistic interest

With regard to the accountability and incidence of IHT reference should be made to pp 26 and 71 above and consideration give, according to the circumstances, to the final form the wording of any such clause should take in the particular will.

96 Powers directed to section 142

I DECLARE that any beneficiary under this Will who is not under age may enter into any deed or other instrument for the purpose of altering the dispositions or provisions of this Will and also may disclaim all or part (including a fraction or percentage of) his or her entitlements in this Will (PLUS IF REQUIRED)
AND I ALSO DECLARE that my Trustees shall have power at their absolute discretion to enter into for the purposes of giving consent any deed or other instrument altering the dispositions or provisions of this Will on behalf of any beneficiary who is under age or a patient within the meaning of the Mental Health Act 1983 or who is unborn or unascertained (or any group or groups of such persons) PROVIDED THAT my Trustees shall exercise such second mentioned power only if satisfied that to do so is for the benefit of such beneficiary or beneficiaries

NOTE
Reference should be made to ch 9, p 98 above. Reference should also be made to Form 76, p 214 in respect of disclaimers.

The first declaration is intended as an aide memoire to the family, the executors and their advisers that it may be appropriate that the likely IHT consequences, both present and future, should be considered in the interests of all those concerned. It is not suggested that without such a declaration the right to vary is not available. While s 142 provides for a two-year period, if the right is to be exercised it should be considered as soon as possible following the death.

The circumstances in which the second declaration could be used, and the need for it, will be a matter of judgment. It presupposes that there is a life tenant and that a general and negotiated re-arrangement of the trusts with the remaindermen, some of whom may not be sui juris, would be beneficial. It is hoped that by this method the need for an application to the court under the Variation of Trusts Act 1958 can be avoided.

97 Indemnity for executors and trustees

IN connection with the administration of my estate and the trusts of this Will none of my Trustees shall be personally liable for any breach of trust or any loss thereby arising to the Trust Fund whether by way of commission or omission done or suffered including any loss suffered by reason of any improper investment or for the negligence or fraud of any agent employed by him or by any other of my Trustees although the employment of such agent was not strictly necessary or expedient unless it shall be proved that he had acted mala fide And in particular without prejudice to the generality of the foregoing provisions none of my Trustees shall be bound to take any proceedings against any person who is or has been one of my Trustees or the personal representatives of any such person for any breach or alleged breach of trust committed or suffered by any such person

NOTE

While this form is included, its use will require careful thought. Its effect is to increase the protection given to trustees by the Trustee Act 1925, s 30(1), and, possibly, to exempt a trustee from liability for a failure to discharge his duties properly. Such a clause may fall foul of the Unfair Contract Terms Act 1977.

98 Executor and trustee charging clauses

ANY of my executors or trustees being a person engaged in any profession or business shall be entitled to charge and be paid all usual professional or other charges for business transacted time expended and acts done by that person or their firm or company or any partner or employee in connection with the administration of my estate and the trusts of this Will including acts which an executor or trustee not being in any profession or business could or might have done personally [And money payable under the foregoing provision shall not be liable to abatement by reason of any legacy gift or direction as to priority of payment of legacies contained under this Will or any Codicil and shall be paid free of all deductions]

or—

ANY of my executors or trustees being a person engaged in any profession or business shall be entitled (a) to charge and be paid all usual professional or other charges for business transacted time expended and acts done by that person or their firm or company or any partner or employee in connection with the administration of my estate and the trusts of this Will including acts which an executor or trustee not being in any profession or business could or might have done personally and (b) to retain or receive whether or not personally any brokerage or commission of a normal nature for any stockbroking or insurance transaction undertaken by that person or their firm or company

NOTE

Remarks of the court in *Re Chapple, Newton v Chapman* (1884) 27 Ch D 584, indicate that a wide charging clause, such as the above, enabling a solicitor-executor or trustee to charge for all the work he does, should only be included in a will on express instructions.

A power to charge is construed as equivalent to a legacy and accordingly the charges should abate rateably with the other general legacies upon a deficiency of assets; *Re Barber, Burgess v Vinnicome* (1886) 31 Ch D 665. The wording of the proviso in the first of such forms, which is aimed at preventing such abatement, is based on wording produced by The Law Society: see *Law Notes* [1919] 138.

The first form is along conventional lines. The second is in wider terms and may be more in keeping with modern conditions and what happens in practice.

99 Testimonium and attestation clauses

IN WITNESS whereof I have hereunto set my hand the day and year first above written

SIGNED by the above-named Testator(trix)

as his (her) Will in the presence of us both present at the same time who in his (her) presence at his (her) request and in the presence of each other have hereunto subscribed our names as witnesses:

or—

SIGNED by the Testator(trix) in our joint presence and then by us in his (her) presence:

NOTE

Where there is property abroad consideration should be given to the following matters, in so far as the execution of the will is concerned:

   a) The need for three witnesses.
   b) The need for the testator and witnesses to sign at the bottom of each page of the will.
   c) The need for the will to be executed under seal.

If there is property abroad, the law of the country concerned will have to be considered, since it may have an effect on the devolution of the property concerned notwithstanding the terms of any will.

The foregoing remarks in relation to the execution of wills may, in fact, be over cautious. The Wills Act 1963, and similar law introduced in other countries which assented to and implemented The Hague Convention on the Conflict of Laws relating to the Form of Testamentary Dispositions was aimed at rationalising generally throughout the world the formalities for the execution of wills. Accordingly, under section 1 of the 1963 Act a will is to be treated as properly executed if its execution conformed to the internal law in force in the territory where it was executed, or in the territory where, at the time of its execution or of the testator's death, he was domiciled or had his habitual residence, or in a state of which, at either of those times, he was a national.

100 Provisions in relation to regular payments under family protection policy

I hold a Family Protection Policy No.   with the
Company Limited under which:
   a) a capital sum of £   becomes payable on the   day of
                       One thousand nine hundred and   or on my
      death prior to that date and
   b) should I die on or before the   day of   One
      thousand nine hundred and   a further capital sum not
      exceeding £   becomes payable by equal quarterly instalments of £

each on the terms as stated in the special provisions contained in the above-mentioned Policy

NOW I DIRECT

i) that the capital sum referred to in (a) above shall be treated as capital and shall fall into and form part of my residuary estate and
ii) that the equal quarterly instalments of £   each referred to in (b) above shall be paid to my wife during her life

NOTE

This form is aimed at preventing the quarterly instalments being treated as capital in the hands of the trustees. In a case where the testator leaves the income of his residuary estate to his wife for her life, unless a clause on the lines of the above example is included in his will she will not receive certain benefits of the family protection policy, even though they would seem to be an important part of such a policy. If no such provision is made all the moneys payable under the policy will be treated as capital. This would, of course, equally apply if the wife had predeceased her husband and the children were under age. If the power of advancement has been suitably enlarged (this could be done either by special wording or adjusting or adding to Form 78, p 215 above) the trustees will have power to use all the instalment benefits for their welfare while they are under age. Nevertheless, unless the interests of the children are indefeasibly vested, there could be income tax complications; see note under that form.

It would appear that according to the present law and Inland Revenue practice there is no liability to income tax on the instalment benefits paid to the wife.

101 Letter about signing will

Dear

I enclose your Will for signature. Will you please read through its terms again to make sure that it is exactly as you would wish.

Assuming everything is in order, you should execute the Will in accordance with the accompanying form of explanation.

If you should have difficulty in finding witnesses you may like to come here to sign your will or go along to a local bank for that purpose.

I look forward to hearing from you when you have executed the Will.

Yours sincerely,

NOTE

This letter is to be sent with a copy of the next form which contains the formalities for execution and other requirements. Reference should also be made to its note.

102 Form setting out formalities for signing will or codicil

1. Two witnesses are needed. They can best be persons of age and should of course be clear sighted. They themselves, and their spouses, should be completely independent and not referred to or in any way interested under the terms of the document whether as a beneficiary or as an executor and trustee. In case of difficulty in finding suitable witnesses a visit to this office may be convenient or alternatively you could go along to a local bank for that purpose.

2. Complete in ink the date in words, not figures, at the beginning/end.

3. There is no requirement or need for the witnesses to read the document although they should be told what it is.

4. Sign in ink by using all your initials and your surname, where indicated at the end, in the presence of the two witnesses.

5. The witnesses should then themselves sign in ink in your presence adding their addresses and occupations. If their writing is difficult to read please supply the necessary details.

6. Accordingly, all three of you should be together and see each other sign in sequence and complete the formalities.

7. It is to be emphasised that nothing must ever be pinned or attached to the document *including by paper clip when returning it to us* as that can lead to future difficulties.

8. A stamped addressed envelope accompanies the document so that you can return it. Two copies will be made, one for your private papers and the other for our file.

9. Please state where you wish the document to be lodged, whether in our strongroom or sent to your bank, in which case please confirm the name of the bank and its address, or returned to you.

Date

NOTE

This form for the signing of the will is in keeping with conventional practice. In fact the requirements are, on close examination, in excess of those under the Wills Act 1837, s 9, but bear in mind the Non-Contentious Probate Rules 1987, SI 1987/2024 r 12. When there is an aged testator or one who has suffered a serious illness, reference should be made to *Re Simpson* (1977) 121 Sol Jo 224; see p 8 above.

There is no mention in the form that where alterations are required they should be made before the will is executed and that they should be initialled by the testator and the two witnesses. Whether or not some reference is made to this point is a matter of choice but it is suggested that even though the solicitor may not in fact be required to retain the completed will it should be returned to him for inspection. He can then check that the formalities have been complied with (see *Ross v Caunters* p 4 above) apart from providing himself with a completed copy for his file. If a copy of the will goes to the client it may be considered good practice if it is endorsed with a note of where the original is kept.

103 Law Society's Personal Assets Log

Record of Will and Important Documents

> This Personal Assets Log is a record issued by Solicitors for you to fill in as a practical reminder of where a Will and related important papers are kept, and of useful people to contact in the event of a death or accident.
> It is not itself a legal document. The answers to the numbered questions should be filled in once you have made your Will.

1. PERSONAL DETAILS

   Name ....

   Address..
   ....
   ....
   Tel: ....

2. SOLICITORS TO CONTACT

   Name ....

   Address..
   ....
   ....
   Tel: ....

[DETAILS OF WILL]

3. Place where original Will is kept

4. Is Cremation requested?

5. Date of Will

6. Date of any Codicils

7. Executors' names, addresses, telephone nos.
   (There may be 1, 2, 3 or 4 Executors)

8. Bank Account with

9. Properties:
   Your House deeds
   Your Mortgage with
   Other Properties

10. Premium Bonds

11. Savings books, Pass books, Savings Certificates

12. Shares Certificates

13. Insurance Policies

14. Birth, Marriage, Adoption etc. Certificates

15. Other

NOTE
This, with adaptation for present purposes, is a reproduction of the four page Personal Assets Log which is available for sale in packs of 50 at £8.95 (inc p & p) per pack to solicitors only, from the Law Society's Publications Department, 50 Chancery Lane, London WC2A 1SX. It is highly recommended and copies of it can usefully be supplied to testators for use when they have completed their Wills.

104 Draft of a bill

(Name and address)
VAT No
Reference   Date

Period 199 to 199	Costs	Tax		Total due
		%	Amount	
To our professional services in connection with the following: a) Advising on the implications and effects of Inheritance Tax and the exemptions available. b) The making of your Will dated 199 including taking instructions and giving general advice, the examination of (documents, accounts, title deeds, policies, etc), the preparation of a draft, its amendment where necessary, engrossing it for your signature and supplying a copy. c) (Additional work arising out of advice on IHT implications involving) d) And all other work in respect of the foregoing, including telephone calls, correspondence and meetings with you and with etc				
Taxable disbursements				
Non-taxable disbursements				
Total amount payable				

Please note that in respect of an account for non-contentious business you have the right to require us within one month to obtain a Remuneration Certificate from the Law Society (under para 1 Article 3 Solicitors Remuneration Order 1972) and to apply to the Court for a taxation of the account (under the Provisions of the Solicitors Act 1974). The Solicitors Remuneration Order 1972 provides that interest is chargeable in respect of non-contentious work commencing one month after the delivery of the account if the account is not paid within that period.

NOTE

The format of a bill and its wording are very much a matter of taste and inclination.

The form of wording used is intended to suggest, particularly with IHT in mind, that the making of a will is either a tax planning exercise itself or can be part of more detailed arrangements.

So that the bill can be used only as a Tax Invoice for VAT purposes the narrative of the bill could be limited to 'Provision of legal services' and a separate statement topped 'Details of legal services referred to in accompanying Tax Invoice (No   )' and tailed 'This detailed narrative has been typed separately to preserve the confidentiality of the matter should it be necessary to produce a tax invoice to Customs and Excise'.

As is usual these days in the case of traders, there could be a suitably prepared tear-off strip at the bottom of the bill and words inserted on the bill like 'Please detach the lower portion and send it with your remittance. If you require a receipt, please return the entire bill'.

105 Common parts of a codicil

I   of   in the County of   DECLARE this to
be a (   ) Codicil to my Will which is dated the   day of
                    19   the former Codicil(s) to which is/are (respectively) dated the
                    day of   19

(2. IN all other respects I confirm my Will and Codicil(s))
IN WITNESS whereof I have hereunto set my hand this   day of
                    199
SIGNED by the above-named Testator (trix)
                    as a Codicil to his (her)
Will in the presence of us both present at the
same time who in his (her) presence at his (her)
request and in the presence of each other have
hereunto subscribed our names as witnesses:

. . . .

. . . .

NOTE

In the case of a will, as appears from, for example, Forms 12, 13 and 14, pp 164 and 165 above, one's personal preference is to include the date of execution at the commencement rather than in the testimonium. On the other hand, in the case of a codicil, one's preference is to include the date in the testimonium, having in mind that in the commencement there will already be at least one date mentioned, being in respect of the will.

Clause 2 is a matter of choice. The effect of a confirmation generally is, subject to any contrary intention, to up-date the date of the will to that of the codicil itself. As a rule of thumb, one's inclination is only to include such confirmation if it be the case that the particular testator has, in fact, been through his will as a whole, and indicated that it is indeed up-to-date in relation to his present wishes.

106　Statement under the Inheritance (Provision for Family and Dependants) Act 1975, section 21

I DECLARE that under the Will that I have signed (to-day) I have not made any financial provision for　　　　　　　　　having taken into account the following circumstances:

A.

B.

C.

NOTE

This form is included as an aide memoire having regard to s 21 which provides that in any proceedings under the 1975 Act a statement made by the deceased, whether orally or in a document or otherwise, shall be admissible under the Civil Evidence Act 1968, s 2, as evidence of any fact stated therein. While it would be possible to include such a statement in a will itself it is suggested that normally it is best made as a separate document since the will becomes public following the grant of probate.

Because of the variety of individual circumstances it is clearly not possible to produce a general precedent. Reference should be made to the commentary on this Act in ch 11, p 110 above. In preparing such a statement a testator should have regard to the matters which the court is required to take into account for the purpose of assessing reasonable financial provision for any possible applicant. The court may consider the testator's statement by virtue of s 3(1)(g).

Part IV. Post-Death Deeds and Miscellaneous
        Precedents

107 Deed of Variation of Will for purposes of Inheritance Tax Act 1984, section 142(1), and Capital Gains Tax Act 1979, section 49(6)

THIS DEED OF VARIATION is made the   day of   One thousand nine hundred and ninety-   BETWEEN   of   in the County of   (hereinafter called 'Mr   ') of the first part and   of   in the County of   and   of   in the County of   (hereinafter together called 'the Beneficiaries') of the second part and   of   in the County of   and   of   in the County of   (hereinafter together called 'the Executors') of the third part SUPPLEMENTAL to the Will dated the   day of   One thousand nine hundred and   (and a Codicil dated the   day of   One thousand nine hundred and   ) of   (hereinafter called 'the Testator') who died on the   day of One thousand nine hundred and ninety-   which Will (and Codicil) was on the   day of   One thousand nine hundred and ninety-   proved by the Executors in the Principal Registry of the Family Division of the High Court of Justice (has not yet been proved and the administration is incomplete)

WHEREAS:

a) By Clause   of the said Will and in the events that have happened it is provided that

And the wording and terms of the said Clause are set out verbatim in the First Schedule hereto

b) For divers good causes and considerations and in order to help (his family and in particular) the Beneficiaries Mr   wishes to enter into this Deed for the purposes and in the manner hereinafter appearing

c) This Deed is also entered into having regard to the terms of Section 142(1) Inheritance Tax Act 1984 (inheritance tax) and Section 49(6) Capital Gains Tax Act 1979 (capital gains tax)

NOW THIS DEED made in pursuance of the said wish WITNESSETH and IT IS HEREBY DECLARED as follows:

1. THE said Will shall be read and construed and take effect and be deemed to have taken effect as from the death of the Testator as if in place of the wording and terms of the said Clause   of the said Will as set out in the First Schedule

hereto there were substituted the wording and terms set out in the Second Schedule hereto

2. FOR the purposes of giving further effect to Clause 1 hereof Mr
and the Beneficiaries HEREBY TOGETHER IRREVOCABLY DIRECT the Executors when administering the estate of the Testator to give effect to the terms of this Deed

3. THE PARTIES hereto HEREBY MAKE the elections set out in the Third Schedule hereto

4. IT IS HEREBY CERTIFIED that this Deed falls within Category M in the Schedule to the Stamp Duty (Exempt Instruments) Regulations 1987
IN WITNESS etc

THE FIRST SCHEDULE above referred to
The wording and terms of Clause   of the said Will of the Testator

THE SECOND SCHEDULE above referred to
The wording and terms of Clause   of the said Will of the Testator as treated as substituted by Clause 1 of this Deed

THE THIRD SCHEDULE above referred to
Elections by the parties hereto under Section 142(2) Inheritance Tax Act 1984 (inheritance tax) and Section 49(7) Capital Gains Tax Act 1979 (capital gains tax)
To the Board of Inland Revenue
> We who are the parties to this Deed hereby give you notice that we jointly elect (as is confirmed by our execution of it) that the terms of Section 142(1) Inheritance Tax Act 1984 and Section 49(6) Capital Gains Tax Act 1979 shall apply. We are instructing our Solicitors to produce this Deed to you within six months after the date hereof.

NOTE
See generally ch 9, p 97 above.

108 Deed of Variation of Will for purposes of Inheritance Tax Act 1984, section 142(1), and Capital Gains Tax Act 1979, section 49(6), following deaths of husband and wife within two years of each other

THIS DEED OF VARIATION is made the   day of   One thousand nine hundred and ninety-   BETWEEN DOREEN JONES of   in the County of   and ABEL SOLICITOR of   in the County of (hereinafter together called 'the late Mrs Smith's Executors') of the first part CHARLES SMITH of   in the County of   and the said Doreen Jones (hereinafter together called 'the Beneficiaries') of the second part and the said Charles Smith and the said Abel Solicitor (hereinafter together called 'the late Mr Smith's Executors') of the third part SUPPLEMENTAL to the Will dated the   day of   One thousand nine hundred and   of Arthur Smith (hereinafter called 'Mr Smith') who died on the   day of One thousand nine hundred and ninety-   which Will was on the   day of   One thousand nine hundred and ninety-   proved by Bertha Smith and the late Mr Smith's Executors in the Principal Registry of the Family Division of the High Court of Justice (has not yet been proved and the administration is incomplete)

WHEREAS:

a) By his said Will Mr Smith having appointed his wife the said Bertha Smith (hereinafter called 'Mrs Smith') and the late Mr Smith's Executors to be his executors and trustees devised and bequeathed all his real and personal property whatsoever and wheresoever (but subject to the payment of his debts and funeral and testamentary expenses) to Mrs Smith if she survived him by one month and failing her so doing there were substitutional gifts and trusts in his said Will

b) Mrs Smith did survive Mr Smith by one month but died on the   day of   One thousand nine hundred and ninety-   that date being within the period of two years following the death of Mr Smith

c) The Will of Mrs Smith which was dated the   day of One thousand nine hundred and ninety-   was on the   day of One thousand nine hundred and ninety-   duly proved by the late Mrs Smith's Executors in the Principal Registry of the Family Division of the High Court of Justice (has not yet been proved and the administration is incomplete)

d) By her said Will Mrs Smith having appointed Mr Smith (who predeceased her) and Mrs Smith's Executors to be her executors and trustees (in the events which have happened and in particular the death of Mr Smith) devised and bequeathed all her real and personal property whatsoever and wheresoever (but subject to the payment of her debts and funeral and testamentary expenses) to such of them her children the said Charles Smith and Doreen Jones as should survive her by one month if both of them in equal shares and failing either or both of them so doing there were substitutional gifts and trusts in her said Will

e) The Beneficiaries (being the said Charles Smith and Doreen Jones) did survive Mrs Smith by one month and both of them are over the age of eighteen years

f) For divers good causes and considerations and in particular to reduce the aggregate amount of inheritance tax payable on the respective deaths of Mr Smith and Mrs Smith the late Mrs Smith's Executors (at the request and concurrence of the Beneficiaries which are testified by their execution hereof) wish to enter into this Deed for the purposes and in the manner hereinafter appearing

g) This Deed is also entered into having regard to the terms of Section 142(1) Inheritance Tax Act 1984 (inheritance tax) and Section 49(6) Capital Gains Tax Act 1979 (capital gains tax)

NOW THIS DEED made in pursuance of the said wish WITNESSETH and IT IS HEREBY DECLARED as follows:

1. THE said Will of Mr Smith shall be read and construed and take effect and be deemed to have taken effect as from the death of Mr Smith as if therein and in priority to the said devise and bequest of his real and personal property he had given two legacies in the wording and terms set out in the First Schedule hereto

[2. FOR the purpose of giving further effect to Clause 1 hereof the late Mrs Smith's Executors and the Beneficiaries HEREBY TOGETHER IRREVOCABLY DIRECT the late Mr Smith's Executors when administering the estate of the late Mr Smith to give effect to the terms of this Deed]

3. THE PARTIES hereto HEREBY MAKE the elections set out in the Second Schedule hereto

4. IT IS HEREBY CERTIFIED that this Deed falls within Category M in the Schedule to the Stamp Duty (Exempt Instruments) Regulations 1987

THE FIRST SCHEDULE above referred to

The wording and terms of the said two legacies deemed to have been contained in the said Will of Mr Smith

'a) I GIVE a legacy of   thousand pounds (£   ) to each of them my children being the said Charles Smith and Doreen Jones

b) PROVIDED that each of the said legacies shall bear its own share of any inheritance tax payable on or by reason of my death

c) MY Executors and Trustees shall have power to appropriate any part of my residuary estate in its then actual condition or state of investment in or towards satisfaction of each of the foregoing legacies without needing the consent of the beneficiary thereof'

THE SECOND SCHEDULE above referred to

Elections by the parties hereto under Section 142(2) Inheritance Tax Act 1984 (inheritance tax) and Section 49(7) Capital Gains Tax Act 1979 (capital gains tax)

To the Board of Inland Revenue

We who are the parties to this Deed hereby give you notice that we jointly elect (as is confirmed by our execution of it) that the terms of Section 142(1) Inheritance Tax Act 1984 and Section 49(6) Capital Gains Tax Act 1979 shall apply. We are instructing our Solicitors to produce this Deed to you within six months after the date hereof.

NOTE
See generally ch 9, p 97 above, in particular at p 100.

109 Deed of Variation of Will for purposes of Inheritance Tax Act 1984, section 142(1), by absolute beneficiary who constitutes discretionary trusts over part of her inheritance

THIS DEED OF VARIATION is made the   day of   One thousand
nine hundred and ninety-   BETWEEN
of
(hereinafter called 'Mrs   ') of the one part
and   of
and   of
(hereinafter called 'the Executors') of the other part

SUPPLEMENTAL to the Will dated the   day of   One thousand
nine hundred and ninety-   of   (hereinafter called 'the Testator')
who died on the   day of   One thousand nine hundred and
ninety-   which Will was on the   day of   One
thousand nine hundred and ninety-   proved by the Executors in the
Principal Registry of the Family Division of the High Court of Justice but the
administration is incomplete

WHEREAS:—

a) By Clause   of the said Will Mrs   is the sole beneficiary of the
   Estate of the Testator And the wording and terms of that clause are set out
   verbatim in the First Schedule hereto
b) For divers good causes and considerations Mrs   wishes to enter
   into this Deed for the purposes and in the manner hereinafter appearing
c) This Deed is also entered into having regard to the terms of Section 142(1)
   Inheritance Tax Act 1984 (inheritance tax)

NOW THIS DEED made in pursuance of the said wish WITNESSETH and IT IS HEREBY
DECLARED as follows:—

1. THE said Will shall be read and construed and take effect and be deemed to
have taken effect from the death of the Testator as if in place of the said wording
and terms of the said Clause   of the Will there were substituted the wording
and terms set out in the Second Schedule hereto

2. MRS   HEREBY IRREVOCABLY DIRECTS the Executors when administering the Estate of the Testator to give effect to the terms of this Deed

3. THE PARTIES hereto HEREBY MAKE the elections contained in the Third Schedule
hereto

4. IT IS HEREBY CERTIFIED that this Deed falls within Category M in the Schedule
to the Stamp Duty (Exempt Instruments) Regulations 1987

IN WITNESS etc

THE FIRST SCHEDULE above referred to
The wording and terms of Clause   of the said Will of the Testator
'I GIVE all my estate both real and personal whatsoever and wheresoever to my
wife   absolutely'

THE SECOND SCHEDULE above referred to
The wording and terms of Clauses   and   to be treated as substituted for those
of Clause   of the said Will by Clause 1 of this Deed

'a) I GIVE to   and   (hereinafter called "the Original
Trustees") the sum of £   to hold upon the trusts and with and
subject to the powers and provisions hereinafter declared concerning the Legacy
Fund PROVIDED ALWAYS that first this gift shall bear its own share of any
inheritance tax and all other like taxes and duties payable on or by reason
of my death and that secondly this gift shall not carry interest until payment

b) CONJOINTLY with my Executors the Original Trustees may have appropriated
to them and receive any part of my residuary property and assets in or towards
satisfaction of the said sum of £
(And in connection with the foregoing power my Executors and the Original
Trustees may jointly fix such value on whatever is so appropriated as they
in their absolute discretion consider fair whether or not following advice from
a duly qualified valuer)

c) IN this Clause the following expressions have the following meanings:
"The Trustees" means the Original Trustees or the trustees and trustee of
these trusts whether original or substituted or added
"The Legacy Fund" means the said sum of £   and the assets for the
time being representing it
"The Trust Period" means the period starting with the date of my death
and ending eighty years later (and that period is the perpetuity period applicable
hereto)
"The Beneficiaries" means those of the following persons living at my death
or born during the Trust Period being my wife   and my
children and my remoter issue and any person who is or has been a spouse
of any child or remoter issue of mine (including of any who have died before
me)

d) THE Trustees shall have power which they may exercise at any time and from
time to time to invest trust moneys in both income producing and non-income
producing assets of every kind and wherever situated and to vary investments
and in those respects to act in the same full and unrestricted manner as if
they themselves were absolutely entitled thereto beneficially

e) THE Trustees shall pay or transfer or otherwise hold (as the case may be)
the Legacy Fund and its income to or for the benefit of any one or more
of the Beneficiaries at such age or time or respective ages or times in such
shares and with and subject to such trusts and dispositive and administrative
powers and provisions (including protective and discretionary trusts and powers
exercisable at the discretion of the Trustees or any other person or persons)

as the Trustees (not being less than two in number) may during the Trust Period by any deed or deeds revocable or irrevocable appoint (regard being had to the law relating to remoteness)

PROVIDED:
  i) that no appointment shall invalidate any prior payment or application of any part or parts of the capital or income of the Legacy Fund
  ii) that no power of revocation reserved to the Trustees in any appointment shall be capable of being exercised after the end of the Trust Period; and
  iii) that the Trustees may during the Trust Period at any time or times by irrevocable deed extinguish or restrict the future exercise of this power of appointment

f) IN default of and until and subject to any appointment by the Trustees under sub-clause (e) of this Clause the Trustees shall hold the Legacy Fund upon the following trusts:
  i) UNTIL the end of the Trust Period UPON TRUST to pay or apply the income of the Legacy Fund with power from time to time to pay or apply the whole or any part or parts of the capital of the Legacy Fund to or for the benefit of any one or more of the Beneficiaries for the time being living PROVIDED THAT the Trustees may (notwithstanding the foregoing discretionary trust in respect of that income) during the period of twenty-one years from my death from time to time accumulate the whole or any part of the income of the Legacy Fund at compound interest by investing it and its resulting income in any investments authorised by sub-clause (d) of this Clause and adding the accumulations to the capital of the Legacy Fund
  ii) SUBJECT as aforesaid UPON TRUST for my wife the said absolutely

g) THE Trustees shall have power at any time or times to appropriate any part of the Legacy Fund in its then actual condition or state of investment in or towards any share in the Legacy Fund (including after any exercise of their power of appointment under sub-clause (e) of this Clause) without needing the consent of anyone

h) ANY of the Trustees who is engaged in any profession or business shall be entitled to charge and be paid all usual professional and other charges for business transacted time spent and acts done by him or any partner or employee of his in connection with the trusts under this Clause including acts which a trustee not being in any profession or business could have done personally

i) ANY of the Trustees may join in exercising any of the trusts and powers under this Clause notwithstanding that he or she is one of the Beneficiaries and will or may benefit as a result

j) I DECLARE but without imposing any binding legal obligation on them that it is my wish first that the Trustees shall regard my wife during her lifetime as the primary beneficiary of both the income and capital of the Legacy Fund and secondly that as soon as possible after the death of my wife the Trustees shall exercise their powers over the capital of the Legacy Fund by distributing it to my children then living if more than one in equal shares but subject to the issue of a deceased child being entitled to the particular share in such proportions and at such time and subject to such trusts and conditions as the Trustees decide

I GIVE all my estate both real and personal whatsoever and wheresoever not otherwise effectively disposed of by this Will to my wife the said   absolutely'

THE THIRD SCHEDULE above referred to
Election by the parties hereto under Section 142(2) Inheritance Tax Act 1984

To the Board of Inland Revenue
We who are the parties to this Deed hereby give you notice that we jointly elect (as is confirmed by our execution of it) that the terms of Section 142(1) Inheritance Tax Act 1984 shall apply. We are instructing our solicitors to produce this Deed to you within six months after the date hereof.

NOTE
See generally ch 9, p 97 above, in particular at p 101.

It is possible to achieve, after the death of the testator, a better result by a deed, under section 142(1), whereby, for example, an adult beneficiary varies the will in such manner that inherited assets are directed to be held upon the trusts of two newly constituted settlements with different dates, for the separate groups of his family. Those settlements commencing on separate days are not related to each other within the terms of section 62(1). In the latter respect, see also observations on p 79 above.

110 Deed for purposes of Inheritance Tax Act 1984, section 142(1), varying disposition of a joint beneficial interest in freehold property which has accrued by survivorship to surviving spouse

THIS DEED OF VARIATION is made the   day of   One thousand nine hundred and ninety-   BETWEEN BERTHA SMITH of   in the County of   (hereinafter called 'Mrs Smith') of the first part CHARLES SMITH of   in the County of   (hereinafter called 'Charles Smith') of the second part and DOREEN JONES of   in the County of   (hereinafter called 'Doreen Jones') of the third part and the said Bertha Smith and ABEL SOLICITOR of   in the County of   (hereinafter together called 'the late Mr Smith's Executors') of the fourth part and the said ABEL SOLICITOR (hereinafter called 'Mr Solicitor') of the fifth part

WHEREAS:

a) Arthur Smith (hereinafter called 'the late Mr Smith') died on the   day
   of   One thousand nine hundred and ninety-
                    and his Will was on the   day of   One
   thousand nine hundred and ninety-   proved by Mr Smith's
   Executors in the Principal Registry of the Family Division of the High Court
   of Justice

b) Immediately prior to his death the late Mr Smith and Mrs Smith were the
   joint owners of the freehold property (hereinafter called 'the Property') known
   as 5 The Close in the City of Barchester and they held it and the future
   net proceeds of sale and any income therefrom until sale in trust for themselves
   as beneficial joint tenants so that in the event of the death of either of them
   the survivor would become the sole owner

c) Accordingly as the result of the death of the late Mr Smith his severable
   share of the beneficial interest in the Property which was included in his estate
   immediately before his death for the purpose of inheritance tax accrued by
   survivorship to Mrs Smith

d) Mrs Smith wishes to vary the disposition of the said severable share of the
   beneficial interest in the Property in the manner hereafter appearing for the
   benefit of her children being Charles Smith and Doreen Jones

e) This Deed is also entered into having regard to the terms of Section 142(1)
   of the Inheritance Tax Act 1984

NOW THIS DEED WITNESSETH as follows:

I. MRS SMITH HEREBY DECLARES as follows:

a) That it shall be deemed to be the case that shortly before the death of the
   late Mr Smith the two of them had by mutual notice in writing to each other
   severed their beneficial tenancy in the Property and its future proceeds of
   sale to the intent that thenceforward they held the Property and its future
   proceeds of sale and any income therefrom until sale in trust for themselves
   as beneficial tenants in common in equal shares

b) That the said Will of the late Mr Smith shall be read and construed and
   take effect and be deemed to have taken effect from his death as if it included
   a gift to take priority over the gift of his residuary estate (to which Mrs Smith
   is entitled) in the wording and terms set out in the First Schedule hereto

2 MRS SMITH and Charles Smith and Doreen Jones HEREBY JOINTLY AND SEVERALLY
COVENANT with the late Mr Smith's Executors and separately with Mr Solicitor
to pay forthwith any additional inheritance tax (including any interest thereon) as
the result of the variation by this Deed of the dispositions of the property comprised
in the estate of the late Mr Smith immediately before his death

3. THE parties hereto including the late Mr Smith's Executors HEREBY MAKE the
election contained in the second Schedule hereto

4. IT IS HEREBY CERTIFIED that this Deed falls within Category M in the Schedule to the Stamp Duty (Exempt Instruments) Regulations 1987

IN WITNESS etc

THE FIRST SCHEDULE above referred to

The wording and terms of the gift deemed to have been included in the Will of the late Mr Smith

'I GIVE free of inheritance tax to my children CHARLES SMITH and DOREEN JONES in equal share my beneficial share in the property known as 5 The Close in the City of Barchester and in its future proceeds of sale and any income therefrom until sale PROVIDED that this gift is subject to the condition that the trust for sale over the said property shall not be enforced during the lifetime of my wife the said Bertha Smith without her consent in writing'

THE SECOND SCHEDULE above referred to

Election by the parties hereto under Section 142(2) Inheritance Tax Act 1984

To the Board of Inland Revenue

We who are the parties to this Deed hereby give you notice that we jointly elect (as is confirmed by our execution of it) that the terms of Section 142(1) Inheritance Tax Act 1984 shall apply. We are instructing our solicitors to produce this Deed to you within six months after the date hereof.

NOTE

See generally ch 9, p 97 above, in particular at p 98.

111 Deed of disclaimer

THIS DISCLAIMER made the   day of   199   BY A N OTHER of
                in the County of   WITNESSETH that the said A N OTHER
HEREBY DISCLAIMS ALL THAT the life interest in a one equal one-third share (including any accrual or accruals thereto) of the residue of the Estate of S O ELSE deceased given to him by the Will dated the   day of
19   of the said S O ELSE who died on the   day of
199   AND the said A N OTHER DECLARES that he has not in any way entered into possession of the said life interest and that he has not done any act or thing that might be or amount to an acceptance of the said life interest

IN WITNESS etc

NOTE

With regard to disclaimers reference should be made to p 101 above.

112 **Assignment and Release over interest in settled property under Inheritance Tax Act 1984, section 57, for purposes of IHT annual exemption**

THIS ASSIGNMENT AND RELEASE is made the   day of   One thousand nine hundred and ninety-   BETWEEN   of
in the County of   (hereinafter called 'Mrs Parent') of the first part
and   of   in the County of   (hereinafter
called 'the Son') of the second part and   of   in the
County of   and   of   in the County of
                    (hereinafter called 'the Trustees') of the third part

WHEREAS:

(A) This Deed is supplemental to a Settlement (hereinafter called 'the Settlement')
dated the   day of   One thousand nine
hundred and   and made between   of the one part and
               and   of the other part

(B) Mrs Parent is entitled during her life to the income of the Trust Fund (which
expression in this Deed bears the same meaning as is assigned to it in the Settlement)

(C) The Son is a child of Mrs Parent and having attained the age of twenty-one
years is entitled subject to the life interest of Mrs Parent to a share (hereinafter
called 'the said share') of the capital of the Trust Fund

(D) The Trustees are the present trustees of the Settlement

(E) The sum of   pounds (£   ) (hereinafter called 'the said
sum') forms part of the capital of the said share

(F) Mrs Parent wishes the Trustees to be able to pay the said sum to the Son

NOW THIS DEED WITNESSETH as follows:
1. In pursuance of her said wish Mrs Parent HEREBY ASSIGNS AND RELEASES unto
the Son ALL THAT her life interest in the said sum to the intent that the Trustees
shall hold the same UPON TRUST for the Son absolutely
2. IT IS HEREBY CERTIFIED that this instrument falls within category L in the Schedule
to the Stamp Duty (Exempt Instruments) Regulations 1987

IN WITNESS etc

NOTE
Reference should be made to the note to the next form.

113 Notice to trustees following deed under 112

Notice under Inheritance Tax Act 1984 Section 57(3) (such Notice must be given within 6 months of the date of transfer).

To . . . . .¹

. . . .

the Trustees of the . . . . .²

. . . .

I . . . . .³
in the knowledge that my beneficial interest in possession in property [in the sum of £   ]⁴ comprised in the above trust was terminated on   ,
hereby give you notice that the amount(s) of
a) £   of the annual exemption⁴
b) £   of the exemption for gifts in consideration of marriage
was/were then available to me and is/are to be applied against the transfer of value deemed to be made by that termination.

Signed . . . .   [FOOTNOTES
Date . . . .   1 Insert full names of the Trustee(s)
                                                   2 State the date and full title of the Settlement. If
                                                     made under a Will or intestacy, or should the settlor
                                                     have died, state the full name and date of death
                                                     of the testator/intestate/settlor.
                                                   3 State full name.
                                                   4 Delete as appropriate.]

NOTE
The above is a modified reproduction of Form 222 which should be used in the particular circumstances. Subject to sub-s (3), under sub-s (1) of s 57, references to transfers of value in s 19 (annual exemption) and s 22 (gifts in consideration of marriage) apply to events under s 52 (charge on termination of interest in possession in settled property).

Under sub-s (3), sub-s (1) does not apply to such a transfer of value unless a notice is given to the trustees of the particular settlement, and except to the extent specified in that notice.

Under sub-s (4), a notice under sub-s (3) shall be in such form as may be prescribed by the Board of Inland Revenue *and shall be given before the end of the period of six months beginning with the date of the transfer of value.* Thus, the giving of the notice and the timing of it, within six months of the release by the life tenant, are a precondition of the application of the two sets of IHT exemptions in such circumstances.

114 Deed of settlement with nominee trusts by parent or other person for minor child

THIS DEED OF SETTLEMENT is made the   day of One thousand
nine hundred and ninety-   BETWEEN of
in the County of   (hereinafter called 'the Settlor') of the one part
and
of
in the County of   and
of
in the County of   (hereinafter together called 'the Trustees' which
expression whenever hereafter used includes the trustees or trustee for the time
being of this Settlement) of the other part

WHEREAS:

I.   (hereafter called 'the Beneficiary') who was born on the
          day of   One thousand nine hundred and ninety-
          is a child/grandchild/godchild of the Settlor

2. WITH a view to the Settlement hereby made the Settlor has paid to the Trustees
the sum of TEN POUNDS ($£$10.00) to be held on the trusts hereof and it is apprehended
that the Trustees may hereafter from time to time receive further sums or property
(whether or not from the Settlor) also to be so held

NOW in consideration of the natural love and affection of the Donor for the Beneficiary
THIS DEED WITNESSETH as follows:

I. THE Trustees may invest the said sum of TEN POUNDS ($£$10.00) in the names
or under the control of the Trustees in the manner authorised by Clause 6

2. THE Trustees shall hold the said sum of TEN POUNDS ($£$10.00) and all further
sums of money and property which may hereafter be paid or transferred to them
to be held on the trusts hereof and the investments for the time being representing
the same (hereafter called 'the Trust Fund') and the income thereof UPON TRUST
for the Beneficiary absolutely

3. SECTION 31 of the Trustee Act 1925 shall not apply to the trusts of this deed
and accordingly the income of the Trust Fund shall as it arises belong to the Beneficiary
And thereafter during any period when the beneficiary is under the age of eighteen
years the Trustees may pay or apply the whole or any part or parts of that income
(whether or not it has been invested in accordance with their power under Clause
6) to or for the benefit of the Beneficiary in such manner as the Trustees shall
from time to time in their absolute discretion think fit

4. THE Trustees shall have the power to pay or apply capital under section 32 of
the Trustee Act 1925 but as if proviso (a) of subsection (1) had been omitted

5. IN exercise of their powers under Clauses 3 and 4 the Trustees may pay or transfer income or capital of the Trust Fund to the parent or guardian of the Beneficiary for the Beneficiary and the receipt of the parent or guardian shall be a good discharge to the Trustees

6. THE Trustees shall have power to invest trust moneys forming part of the capital or income of the Trust Fund in both income producing and non-income producing assets of every kind and by placing them on deposit at banks and other financial bodies with power to vary investments and in those respects to act in the same full and unrestricted manner as if they themselves were absolutely entitled thereto beneficially

7. ANY trustee (excluding the Settlor and any wife/husband of the Settlor) being a Solicitor Accountant or other person engaged in any profession or business shall be entitled to charge and to be paid all usual professional or business charges for business transacted time spent and acts done by him or her or any partner or employee of theirs in connection with the trusts hereof including acts which a trustee not being in any profession or business could have done personally

8. NO part of the Trust Fund or the income thereof shall in any circumstances whatsoever be paid or lent to or applied for the benefit of and no power or discretion vested in the Trustees shall be capable of being exercised in such a manner as to benefit either directly or indirectly the Settlor or any person who is the wife/husband of the Settlor

9. THE power of appointing new trustees hereof is vested in the Settlor during his/her life

IN WITNESS etc.

NOTE
See observations on p 62 above.

115 Severance notice under the Law of Property Act 1925, section 36(2)

Mutual Notice of Severance
in respect of Joint Tenancy over

. . . .

1. a) We are the joint owners of the freehold property ('the property') known as
in the County of
b) The property was conveyed to us by a Conveyance dated the
day of   19   made between   and ourselves

or—b) The property is registered at HM Land Registry under Title Number
with Title Absolute
  c) We hold the property and the future proceeds of sale on behalf of ourselves
as beneficial joint tenants so that in the event of the death of either of us
the survivor will become the sole owner
  d) The property is subject to a Legal Charge dated the   day of
19   made between ourselves and

2. We have been advised by Messrs   that having regard to considerations
of inheritance tax and in particular arising out of the possibility of our both dying
following a joint calamity it would be better that we should change our beneficial
joint tenancy into a tenancy in common so that we would each have the right in
the future to dispose of our individual interest in the property and its proceeds
of sale including by our respective Wills

3. Accordingly, by virtue of the proviso to Section 36(2) Law of Property Act 1925
each of us hereby gives notice to the other of our desire to sever as from the date
hereof our joint tenancy in equity over the property and we hereby separately declare
that the joint tenancy is thereby duly severed in equity to the intent that henceforward
we shall hold the property and the future proceeds of sale as tenants in common
in equal shares

4. We hereby instruct Messrs   to endorse on the said Conveyance a
Memorandum recording the severance effected by this Notice
or—
4. We hereby instruct Messrs   to apply, on our behalf, to the Chief
Land Registrar to place the appropriate restriction on our Title to the Property
having regard to the terms of this Notice

Dated this   day of   199

. . . .
(   ) (   )

NOTE
Application should be made to HM Land Registry on Form 75, in the case of the second alternative
No 4 above, to register a restriction under the Land Registration Act 1925, s 58 (rr 235 and 236,
Land Registration Rules 1925). That restriction could be in the following terms:—
    'No disposition by one proprietor of the land (being the survivor of joint proprietors and
    not being a trust corporation) under which capital money arises is to be registered except
    under an order of the registrar or of the Court.'

116 Deed severing joint tenancy over matrimonial home including for the purpose of enabling each joint tenant to make a bequest to third parties

THIS DEED OF SEVERANCE AND COVENANT is made the   day of
One thousand nine hundred and ninety-   BETWEEN
of
of the one part and his wife
of the other part

WHEREAS:—

(A) i) The parties hereto are the joint owners of the freehold property ('the property') known as   in the County of   which they acquired as their permanent matrimonial home

    ii) The property was conveyed to them by a Conveyance dated the   day of   One thousand nine hundred and   and made between   of the one part and themselves of the other part

—OR—

    ii) The property is registered at HM Land Registry under Title Number   with Title Absolute

    iii) The parties hereto hold the property and its future proceeds of sale and the net income (if any) until sale upon trust for themselves as beneficial joint tenants so that in the event of the death of either of them the survivor will become the sole owner of the same

    iv) The property is subject to a Legal Charge dated the   day of One thousand nine hundred and   and made between themselves of the one part and   of the other part

[( ) The parties hereto have been advised by Messrs   that having regard to considerations of Inheritance Tax in particular arising out of the possibility of their both dying because of a joint calamity it would be better that they should change their beneficial joint tenancy into a tenancy in common so that each of them would have the exclusive right in the future to dispose of their individual interests in the property and its future proceeds of sale including by their respective Wills in such manner as they separately decide]

( ) The parties hereto accordingly wish to enter into this Deed for the purposes of severing their beneficial joint tenancy and declaring their respective interests in the property and their respective rights over it

NOW THIS DEED WITNESSETH as follows:—

1. By virtue of the proviso to Section 36(2) of the Law of Property Act 1925 each of the parties hereto HEREBY GIVES notice to the other of their respective desire

to sever as from the date hereof their joint tenancy in equity over the property and they together HEREBY DECLARE that from the date hereof they shall hold the property upon trust subject always to the said Legal Charge and to the terms of their covenants under Clause 2 hereof to sell the same and to hold its future proceeds of sale and the net income (if any) until sale for themselves as tenants in common in equal shares and accordingly:—

They hereby agree to instruct Messrs   to apply on their behalf to the Chief Land Registrar to place the appropriate restriction on the Title to the Property having regard to the terms of this Clause

—or—

They hereby agree to instruct Messrs   to endorse on the said Conveyance a Memorandum recording the severance effected by this Clause

2. The parties hereto HEREBY COVENANT with each other on behalf of themselves and their respective successors in title as owners of their legal estates in or of (or of any part of) their respective beneficial interests in the property and its future proceeds of sale as follows:—

     a) That so long as both of them are alive and one at least retains some beneficial interest in the same the property shall not be sold without their joint written consent

     b) That so long as the survivor of them retains some such interest the property shall not be sold without the written consent of the survivor

IN WITNESS etc

NOTE

Reference should be made to the note under the preceding form when the title of the property is registered.

117 Declaration recording prior gift of articles by delivery

I   of   in the County of   Solicitor HEREBY SOLEMNLY AND SINCERELY DECLARE as follows:

1. ON the   day of   One thousand nine hundred and ninety-   I was present at a meeting which took place at   in the County of   between   ('the Donor') and   ('the Donee')

2. AT that meeting I did see and hear the Donor touch or otherwise clearly indicate each and all of those chattels which are described in the Schedule hereto and express himself/herself as irrevocably transferring by delivery his/her ownership and all that his/her right title and interest in the said chattels by way of absolute gift to the Donee And I also saw and heard the Donee indicate and express herself/himself

as accepting delivery of the same in the manner indicated and expressed by the Donor

AND I make this solemn Declaration conscientiously believing the same to be true and by virtue of the provisions of the Statutory Declarations Act 1835

THE SCHEDULE before referred to

DECLARED at etc

NOTE
Reference should be made to the comment on p 64 above.

118 Deed of gift of articles

THIS DEED OF GIFT is made the   day of   One thousand nine hundred and ninety-   BETWEEN   of   in the County of
                    (hereinafter called 'the Donor') of the one part and
(hereinafter called 'the Donee') of the other part

WITNESSETH as follows:

1. IN consideration of his/her natural love and affection for the Donee the Donor HEREBY ASSIGNS his/her ownership and all that his/her right title and interest in the chattels which are described in the Schedule hereto by way of absolute gift to the Donee

2. IT IS HEREBY CERTIFIED that this instrument falls within category L in the Schedule to the Stamp Duty (Exempt Instruments) Regulations 1987

IN WITNESS etc

THE SCHEDULE before referred to

NOTE
Reference should be made to the comment on p 65 above.

119 IHT indemnity by beneficiary of PET for benefit of donor's estate should donor die within subsequent seven years

THIS DEED OF COVENANT AND INDEMNITY is made the   day of
                    One thousand nine hundred and ninety-
BETWEEN   of   in the County of   (hereinafter
called 'the Beneficiary') of the one part and   of   in the
County of   (hereinafter called 'the Donor') of the other part

WHEREAS:

(A) In this deed:
   i) The expression 'IHT' means inheritance tax and includes any interest thereon
   ii) The expressions 'potentially exempt transfer' and 'chargeable transfer' have
      the same meanings as are respectively assigned to them in the Inheritance
      Tax Act 1984
   iii) Any statutory references are to sections sub-sections and paragraphs in the
      said Act

(B) On or about the   day of   One thousand nine hundred
and ninety-   the Donor made an absolute gift to the Beneficiary of assets or cash
details of which are contained in the Schedule hereto

(C) It was a condition of the said gift that the Beneficiary or his estate should
discharge any liability for IHT in the event of it becoming a chargeable transfer
whenever that liability might arise and become payable (including by instalments)

(D) The parties hereto have been advised that the said gift is a potentially exempt
transfer for the purposes of Section 3A and that under sub-section (4) of that Section
it will become a chargeable transfer thus giving rise to a liability for IHT in the
event of the death of the Donor during the period of seven years following the
making of his said gift And in order to calculate the amount of that liability it
will be necessary to take into account the value of other chargeable transfers (whether
or not originally potentially exempt transfers) made on the same day as the said
gift or during the period of seven years prior thereto and also the number of completed
years that the Donor will have survived during the said seven years following the
making of his said gift for the purposes of the benefit of the taper relief under
Section 7

(E) As the result of the provisions of Section 199(1) and (2) in the event of the
death of the Donor during the period of seven years following the making of it
both the personal representatives of the Donor and the Beneficiary are liable for
IHT on the value transferred by the said gift but by Section 204(8)(b) the liability
of the personal representatives of the Donor is limited to the extent that the IHT
remains unpaid twelve months after the end of the month in which the death of
the Donor occurs

(F) It was a further condition of the said gift that the Beneficiary having regard to his primary liability to discharge the said IHT liability should enter into this deed for the protection of the estate of the Donor

NOW THIS DEED WITNESSETH as follows:—
1. The covenants and authority that hereinafter appear are made by the Beneficiary on behalf of himself and his personal representatives for the benefit of the estate of the Donor

2. The Beneficiary HEREBY COVENANTS with the Donor that in the event of the death of the Donor he will pay to the Commissioners of Inland Revenue any liability for IHT which may then arise in respect of the said gift or the property comprised in it as and when the same may become due for payment and that he will indemnify and keep indemnified the Donor and his personal representatives against all demands proceedings costs claims and expenses in respect of the said liability

3. Without prejudice to the foregoing terms of this deed:
   a) The Beneficiary HEREBY COVENANTS with the Donor that he will on written demand by the personal representatives of the Donor repay to them the amount of any IHT which they may have paid to the Commissioners of Inland Revenue in respect of the said liability
   b) The Beneficiary HEREBY AUTHORISES the personal representatives of the Donor to raise by sale or mortgage or otherwise out of any property forming part of the estate of the Donor to which the Beneficiary becomes entitled on the death of the Donor the necessary amount of cash for the purposes of making the said payment for IHT to the Commissioners of Inland Revenue or making any such repayment as is referred to in (a) of this Clause

IN WITNESS etc

THE SCHEDULE above referred to
The Subject Matter of the said Gift made by the Donor

NOTE
See comment, about the need for such a deed, in sub-chapter C of ch 5, p 47 above.

120 Client Memorandum; About Powers of Attorney, particularly Enduring Powers of Attorney

We have made this Memorandum because, in our opinion, every adult should make an enduring power of attorney to take advantage of the Enduring Powers of Attorney Act 1985.

Under an ordinary power of attorney a person ('the Donor') can grant another ('the Attorney') authority to do what the Donor can himself or herself otherwise do. It follows that in the event of the Donor suffering mental incapacity and thus being rendered incapable of managing his or her affairs an ordinary power of attorney is automatically revoked, at a time when many people would think it to be of its greatest importance and use. In those circumstances it was necessary for someone, usually a member of the family, to be appointed receiver by means of a formal, although reasonably convenient, procedure and thereafter to act under the supervision of the Court of Protection. Nevertheless, many families did not welcome the making of such an application to the Court of Protection and often instead the Attorney carried on under the power of attorney illegally. As the result of the 1985 Act there is a satisfactory alternative available provided of course that the person concerned, being the Donor, is when in normal health prepared to make an enduring power of attorney.

Although circumstances of mental incapacity usually arise towards the latter part of a person's life, it is not difficult to envisage very sad circumstances when a much younger person suffers mental incapacity as the result of a dreadful accident or illness, causing not only anguish but also severe practical and legal difficulties in relation to his or her personal and financial matters and for the family. It is because of this that we are of the opinion that every adult should make an enduring power of attorney to take advantage of the 1985 Act.

Under the 1985 Act it is possible to create a power of attorney which is effective from its creation and which will survive, subject to safeguards, when the Donor becomes mentally incapable of handling his or her affairs provided it is *registered* at that time in accordance with the provisions of the Enduring Powers of Attorney Act 1985. The enduring power of attorney should of course be made in advance when the person making it is fit.

1. In accordance with the 1985 Act an enduring power of attorney must be made in a prescribed form and manner.

2. The Donor may confer on the Attorney general authority to act on his or her behalf. Likewise, it is possible to confer authority in relation to a specified part of the property and affairs of the Donor or to confer on the Attorney authority to do specified things on the Donor's behalf. Any authority may also be conferred subject to conditions and restrictions. In our opinion there is a strong case for the Donor making the power unrestricted to enable the Attorney generally to take any necessary action on behalf of the Donor, not necessarily to be foreseen when the enduring power of attorney is made.

3. An enduring power of attorney can be treated and operate as an ordinary power of attorney when made. Nevertheless a restriction or condition can be included if desired to the effect that the Attorney is to have no authority unless and until he has reason to believe that the Donor is or is becoming mentally incapable. Alternatively

the Donor could state that the enduring power of attorney shall not take effect until it has been registered with the Court of Protection.

4. Subject to any conditions or restrictions the Attorney may also act in relation to the duties of the Donor in respect of trusts of which he or she is a trustee. This fiduciary authority would in fact overcome certain technical difficulties where a matrimonial home was jointly owned and it was intended to sell it.

5. We emphasise that the granting of a power of attorney which has immediate effect when made does not, of course, exclude the Donor carrying on, as before, dealing with business matters, signing cheques and so on, unless or until he or she becomes mentally incapable. The intention behind any power of attorney is, in our opinion, for it to be of help in case of need and when desired.

6. It must of course be accepted that the Donor, before granting any kind of power of attorney, must have the fullest confidence in his Attorney or, if more than one, his Attorneys.

7. a) It is possible to grant a power of attorney to more than one person in such manner that:—
   i) The Attorneys' powers are joint. Here, all the Attorneys would need, for example, to sign any documents.
   ii) The Attorneys' powers are joint and several. Thus the Attorneys can act, in the alternative, and therefore either as per (i) above, or separately.
   Having regard to the purposes of an enduring power of attorney, in our opinion it should be granted to at least two attorneys who can act jointly *and* severally. That is because the death or bankruptcy of an attorney cancels his use of the power of attorney and the power of attorney as a whole where there is joint authority only.
   b) Clearly where there is more than one Attorney, as in the case of the alternatives we have mentioned, to avoid complication and misunderstanding there would need to be settled procedures on the part of those concerned so that the left hand knows what the right hand is doing, but these are practical considerations rather than legal ones.

8. The usual way for an Attorney to sign on behalf of the Donor is:—

A.B. Donor	X.Y. Attorney
by her Attorney or	as Attorney for
X.Y. Attorney	A.B. Donor

9. When the Attorney believes that the Donor has become or *is becoming* mentally incapable, the Attorney is required to register the enduring power of attorney with the Court of Protection before she or he can continue to act under it. Once the Donor has become incapable the authority of the Attorney, before registration of the power, is very limited.

10. Once registered the terms of the power of attorney are fixed and cannot be varied by the Donor. Nevertheless, in case of necessity, an Attorney may apply to the Court of Protection for additional consent or authority.

11. To register, the Attorney is required to give formal notice to the Donor personally and also to certain close relatives of the Donor and any other Attorney(s) and must thereafter apply to the Court of Protection for registration.

12. An objection to the registration of the power of attorney may be made to the Court of Protection alleging for example that the enduring power of attorney is not valid or that the Donor is mentally capable or that the Attorney is unsuitable. If the objection is made within 5 weeks of receiving the application to register the Court will not register the power of attorney before making its own enquiries.

In order to assist the explanations in this Memorandum and as an enduring power of attorney must be made in the prescribed form we show below, *for the purposes of illustration only*, a copy of the prescribed form with its explanatory information.

Date: 199

ENDURING POWER OF ATTORNEY

Part A: About using this form

1. You may choose one attorney or more than one. If you choose one attorney then you must delete everything between the square brackets on the first page of the form. If you choose more than one, you must decide whether they are able to act:
- Jointly (that is, they must all act together and cannot act separately) or
- Jointly and severally (that is, they can all act together but they can also act separately if they wish).

On the first page of the form, show what you have decided by crossing out one of the alternatives.

2. If you give your attorney(s) general power in relation to all your property and affairs, it means that they will be able to deal with your money or property and may be able to sell your house.

3. If you don't want your attorney(s) to have such wide powers, you can include any restrictions you like. For example, you can include a restriction that your attorney(s) must not act on your behalf until they have reason to believe that you are becoming mentally incapable; or a restriction as to what your attorney(s) may do. Any restrictions you choose must be written or typed where indicated on the second page of the form.

4. If you are a trustee (and please remember that co-ownership of a home involves trusteeship), you should seek legal advice if you want your attorney(s) to act as a trustee on your behalf.

5. Unless you put in a restriction preventing it your attorney(s) will be able to use any of your money or property to make any provision which you yourself might be expected to make for their own needs or the needs of other people. Your attorney(s) will also be able to use your money to make gifts, but only for reasonable amounts in relation to the value of your money and property.

6. Your attorney(s) can recover the out-of-pocket expenses of acting as your attorney(s). If your attorney(s) are professional people, for example solicitors or accountants, they may be able to charge for their professional services as well. You may wish to provide expressly for remuneration of your attorney(s) (although if they are trustees they may not be allowed to accept it).

7. If your attorney(s) have reason to believe that you have become or are becoming mentally incapable of managing your affairs, your attorney(s) will have to apply to the Court of Protection for registration of this power.

8. Before applying to the Court of Protection for registration of this power, your attorney(s) must give written notice that that is what they are going to do, to you and your nearest relatives as defined in the Enduring Powers of Attorney Act 1985. You or your relatives will be able to object if you or they disagree with registration.

9. This is a simplified explanation of what the Enduring Powers of Attorney Act 1985 and the Rules and Regulations say. If you need more guidance, you or your advisers will need to look at the Act itself and the Rules and Regulations. The Rules are the Court of Protection (Enduring Powers of Attorney) Rules 1986 (Statutory Instrument 1986 No 127). The Regulations are the Enduring Powers of Attorney (Prescribed Form) Regulations 1990 (Statutory Instrument 1990 No 1376).

10. Note to Attorney(s)
After the power has been registered you should notify the Court of Protection if the donor dies or recovers.

11. Note to Donor
Some of these explanatory notes may not apply to the form you are using if it has already been adapted to suit your particular requirements.
   You can cancel this power at any time before it has to be registered

Part B: To be completed by the 'donor' (the person appointing the attorney(s))

Don't sign this form unless you understand what it means

Please read the notes
in the margin which
follow and which are
part of the form itself.

Donor's name and address.

I . . . .

of . . . .

Donor's date of birth.

born on . . . .

See note 1 on the front of
this form. If you are
appointing only one
attorney you should cross
out everything between the
square brackets. If
appointing more than two
attorneys please give the
additional name(s) on an
attached sheet.

appoint . . . .

of . . . .

● [and . . . .

of . . . .

Cross out the one which
does not apply (see note 1
on the front of this form).

● jointly
● jointly and severally]

to be my attorney(s) for the purpose of the Enduring
Powers of Attorney Act 1985

Cross out the one which
does not apply (see note 2
on the front of this form).
Add any additional powers.

● with general authority to act on my behalf
● with authority to do the following on my behalf:

If you don't want the
attorney(s) to have general
power, you must give
details here of what
authority you are giving the
attorney(s).

in relation to

Cross out the one which
does not apply.

● all my property and affairs
● the following property and affairs:

Part B: continued

Please read the notes in the margin which follow and which are part of the form itself.

If there are restrictions or conditions, insert them here; if not, cross out these words if you wish (See note 3 on the front of this form).

If this form is being signed at your direction:—
• the person signing must not be an attorney or any witness (to Parts B or C).
• you must add a statement that this form has been signed at your direction.
• a second witness is necessary (please see below)

Your signature (or mark).

Date.

Someone must witness your signature.

Signature of witness.

Your attorney(s) cannot be your witness. It is not advisable for your husband or wife to be your witness.

• subject to the following restrictions and conditions:

I intend that this power shall continue even if I become mentally incapable.

I have read or have had read to me the notes in Part A which are part of, and explain, this form.

Signed by me as a deed . . . . and delivered

on . . . .

in the presence of . . . .

Full name of witness . . . .

Address of witness . . . .

. . . .

. . . .

A second witness is only necessary if this form is not being signed by you personally but at your direction (for example, if a physical disability prevents you from signing).
Signature of second witness.

in the presence of . . . .

Full name of witness . . . .

Address of witness . . . .

. . . .

. . . .

Part C: To be completed by the attorney(s)

Note 1. This form may be adapted to provide for execution by a corporation.

2. If there is more than one attorney additional sheets in the form as shown below must be added to this Part C.

Please read the notes in the margin which follow and which are part of the form itself.	I understand that I have a duty to apply to the Court for the registration of this form under the Enduring Powers of Attorney Act 1985 when the donor is becoming or has become mentally incapable.
Don't sign this form before the donor has signed Part B or if, in your opinion, the donor was already mentally incapable at the time of signing Part B.	I also understand my limited power to use the donor's property to benefit persons other than the donor.
	I am not a minor
If this form is being signed at your direction:— ●the person signing must not be an attorney or any witness (to Parts B or C). ●you must add a statement that this form has been signed at your direction. ●a second witness is necessary (please see below).	
Signature (or mark) of attorney.	Signed by me as a deed . . . . and delivered
Date.	on . . . .
Signature of witness.	in the presence of . . . .
The attorney must sign the form and his signature must be witnessed. The donor may not be the witness and one attorney may not witness the signature of the other.	Full name of witness . . . . Address of witness . . . .
A second witness is only necessary if this form is not being signed by you personally but at your direction (for example, if a physical disability prevents you from signing).	
Signature of second witness.	in the presence of . . . . Full name of witness . . . . Address of witness . . . .

Appendix. IHT Tables

A. Table of rates of IHT

As explained on page 16 above from each 6 April for the following 12 months, the table of rates is changed in line with the retail prices index. For the 12 months to 5 April 1992 the table in Schedule I of the Inheritance Tax Act 1984 is as below

Portion of value		Rate of tax
Lower limit	Upper limit	Per cent
£	£	
0	140,000	NIL
140,000	—	40

The above are the rates of *transfers on death*.

In the case of *lifetime transfers* because PETs are when made not chargeable transfers (see p 46 above) there are few lifetime transfers which are chargeable transfers and which on their making give rise to a liability to IHT. The latter would include a lifetime transfer into a settlement without an interest in possession (effectively a discretionary trust) or to a company.

The IHT rates on such lifetime chargeable transfers are one-half of the rates shown in the above table. Nevertheless in the event of the death of the transferor within seven years of the transfer the IHT liability will be recalculated to take into account the then death rate, the effect of taper relief, see page 46 above, and giving credit for the IHT paid when the chargeable transfer was made.

B. Grossing table for net lifetime transfers

As mentioned in Appendix A there are few lifetime transfers which are chargeable transfers and which on their making give rise to a liability to IHT. The latter would include a lifetime transfer into a settlement without an interest in possession (effectively a discretionary trust) or to a company.

When the beneficiary of such a chargeable transfer receives his gift net of IHT it is necessary to gross up the value of the transfer in order to assess the value which, after deduction of IHT, is the net value of the transfer; see page 53 above.

The figures below are for the 12 months to 5 April 1992.

Rate of IHT for transfers taxed at half of death rate (for example a lifetime chargeable transfer into a discretionary trust):

20% on excess over £140,000.

Example
In December 1991, a donor who has made no previous chargeable transfers (which if there were would need to be taken into account for cumulation purposes) but has used his annual IHT exemptions, places £200,000 into a discretionary trust and agrees to discharge the IHT liability on his chargeable transfer

$$£140,000 + \left(£60,000 \times \frac{100}{80}\right) = £215,000$$

£200,000 is received by the trust and £15,000 is paid by the donor for IHT. For future purposes the donor's gross cumulative total is £215,000.

C. Grossing table for use on death where specific gifts do not bear their own IHT for purposes of Inheritance Tax Act 1984, sections 36 to 42.

Reference should be made to G of chapter 6, page 73 above.

The figures and example below are for the 12 months to 5 April 1992.

Grossing-up for transfers on death amounting to £140,000 or over:
£140,000 plus ⅔ for each £1 over £140,000.

Example
Gross equivalent of £160,000 = £140,000 + ⅔ (£160,000 – £140,000)
$$= £173,333$$

NOTE
(a) If there have been chargeable lifetime transfers during the seven-year period prior to the death the following steps are necessary:
 1 from the gross lifetime cumulation, deduct tax at death rates;
 2 add that net figure to the figure for specific gifts;
 3 find the gross equivalent of that total;
 4 from the gross equivalent deduct the (gross) value of the lifetime cumulation: the resulting figure is the gross value of the specific gifts.
(b) A second grossing is necessary where s 38(4) and (5) applies.

Index